JOHNSON'S CRITICAL PRESENCE

Johnson's Critical Presence demonstrates how Johnson's criticism has for long been divided from the issues of modern criticism by historical narratives that have marked the progress of criticism from 'classic to romantic'. The image of Johnson constructed by his immediate antagonists has been preserved by the routines of historical representation, and mediated to the present day, most recently, by the characterizations of 'radical theory'.

By an in-depth analysis of major works by Johnson, Smallwood argues that the historicization of eighteenth-century criticism can be more fruitfully understood in the light of the 'dialogic' and 'translational' historiography of such thinkers as Collingwood and Ricoeur, and that the contexts of Johnson's criticism must include the poetry he read as well as the theories he espoused. In this way the book reinstates Johnson's 'presence' as critic while displacing the 'history of ideas' as the leading paradigm for conceptualizing the history of criticism.

Philip Smallwood is Professor of English at the University of Central England and has written widely on Samuel Johnson and on the theory, practice and history of literary criticism. His books include *Modern Critics in Practice* (1990), *Johnson Re-Visioned*, an edited collection of new essays on Johnson *(*2001), and *Reconstructing Criticism: Pope's 'Essay on Criticism' and the Logic of Definition* (2003). He is the editor of *Critical Pasts*, a collection of essays on approaches to critical history, and co-editor of the unpublished manuscripts on critical and aesthetic themes of the British philosopher R.G. Collingwood.

NATUS
SEPT. VII
1709.

MORTUUS
13 DECEM.
1784.

SAMUEL JOHNSON L.L.D.

Johnson's Critical Presence

Image, History, Judgment

PHILIP SMALLWOOD
University of Central England

ASHGATE

Published by
Ashgate Publishing Limited
Gower House
Croft Road
Aldershot
Hampshire GU11 3HR
England

Ashgate Publishing Company
Suite 420
101 Cherry Street
Burlington, VT 05401-4405
USA

Ashgate website: http://www.ashgate.com

British Library Cataloguing in Publication Data
Smallwood, P.J.
    Johnson's critical presence : image, judgment, and critical
    history. - (Studies in early modern English literature)
    1. Johnson, Samuel, 1709-1784 - History and criticism
    2. Johnson, Samuel, 1709-1784 - Knowledge - Literature
    3. Literature - History and criticism - Theory, etc.
    4. Criticism - England - History - 18th century
    I. Title
    828.6'.09

Library of Congress Cataloging-in-Publication Data
Smallwood, Philip.
    Johnson's critical presence : image, history, judgment / Philip Smallwood.
        p. cm – (Studies in early modern English literature)
    Includes bibliographical references (p.) and index.
    ISBN 0-7546-3357-8 (alk. paper)
      1. Johnson, Samuel, 1709-1784–Knowledge–Literature. 2. Criticism–Great
Britain–History–18th century. 3. Great Britain–Intellectual life–18th century. 4. Canon
(Literature) I. Title. II. Series.

    PR3537.L5S63 2003
    828'609–dc22

                                                                    2003065059

ISBN 0 7546 3357 8

Series cover design after *Dr Thomas Morell* by William Hogarth

Printed and bound in Great Britain by MPG Books Ltd, Bodmin, Cornwall

Contents

List of Illustrations		*vi*
General Editor's Preface		*vii*
Preface		*viii*
Acknowledgments		*xiv*
List of Abbreviations		*xvi*

1 Samuel Johnson, Critical Presence and the Theory of the History of Criticism — 1

2 'Only Designing to Live': Personal History and the Non-Reductive Context of Johnsonian Criticism — 15

3 Historicization and the Judgment of Shakespeare — 38

4 Historicization and Literary Pleasure: Johnson Reads Cowley — 64

5 Voice and Image: Critical Comedy, the Johnsonian Monster, and the Construction of Judgment — 95

6 From Image to History: Johnson's Criticism and the Genealogy of Romanticism — 117

7 Conclusion: Johnson's Transfusion of the Critical Past and the Making of the Literary Canon — 137

Bibliography — *157*
Index — *166*

List of Illustrations

Frontispiece: *Samuel Johnson*. John Hall after Joshua Reynolds (1787)

5.1   *Old Wisdom Blinking at the Stars*. James Gillray (1782)   103

5.2   *Samuel Johnson*. Joshua Reynolds (1769)   105

5.3   *Apollo and the Muses, Inflicting Penance on Dr Pomposo, Round Parnassus*. James Gillray (1783)   108

General Editor's Preface

Studies in Early Modern English Literature

The series focuses on literary writing of the seventeenth and eighteenth centuries. Its objectives are to examine the individuals, trends, and channels of influence of the period between the Renaissance and the rise of Romanticism. During this period the English novel was invented, poetry began to tackle its unsteady relationship with non-literary discourse, and post-Shakespearean drama reinvented itself.

Alongside studies of established figures, the series will include books on important but lesser-known writers and those who are acknowledged as significant but given slight attention: typically, William Cartwright, James Shirley, John Denham, Edmund Waller, Isaac Watts, Matthew Prior, William D' Avenant, Mark Akenside and John Dyer. Also of particular interest are studies of the development of literary criticism in this period, monographs which deal with the conditions and practicalities of writing including the practices of the publishing trade and financial and social circumstances of writing as a profession and books which give special attention to the relationship between literature and other arts and discourses.

Monographs on a variety of writers and topics will be accepted; authors are invited to combine the best traditions of detailed research with astute critical analysis. The use of contemporary theoretical approaches will be acceptable, but every book will be founded primarily upon historical, biographical and textual scholarship.

Professor Richard Bradford
University of Ulster

Preface

My judgments themselves characterize the way I judge, characterize the nature of judgment. (Ludwig Wittgenstein, *On Certainty*, 22e)

This book asks how far Johnson's literary criticism might still matter *as* criticism at the present time; and in ways that I hope will be clear from the outset, its focus is textual and critical as distinct from cultural and material. The 'history' I wish to explore is not primarily a social or political history of criticism,[1] but is concerned with the history that values criticism's past engagement with literary texts and - at its most lively and profound - with other criticism. The argument I set forth in this study is that despite concerted scholarly efforts toward critical recuperation over many years, Johnson's criticism continues to be read by historians of criticism as a body of theory that is now largely unappreciable as criticism and has lost its persuasive power; it cannot be taken seriously by the modern critical scene, or by present readers of literature, because of the lingering narrative archetypes used by historians to dramatize the progress of criticism from 'classic to romantic'. I suggest that needs dictated by the favoured emplotment of critical history, its accompanying point of view, its sanctioned categories, and the necessity for Johnson to be interpreted as a representative critic of his age, have preserved an image of Johnson exaggerated or distorted in discernibly conventional, highly institutionalized ways. For all his 'historical' importance Johnson is no longer judged likely to awaken the spirit of contemporary curiosity or excitement about the literature of his own day, the literature of our time, or the responses, theories and ideas they inspire.

This image has been mediated to the present day by a combination of forces none of which is unequivocally hostile to him, but all of which are in different ways monuments to Johnson's *past* importance - from Macaulay's Johnson, through the ambivalence of F.R. Leavis in the twentieth century,[2] to the recent 'culturalization' of eighteenth-century studies and the prestige of the 'history of ideas'. Most recently, there have arisen the culturally radical and 'postmodern' responses to evaluation, and canonization, within the modern theory of criticism itself.[3] As a critical balance to this trend, I bring forward in this book examples of Johnsonian judgment which suggest the currency he might nevertheless have as a critic alongside his 'historical' value 'for his time', and it is in this sense that this book argues for the presence of Johnson's critical text against the cultural and historical obstacles to its current recognition. In so doing it sets major critical writings by Samuel Johnson in the light of his critical image in the past and present. I examine some unconventional aspects of how this image was constructed, focus upon Johnson's conception of judgment (as an aspect of our judgment of him), and suggest the tension between Johnson's conception of critical history, and our prevailing modern conception, as this is evident from discussions of Johnson's own historical role. The study of Johnson, and the work of theorizing history, are here seen as interdependent, mutually necessary, activities.

The image of Johnson compounded by three centuries of critical reception is necessarily complex;[4] but the pervasive assumption of Johnson's obsolescence as a critic is reinforced at every stage by teleological constructs, contestable classifications, conventional taxonomies and an emphasis on kinds of historical context which assume the limitations of the critical text. These fixities of structure and content have been adopted by major critical historians in their treatment of Johnson in the last one hundred years, and the criticism of Johnson remains the subject of a cultural politics whose foundations are so deep-seated they are taken for granted. Saintsbury's Johnson of 1905 is a figure from eighteenth-century costume drama. His tale of criticism, running to three large volumes, is a rambling picaresque. Wellek's Johnson, who makes his appearance in the first volume of Wellek's magnum opus, is the psychiatric patient of 1955. The *Cambridge* historians in turn supply the decomposed and de-centred subject of 1997.[5] But what seems lost in the contextual and co-textual material of all three histories, I shall suggest, is a sense of the historical significance of critical moments which seem to fall outside the scope of the history of criticism as a history of ideas (and any kind of narrative development grounded on this). Thus, by a reference back to the form, tone, and terminology of the Johnsonian text, different contexts can be construed and brought into play; these can be related in different ways to the critical text or the text can be lifted from them entirely; different expectations can be aroused; the potentialities within the present of criticism can be extrapolated from the critical past, and the process of historicization can be opened up.

To this end I address in this study the enduring comic irony of Johnson's criticism and (by comparison) the often unappreciated irony of its historical role, his criticism's penetration by an emotional agency, and the visual drama of eighteenth-century satirical caricature - of which Johnson is here the *victim*. The vitality of the caricaturists' view of Johnson rests upon the same conception of his authoritarian limits, rigidity and conservatism, as that assumed by modern historians of his criticism, and by recent 'radical' theorists; and the best eighteenth-century visual satirists of Johnson, his historians and his modern 'revolutionary' detractors have in their different ways institutionalized Johnson as the paradigmatic critical judge. But along with other kinds of re-readings, the caricaturists' Johnson also provides in this study a context of welcome aesthetic experience for comprehending the radical energy of the critical past and the kinds of creative responses it can provoke. Emphasizing the satirical critique of judgment, such caricatures exemplify an artistic alternative to the 'history of ideas' as the organizational key to the history of eighteenth-century criticism. Ultimately, my method sets out to restore some basic but forgotten potentialities within Johnson's meanings and Johnson's words, and to cast a critical light on the ideas currently used to organize the critical past from the perspective of a notionally 'radical' present. I seek to relate an inadequacy in the shape of the critical past to an inadequacy in the current state of critical understanding.

Focusing initially on Johnson's pity and pain at the death of Shakespeare's Cordelia, Chapter 1, 'Samuel Johnson, Critical Presence and the Theory of the History of Criticism', opens with a systematic account of the theory of the history of criticism, its peculiar problems and paradoxes, extending into an assessment of how three major critical histories of the twentieth century have dealt in substantially similar and symptomatic ways with the complex thought and emotional content of Johnson's literary criticism. The deficiencies of the developmental model of critical history, I argue here, call for a varying of the permissible patterns of historical relation if Johnson's value as a critical presence is to be understood.

Chapter 2, '"Only Designing to Live": Personal History and the Non-Reductive Context of Johnsonian Criticism', interrogates the claims of those critics who have sought the source of Johnson's critical practice in the acquired prejudices of his early career, and it is here that I suggest the first of several means by which the historicized reading of a Johnsonian 'life in criticism' can be re-charted. I turn, however, not exclusively to the excerptible contents of the inherited 'rules' of criticism thought to have weighed Johnson down, but to metacriticism, and to the mock-heroic construction of the critic to be found in Johnson's periodical papers - from the early *Ramblers* to the portrait of Dick Minim in the *Idler* of Johnson's middle years. The chapter suggests how far Johnson developed in response to new experience; in what ways the early criticism anticipates the later work and in what ways it does not; how Johnson had pre-empted, by self-satire, later attempts to represent his criticism satirically; and how from the start of his career he articulates his own mixed satirical and heroic consciousness of the cultural role of the critic.

The second part of the chapter brings the comedy and humanity of *Rasselas* into the evaluation of Johnson's personal critical history. Far from being hemmed in or confined by an adhesion to the neoclassicism against which he strained, degrading the authority and even discussability of his critical views, Johnson's creative work at its best must encourage us to expect a great deal more of the Shakespearean criticism written by Johnson than most other contexts allow - as must a re-interpretation of the critical role of Dryden's translated poetry, the comedy of praising folly available from long-standing humanist traditions, or the fluid essays of Montaigne. I thereby commend a more subtle relationship between Johnson and the contexts of his criticism.

Chapter 3, 'Historicization and the Judgment of Shakespeare', extends the process of re-visualizing Johnsonian judgment, here by realizing meanings within the critical text that are conventionally blurred by historical representation. Putting into practice the historiographical concepts of Collingwood, Berlin, Jauss, Gadamer, Ricoeur and Perkins recalled in Chapter 1, the chapter is devoted to the axial role of Johnson's criticism of Shakespeare, its significance in defining Johnson's internal critical biography, and the influence exerted upon the *Lives of the Poets* of its radical criteria of judgment. Re-historicizing the idea of judgment, it is suggested here, involves the appreciation of the close, 'tiered' relationship between Johnson's critical generalizations in the *Preface* and the particulars of his notes to Shakespeare's plays. The proximity of these generalizations to the textuality of the plays - directly or via the notes - again provides a non-reductive relationship with the critical past - both the past of Johnson and Johnson in the past. Where others have focused on the importance of the 'Intellectual Context of the Preface to Shakespeare',[6] I suggest that the challenge of the critical past is often the challenge of an *emotional* agency. Its primary historical context is a literary field. Thus it is that to tackle the criticism of Johnson historically is always to grapple with the thoughts and the emotions of Johnson first hand. These thoughts and emotions are usually as substantially the subject of critical enquiry, controversy and debate, I argue, as they were in his day, and as far as they are not, Johnson has no place in a properly constituted history of criticism.[7]

Chapter 4, 'Historicization and Literary Pleasure: Johnson Reads Cowley', expands this argument by turning from the criticism of the greatest writer in English to a leading critical preface by Johnson in the *Lives*, this time with reference to a relatively obscure seventeenth-century poet, and involving a different kind of critical occasion. Here, homogenizing historicizations of Johnson's criticism are once again confuted in the particular case by a detailed reading of the 'Life of Cowley'. This reading is set against the poems by Cowley on which the 'Life of Cowley' is built. The chapter considers the proximate poetic context of the 'Life' as against its historical role in eighteenth-century taxonomic and conceptual change. The criticism of Johnson, and the poetry upon which he writes, are seen as interdependent experiences and jointly necessary to historical knowledge about the critical past. They resist historical taxonomies by emphasizing the role of emotion in literary criticism, and expose the difficulty of comprehending critics' emotional responses to literature within the history of ideas. In place of the tendency of historians to assume within later criticism higher levels of sophistication and greater theoretical profundity, such criticism can suggest variant narratives of prospective validity - that of rise and decline, or more simply decline.

Chapter 5, 'Voice and Image: Critical Comedy, the Johnsonian Monster, and the Construction of Judgment', returns to contemporary responses to controversial Johnsonian judgments and their reception by history; but I do so, as suggested above, by bringing to the fore two further non-reductive aspects of the history of criticism within the figure and personality of Johnson. First I recall the comedy of Johnson's criticism, initially evident in the *Rambler*, but also pervading the tonal qualities and judgmentalism of the text of the *Lives of the Poets*; secondly, I draw attention to the role of the visual as an organic part of the textual context of eighteenth-century criticism. Such perspectives place in a textually and contextually problematic light the critical and cultural milieu in which Johnson's criticism was conceived and received. Thus the chapter surveys eighteenth-century satirical caricatures of the critic, of critical magisterialism, and of Johnson himself, and it offers a close contextualizing 'reading' of two symptomatic satirical treatments of Johnsonian judgment by James Gillray (in his complex travesty of an idealized portrait of Johnson by Reynolds and as the model of critical stupidity corporate in the penitent 'Dr. Pomposo').

Chapter 6, 'From Image to History: Johnson's Criticism and the Genealogy of Romanticism', moves from this travestied image of Johnson's criticism back to the wider narrative of historical change, and defines an underlying irony of history.

The chapter discusses the resistance to Johnson of major romantic critics on the topics of Shakespeare, Dryden, Pope and poetical diction, and a revisionary account is given of the 'anxiety of influence' linking Johnson's criticism to such major English and European figures as Wordsworth, Coleridge, Hazlitt, A.W. Schlegel and Stendhal. While ironically submissive to the force of Johnson's influence as a critic, such writers most often conspired to reproduce an influentially distorted 'image' of Johnsonian judgment. It is this post hoc mis-figuration of Johnson - and not the failure of the critical text itself - which I argue has done most to deny presence and intrinsic significance to the criticism of the past and has continued to dictate the shape of its history.

The final chapter returns to the theoretical problem of critical history from which this enquiry arose. I conclude that Johnson's major works of criticism express not a crucial moment in the shift from a 'classic' to a 'romantic' system, or any system of generalized entities whatever, but potentially important, if difficult and challenging accounts of what certain authors have to say. Only the accumulation of cultural-historical data has made it seem otherwise. Johnson's own approach to the past of criticism is that of a critic who has no truck with a succession of systems. His relationship with earlier critics, as for example Dryden, is translational, and it extends into the domain of critical writing Dryden's own historical relations as a poetical translator. The critics who come after Johnson, the cultural radicals, and anti-canonists, along with the occasional recreators of the figure of Johnson as critic and eccentric in the modern novel, owe much to the caricaturists' Johnson. In imagining the realities of the critical past from our present point, we are left with the mythical figure of Johnson, the romantic image that combines a developmental history of criticism with discontinuity, a reductive contextualism with a symbol of inevitable failure.

Notes

---

[1] Recent controversies over Johnson's putative 'Jacobite' leanings, which I do not wish to extend, have tended to accelerate this trend. See, for example, Jonathan Clark and Howard Erskine-Hill, eds., *Samuel Johnson in Historical Context* (Houndmills: Palgrave, 2002).
[2] The two essays in question are 'Johnson as Critic', *Scrutiny* 12, no. 3 (1944): 187-200 and Leavis's review of J.W. Krutch's *Samuel Johnson* (New York: Harcourt Brace, 1944). The latter is entitled 'Doctor Johnson' and was printed in the *Kenyon Review* 8 (1946): 637-57. In the former essay Leavis credited Johnson with an *immediate* critical value - his essays 'compel, and they repay, a real and disinterested reading, that full attention of the judging mind' and are 'alive and life giving' ('Johnson as Critic', 187) - that he went on to withdraw in the later piece. Here Johnson was 'very much at home in a cultural tradition that lays a peculiarly heavy stress on the conventional and social conditioning of individual achievement', and was now 'representative in his inability to appreciate the more profoundly creative uses of language - for that was his case' ('Doctor Johnson', 646; 651-52). I suggest that a conviction of Johnson's pre-eminently negative relation to his age supervenes in the later essay, and that Leavis's mode of devaluing is the product of a reductively determinist historicization even when other ideas of history are available to him

and are put into practice elsewhere. Leavis now does little, for example, to credit Johnson with the spirit of historical present value such as pervades his own study of the poetical past in *Revaluation*.

[3] As Kevin Hart has shown when he combines post-materialist concepts and tropes, the terminology of deconstruction, and an approach to Johnson via Boswell, the elements of later critical movements within this amalgam have not always displaced its former phases but may often have revived and strengthened them. See *Samuel Johnson and the Culture of Property* (Cambridge: Cambridge University Press, 1999).

[4] For an authoritative account of Johnson's reception to 1970 see James L. Clifford and Donald J. Greene, *Samuel Johnson: A Survey and Bibliography of Critical Studies* (Minneapolis: University of Minnesota Press, 1970), 3-33; and for a more recent, focused, equally authoritative overview, Steven Lynn's essay 'Johnson's Critical Reception', in *The Cambridge Companion to Samuel Johnson*, ed. Greg Clingham (Cambridge: Cambridge University Press, 1997), 240-53.

[5] See George Saintsbury, *A History of Criticism and Literary Taste in Europe*, vol. 2: *From the Renaissance to the Decline of Eighteenth Century Orthodoxy*, 2nd ed. (Edinburgh and London: William Blackwood and Sons, 1905); René Wellek, *A History of Modern Criticism*, vol. 1: *The Later Eighteenth Century* (London: Jonathan Cape, 1955); *The Cambridge History of Literary Criticism*, vol. 4: *The Eighteenth Century*, ed. H.B. Nisbet and Claude Rawson (Cambridge: Cambridge University Press, 1997).

[6] I have particularly in mind R.D. Stock's learned but symptomatic volume, *Samuel Johnson and Neoclassical Dramatic Theory: The Intellectual Context of the* Preface to Shakespeare (Lincoln: University of Nebraska Press, 1973).

[7] What can be said of the history of criticism with respect to Johnson can be said of the history of philosophy with respect to the ancient or non-contemporary philosophers. See, on this issue, Roger Scruton, *A Short History of Modern Philosophy*, 2nd ed. (London and New York: Routledge, 2002), 10. One difference would be that whereas historians of philosophy will be concerned with the currency of 'ideas', historians of criticism will need to take account of other elements within the sum total of 'criticism' - appreciations, depreciations, emotional reactions and so forth, these apprehended in relation to the literary text the critic is concerned immediately or more distantly with.

Acknowledgments

I am grateful to the following for permission to draw upon copyright material I have published in articles and essays elsewhere:

Cambridge University Press for permission to adapt parts of my essay 'Shakespeare: Johnson's Poet of Nature', in *The Cambridge Companion to Samuel Johnson*, ed. Greg Clingham (Cambridge: Cambridge University Press, 1997), 143-60.

Associated University Presses for permission to use parts of my essay 'Ironies of the Critical Past: Historicizing Johnson's Criticism' in *Johnson Re-Visioned: Looking Before and After*, ed. Philip Smallwood (Lewisburg and London: Bucknell University Press/Associated University Press, 2001), 114-33.

Edinburgh University Press for permission to adapt passages from my article 'Dryden's Criticism as Transfusion', in the Dryden tercentenary number of *Translation and Literature* (Edinburgh: University of Edinburgh Press, 2001), 78-88.

The editor of *The British Journal for Eighteenth-Century Studies* for permission to draw upon my article 'The Johnsonian Monster and the *Lives of the Poets*: James Gillray, Critical History and the Eighteenth-Century Satirical Cartoon', *The British Journal for Eighteenth-Century Studies*, 25, no. 2 (Autumn 2002): 217-45.

Gillray's *Old Wisdom Blinking at the Stars* and his *Apollo and the Muses, Inflicting Penance on Dr Pomposo, Round Parnassus* are reproduced courtesy of the Print Collection, Lewis Walpole Library, Yale University. Reynolds's 1769 portrait of *Samuel Johnson* is held in a private collection and is reproduced here courtesy the National Trust Photographic Library/John Hammond. The Frontispiece, an etching by John Hall after Joshua Reynolds's 'Blinking Sam', is reproduced by courtesy of the National Portrait Gallery, London.

I must thank the Arts and Humanities Research Board for support under the Research Leave Scheme which enabled me to complete this study; Yale University for the award of a Visiting Fellowship which facilitated work on caricature representations of Johnson at the Lewis Walpole Library; and my Faculty and the School of English at the University of Central England for support in attending conferences at which versions of parts of this study have been read. I should like to thank Dr. Robert Eaglestone for his kind invitation to me to address the Ethics and Aesthetics Seminar at the School of Advanced Study, University of London, on the topic of Johnson and Cordelia. Above all, I should like to thank Greg Clingham of Bucknell University whose original and comprehensive study of Johnson's *Lives*,

Johnson, Writing, Memory, was published in 2002. I am grateful to Professor Clingham for his learned and ready support, valued friendship and intellectual encouragement in all matters Johnsonian, and for the many conversations about Johnson, criticism and history I have enjoyed in his company. Dr. Susan Butterfield, until lately of Birmingham University, and Dr. Mark Pedreira of the University of Puerto Rico, San Juan, both generously gave of their valuable time to read the whole manuscript and to make many astute suggestions for improvement. I am indebted to them both, as I am to the anonymous Ashgate readers for their indispensable advice, and to Dr. Tom Mason and Professor David Hopkins of Bristol University for their inspiration and wise counsels over the years.

List of Abbreviations

Works by Johnson from *The Yale Edition of the Works of Samuel Johnson*, General Editor: John H. Middendorf (New Haven and London: Yale University Press, 1958-) are cited parenthetically throughout in abbreviated form as follows:

Diaries   *Diaries, Prayers, and Annals*, ed. E.L. McAdam Jr., with Donald and Mary Hyde (1958).

Idler   *The Idler* and *The Adventurer*, ed. W.J. Bate, John M. Bullitt, and L.F. Powell (1963).

Poems   *Poems*, ed. E.L. McAdam Jr., with George Milne (1964).

Rambler, 3-5   *The Rambler*, ed. W.J. Bate and Albrecht B. Strauss, 3 vols. (1969).

Shakespeare   *Johnson on Shakespeare*, ed. Arthur Sherbo, introduction by Bertrand H. Bronson, 2 vols. (1969).

Rasselas   Rasselas *and Other Tales*, ed. Gwin J. Kolb (1990).

Other work by Johnson is cited parenthetically as follows:

Lives   *Lives of the English Poets*, ed. George Birkbeck Hill, 3 vols. (Oxford: Clarendon Press, 1905).

Works by Pope from *The Twickenham Edition of the Poems of Alexander Pope*, General Editor: John Butt (London and New Haven: Methuen and Yale University Press, 1939-1969) are cited parenthetically throughout in abbreviated form as follows:

Imitations   *Imitations of Horace with an Epistle to Dr Arbuthnot and the Epilogue to the Satires*, ed. John Butt (1939).

Epistles   *Epistles to Several Persons (Moral Essays)*, ed. F.W. Bateson (1951).

Essay   *Pastoral Poetry and an Essay on Criticism*, ed. E. Audra and Aubrey Williams (1961).

Homer, 7-10   *Homer's Iliad and Odyssey*, ed. Maynard Mack (1967).

Dunciad   *The Dunciad*, ed. James Sutherland (1965).

Other abbreviations:

AJ   *The Age of Johnson: A Scholarly Annual*

BJA   *The British Journal of Aesthetics*

BJECS   *The British Journal for Eighteenth-Century Studies*

CQ   *The Cambridge Quarterly*

ELH   *English Literary History*

HLQ   *The Huntington Library Quarterly*

N&Q   *Notes and Queries*

PMLA   *Publications of the Modern Language Association of America*

PQ   *Philological Quarterly*

Chapter 1

Samuel Johnson, Critical Presence and the Theory of the History of Criticism

> The important critic is the person who is absorbed in the present problems of art, and who wishes to bring the forces of the past to bear upon the solution of these problems. (T.S. Eliot, 'Imperfect Critics', *The Sacred Wood*, 37-38)

> The problem for the historian of criticism would seem obvious: how does one write a history of a radically heterogeneous and internally dialogised 'object'? One way to simplify one's task is to simplify one's story.... Different critical perspectives convert the plot into different stories. (Dominick LaCapra, 'On Writing the History of Criticism Now?' *History and Criticism*, 99)

Presence, History and Emotional Agency

In what sense does the following statement by Samuel Johnson become part of what we know as 'the history of criticism'? How can this utterance, of all the things that constitute criticism, be historicized?

> Cordelia, from the time of Tate, has always retired with victory and felicity. And, if my sensations could add any thing to the general suffrage, I might relate, that I was many years ago so shocked by Cordelia's death, that I know not whether I ever endured to read again the last scenes of the play till I undertook to revise them as an editor. (*Shakespeare*, 8: 704)

The shockability of earlier generations when faced with works of art we now value and believe we understand is much canvassed, and the sense of estrangement, experienced at the same time, when comparisons are made with the past, must often accompany our sense that a critical text is part of history. But by giving the critical text historical status we also see it as time-hallowed, as enjoying a certain kind of cultural esteem. The Johnson I should like to focus on in this study is not the Johnson whose criticism seems simplistically to register only a profound difference from the present that only the blind could fail to see, but one whose distance from the concerns of modern critics, and the tastes of modern readers, must cause us to think historically about literary criticism in a correspondingly more searching way, and to open up the historicization of Johnson to theoretical scrutiny.

In pursuit of this aim, I shall in this study rely less on the practice of historians who select their facts from an eighteenth-century context of ideas, politics and society, but draw freely on the vitality of modern historical theory operating within an Hegelian, 'idealist' and hermeneutic or 'reader-reception' tradition, and build my argument on a framework derived from theorists of history such as R.G. Collingwood and Paul Ricoeur. For despite the revolutions in, and debates about, history over the last thirty years (including arguments over traditional 'history as reality' versus postmodernist 'history as text'), the history of criticism, and in consequence the historical representation of Johnson's criticism, has been touched only superficially by the tide of historiographical change. In its qualities of re-presentation, the history of eighteenth-century criticism has thus disguised the complex ways in which Johnson's criticism is fitted to speak directly to the modern reader of literature, and in Michel de Certeau's telling phrase at times to 'menace our knowledge'.[1] In particular, I shall suggest that the conventions of historical writing about criticism have failed to chart the context of *significant* dissimilarity that enables us to focus on the unique value and distinctive limits of our own experience as critics. Before trying to solve problems specific to the pastness of Johnson's criticism, we therefore need to look more closely at the theoretical problems of the history of criticism as difficulties in their own right, and in this first chapter my aim will consequently be to address in preparatory terms some neglected aspects of the relationship between what criticism is and what criticism was, between literary criticism and its history.

'Not for Direct Instruction in Critical Thinking'

In one understanding, the past of criticism is all the criticism there has ever been; more often, however, when we think of the critical past we are thinking of criticism written in advance of the present by more than fifty or one hundred years. We have in mind criticism written beyond one generation ago, or by critics who are dead but not completely forgotten, the Drydens, Johnsons, Coleridges and Arnolds of worlds that are no more. We are thinking about criticism in relation to which historical thought of some kind seems possible or necessary. Many general studies of literary criticism or literary theory adopt a roughly chronological arrangement for organisational or explanatory purposes and there is a sense in which to analyse criticism at all is to re-write its history.

An effect of traditional historical categories when applied to the past of criticism is that they seem to impose a condition of cultural distance on the way past texts of criticism are perceived, the further effect of which is at once to immortalize and to disable the critic. Nowhere is this historicity more confidently present than in modern historical commentary on the English critics and criticism of the later seventeenth and eighteenth centuries. Dryden, according to Pat Rogers, writing in volume 4 of the *Cambridge History of Literary Criticism*, was not 'great' *per se*, but 'the greatest practising critic of the later seventeenth century';[2] Pope, according to other contributors to this volume, was locked into the conventional attitudes and prejudices of his time.[3] The broad perspectives of critical historians on the Augustan writers are reflected with equal negativity in the perspectives of modern critics on the precise historical value of Johnson. Thus Johnson, wrote Leavis famously in an influential essay published in the 1940s, is 'not for direct instruction in critical thinking'.[4] 'His mind', says John Wain, in an Introduction to a collection of Johnson's criticism published around thirty years later, 'was not a modern mind'.[5] Even a specialist student of Johnson such as William Edinger has recently claimed that Johnson's taste is 'not only radically discontinuous with our own preferences but also frustratingly beyond the reach of sympathetic imagination' and exhibits (in his 'Life of Cowley') the 'unbridgeable gulf of paradigmatic difference' between Johnson and ourselves.[6]

But this question of what value criticism has when it is 'not for direct instruction in critical thinking', a suggestion conscious of its own low risk as an incitement to antithetical views, seems to depend on how far we are inclined to see the culture of the present and the culture of the past in oppositional terms, and on how far we can be persuaded that the critical past can sometimes mingle directly and freely with the thoughts and feelings of the critical present, to improve and refine it. My proposition in this study, with reservations I shall shortly explore in this chapter, is that in order to understand the relationship between the past of criticism and the critical present, between what used to be done in the name of criticism and what is called criticism today, Ricoeur's notion of the 'reality of the past', and Collingwood's notions of history as 're-enactment', and as 'self-knowledge',[7] can be most usefully revived. Making sense of the past of criticism, I shall argue, calls for what once was termed an 'idealist' conception of history; it admits into the study of critical history what Hans Robert Jauss has termed an 'aesthetics of reception'.[8] Implicit within this is a humbling recognition of one's own imminent historicization - as Johnson himself recalls when commenting on the aggression of the earlier eighteenth-century editors of Shakespeare toward their dead predecessors:

> I know not why our editors should, with such implacable anger, persecute their predecessors. *Οἱ νεκροὶ μὴ δάκνουσιν,* the dead it is true can make no resistance, they may be attacked with great security; but since they can neither feel nor mend, the safety of mauling them seems greater than the pleasure; nor perhaps would it much misbeseem us to remember, amidst our triumphs over the 'nonsensical' and the 'senseless', that we likewise are men; that *debemur morti,* and as Swift observed to Burnet. shall soon be among the dead ourselves. (*Shakespeare,* 8: 985)[9]

What is a History of Literary Criticism?

Let us begin by considering more closely some of the senses in which history and criticism penetrate each other. In the normal course, though not uncontroversially, the study of past literature is in some sense an effort of historical comprehension. Criticism includes the study of the history of literature, its contexts outside literature in the passage of political and social events, its literary continuities, its revolutions and laws. However the articulation of criticism and history that best lends itself to critical investigation is to be found in the history of criticism as a literary genre. What Michel de Certeau has termed 'the writing of history', and the connections between historical composition and literary creation, especially fictional narrative, have received an unusual quantity of attention from literary theorists in the last few years. 'Recently', writes David Perkins of the institutions of literary history:

> our awareness of the omnipresence of rhetoric in discourse has been growing. Thirty years ago, literary studies and the social sciences were in separate compartments; in each, the work of the other was more or less ignored. Literary critics studied rhetoric and fictional representation, and historians (and even literary historians) made representations of the past without considering that these were rhetorical in form and were even, in many cases, like literary fictions. Now, however, we increasingly see that the past is necessarily transformed in the effort to represent it discursively.[10]

The generic characteristics of the writing of critical history can, in their turn, transform the past of criticism, and its meaning for the present, by different uses and variant interpretations of historical form. In different ways and at different lengths, Terry Eagleton's short book *The Function of Criticism*, George Watson's earlier introductory volume *The Literary Critics*, George Saintsbury's great pioneering work, or the substantial histories of J.W.H. Atkins, J.E. Spingarn, René Wellek, or René Bray's *La formation de la doctrine classique en France* all capture the 'shape of the past' in its critical aspect. And since this past of criticism - like that of everything else in the world - lengthens with time, the past portrayed by histories of criticism is endlessly open to addition and to change. But amongst the reasons for change is also that different things within the past are valued as criticism by different historians. The past of criticism is subjected *to* criticism, and this critical perspective upon the past is defined by the operation of value judgments: some things are counted into the history of criticism and some things out. Selection is an indispensable requirement in the construction of historical narrative, a necessity of its discursive impetus and pace.

A further influence on the shape of the critical past occurs with the burgeoning industries of academic research. As time goes by more things are brought into the sum total of criticism by research or are revived in its hothouse. George Saintsbury's turn-of-the-century history of criticism ran to three large volumes. The new *Cambridge History of Literary Criticism* has nine. The shape of the past of criticism thus changes with its expanding bulk. The 'theory explosion' of the last three decades, the huge development of critical writing in colleges and schools for educational and assessment purposes (what university department of English does *not* have a program in critical theory or critical thought?), the proliferation of literary journalism in newspapers and magazines of all kinds, all 'end-load' the shape of the critical past in ways the historian cannot ignore.

Among the problems of critical history that need most to concern us in studying Johnson (aesthetically and historiographically) is how, precisely, historians regard the material of criticism and how they relate this material to the critical present from which perspective they are surveying the past. In Chapter 6 of the third volume of *Time and Narrative*, Paul Ricoeur confronts the problem of what we are saying 'when we say that something "really" happened in the past'.[11] Proposing an analytical framework composed of the 'Same', the 'Other', and the 'Analogous', Ricoeur turns to Collingwood's *Idea of History* and the argument that the historian must re-enact the past in the present, and must do so through an effort of historical imagination which is *both* a process of self-realization (consciousness of one's own thought) and an interrogation of the historical texts. 'Re-enactment', Collingwood had written, is 'not a passive surrender to the spell of another's mind; it is a labour of active and therefore critical thinking'.[12] Are we not, asks Ricoeur in the same vein, 'ourselves made contemporaries of past events by a vibrant reconstruction of their intertwining? In short, is the past intelligible any other way than as persisting in the present?'[13] But if this conception of historical re-enactment, or reconstruction, is to organize the materials of critical history, we must, with Ricoeur, also juxtapose the 'Sign of the Same' with the 'Sign of the 'Other', and move from a position of empathy with the leading principles of Collingwood's theory of re-enactment to Ricoeur's 'Negative Ontology of the Past' where 'many contemporary historians see in history an affirmation of otherness'.[14] The past of criticism might be esteemed historically according to the value we place on the extended community of *other* people; but, warns Ricoeur, '[w]hen curiosity gains the upper hand over sympathy, the stranger becomes alien', and '[t]he difference that separates gets substituted for the difference that binds together'.[15]

The history of criticism may in this light tend to conflate the critical past too often with a history of dead (unre-enactable) ideas. The classification and emplotment of largely redundant theories within intellectual history, playing no immediate role in critical speculations or decisions of the present day, will suggest only 'the difference that separates' and not 'the difference that binds together'. The ideas are neither the 'Same' as those of the present, nor do they persist into the present because they are 'Other' in the sense that Ricoeur seeks to define - as parts of the past from which the present might learn, as readers today might learn about ancient and modern literature from the community of past critics. Most historicizations of Johnson's criticism are like this, and have been defended as such. 'It should be frankly recognized', writes René Wellek:

> that the history of criticism is a topic which has its own inherent interest, even without relation to the history of the practice of writing: it is simply a branch of the history of ideas which is in only loose relationship with the actual literature produced at the time. No doubt one can show the influence of the theory on the practice and, to a minor degree, of the practice on the theory, but this is a new and difficult question which should not be confused with the internal history of criticism .... The historian of criticism need only ask what Wordsworth meant by his doctrine, whether what he said makes sense, and what were the context, the background, and the influence on other critics of his theory....[16]

But not only are works of literature (as here) themselves not easily summarized merely as acts of thought - the emotional life or content of such works being notoriously regarded as their inspiration - the capacity to engage with the particulars of literary works, and sympathize with intense emotion, is also the distinctive role of the literary critic. The critic, according to Leavis (in an essay replying to Wellek's review of Leavis's *Revaluation*), is distinguished from the philosopher by an emotional intelligence where:

> His first concern is to enter into possession of the given poem ... in its concrete fulness, and his constant concern is never to lose his completeness of possession, but rather to increase it. In making value-judgements (and judgements as to significance), implicitly or explicitly, he does so out of that completeness of possession and with that fullness of response.[17]

The critic, wrote D.H. Lawrence, is not a scientist but must be able to '*feel* the impact of a work of art in all its complexity and its force'.[18]

But in Wellek's argument from the history of 'thought', the problem in the study of Johnson's criticism must also be the classificatory constructions or '"super-personal" entities or "forces"', as Isaiah Berlin terms them, 'whose evolution is identified with human history'.[19] Most of these entities are ' - isms', collections of texts and critics into 'schools and movements' or cultural gestalts, and they seem in one respect to have us see different ages as self-enclosed, or externally related: we are at the end of a scale or series marked by spaces on an imaginary line. My suggestion is that this commitment to the history of criticism as a history of systems, their elements selected heuristically according to the cultural generalization supposed to prevail at the time, has tended to obscure the inter-cultural grounds of emotional agency in the dead critics (Ricoeur's 'other' people) whose quite different imaginative worlds one might want to inhabit - Dryden's belief that Juvenal gives ... [him] 'as much pleasure as ... [he] can bear'; Pope's love of 'that unequal'd Fire and Rapture, which is so forcible in *Homer*'; Johnson's own pity and pain at the death of Cordelia.[20] Accordingly the reconsideration of Johnson's criticism in the chapters that follow will focus primarily upon Johnson's de-structuring responses to, and judgments upon, actual authors and actual works. Particular responses and judgments are explored in some detail as an antidote to the narrative of a developmental history and reductive historical contextualism, and as the most frequent casualty within the stubbornly 'neo-positive' historical construction of criticism. The re-reading of Johnson that takes place in this book is thus offered as a response to the problem of major historical form.

To suggest what might in practice be meant by 'emotional agency' as an element within the history of criticism, I will quote a second example from Johnson's Shakespearean work:

> V.ii.66 OTHELLO. Oh perjur'd woman! thou dost stone my heart,
>   And mak'st me call, what I intend to do,
>   A murder, which I thought a sacrifice.

> This line [68] is difficult. 'Thou hast hardened my heart, and makest me' kill thee with the rage of a 'murderer', when 'I thought to have sacrificed' thee to justice with the calmness of a priest striking a victim.

It must not be omitted, that one of the elder quartos reads, 'thou dost stone *thy* heart'; which I suspect to be genuine. The meaning then will be, 'thou forcest me' to dismiss thee from the world in the state of the 'murdered' without preparation for death, 'when I intended' that thy punishment should have been 'a sacrifice' attoning for thy crime.

I am glad that I have ended my revisal of this dreadful scene. It is not to be endured. (*Shakespeare*, 8: 1045)

Since the nineteenth century in one sense invented developmental history, it should not be surprising that conceptions of the critical past in an age of theory encode, or allegorize, nineteenth-century cultural and narrative norms and that they encourage a contextualism whose tendency is to anchor the text in the past. But such direct Johnsonian testimony - with reference here to the major tragedy he had used in the *Preface* to refute the criticisms of Shakespeare made by Voltaire - resists the history of criticism organized as a sequence of synthetic cultural types, epistemes or traditions that unfold through time, and it cuts across the narrative of rational progress leading to the rejection of reason: structuralism to poststructuralism, modernism to postmodernism, classic to romantic. Johnson's 'It is not to be endured' - the 'full-outness' of which terminates the editorial comment in mid stream - precisely reflects the twentieth-century demand of D.H. Lawrence for the critic's 'sincere and vital emotion',[21] as it does Leavis's call for the critic ideally to 'possess' in re-created form the experience of a work. Its value is the paradox that while criticism is set at a distance of dignified neutrality by history, the facts of its past may be more than the sum of its theories, and make sense in a 'world' not dominated by teleology and causality leading to the golden dawn of the romantic age or the enlightened 'anti-enlightenment' of cultural postmodernity. Later theorists seem once again to have found the right formula here. In the terms that Hans-Georg Gadamer defined the meaning of the 'classical' (and by implication refreshed our sense of what the 'neoclassical' is) Johnson, as this book aims to suggest, can '[say] something to the present as if it were said specifically to it'.[22]

Johnson's Criticism and Historical Representation in Practice

Readers who looked for information on Samuel Johnson in a history of criticism might want to know what 'criticism' Johnson wrote and when it appeared; they might want summaries of his critical opinions and examples of his literary tastes, or to discover what influence he had in his time and who influenced him. But in meeting these needs - as Perkins has argued of the history of literature - the history of criticism is no more a transparent medium than other kinds of historical or literary text. Historiographical theory has uses in reminding us of the textuality, the inescapable 'literariness', of historical writing, and its perception, I have suggested, can be extended to the writing of critical history. Histories of criticism construct their narratives out of generalized entities, groups of critical texts, schools, movements, theories and rules, dramas of decorum or revolution, according to a complex system of textual transformation, interpolation, illustration and motivation appropriate to the archetype they are working within. They exhibit by these means their 'point of view' on the critical past. While, in Paul Ricoeur's terms, all histories owe an unexpired 'debt' to the past that works of fiction do not, histories of criticism are in their own way creative works. They have a foot in the story-telling tradition, in tragedy, romance or comedy, and in the making, maintenance and exploitation of powerful images or conceptual myths.[23] They may register a rise or decline in the health or value of criticism. They may be philosophically optimistic or convey a pessimistic view.

The textuality of the history of criticism thus conditions the 'presence' of Johnson's criticism, and imposes important restraints on its conception *as* criticism as we read it today: representations of Johnson's criticism in histories of criticism over the last one hundred years have not changed in essentials, and they project an image of Johnsonian criticism that is invariably designed to justify the revolt of the romantic critics and the ascendancy of the 'Romantic Age'.[24] All three major twentieth-century histories of criticism that give space to Johnson in different intellectual climates (Saintsbury's of 1905, René Wellek's of 1955 and the recently published volume 4 of *The Cambridge History of Literary Criticism* of 1997), can confidently utilize 'neoclassicism' as the temporal and dialectical priority of their narrative scheme. In so doing they reinforce the consciousness of 'rules' (and a rule-governed mentality of a more general kind) against which the history of criticism must assert its self-consequence and success and must define its progress toward an unassailable present. Under the rubric of 'Eighteenth-Century Orthodoxy', Saintsbury can, for example, claim that Johnson's tastes and attitudes as critic were formed by a 'limited theory of English verse' derived from Dryden and from Pope, and that 'the critical school in which he had been brought up was strictly neo-classic'. Johnson's 'general critical attitude' was one of rigidity from which he could never entirely escape:

> in the four great documents of *The Rambler*, *Rasselas*, the Shakespeare *Preface*, and the *Lives*, we see it in the two first rigid, peremptory, in the *Preface*, curiously and representatively uncertain, in the last conditioned by differences which allow it somewhat freer play, and at some times making a few concessions, but at others more pugnacious and arbitrary than before.[25]

Wellek, too, is inclined to award Johnson marks according to his freedom from neoclassic rules: 'While Johnson ... is liberal in the matter of decorum in characterization, he holds firmly to neoclassical views about decorum in language'.[26] Once again, Johnson's critical attitudes are explained by early influences: 'Dr Johnson's ear must have been early attuned only to the heroic couplet, whose niceties and differences he was obviously very well able to perceive and to describe', so that 'Johnson is ... firmly rooted and even enclosed in the taste of his own age'.[27]

Somewhat more surprising (given the volume's otherwise clear ambitions to be up to date on matters of historical organization and its contrasting commitment to encyclopaedic form), is that a developmental narrative of liberation from bondage and enchainment can at times govern how Johnson's criticism is talked about in the 1997 *Cambridge History* - where we find the following:

> although Johnson lends his authority to the challenge to the unities, he forgoes the appeal to the imaginative participation in dramatic illusion which was to be so essential to those younger dramatists and critics who came to see themselves as renewers of the Shakespearean tradition. In other respects his criticism tended to adhere to neo-classical principles of generic purity, decorum and poetic justice which had been dominant over the extended period he had devoted to the work of editorship, and which continued to play a part in dramatic criticism, alongside the various innovations, until the turn of the century.[28]

Two observations regarding the historical representation of Johnson's criticism can now be made: (i) the extraordinary *inertia* of historical accounts of past literary criticism whereby a history published in 1997 can - with all the differences of cultural situation, formal variation and contemporary context that hold them apart - adopt more or less the same interpretive framework as a history published in 1905; (ii) the sense of *superiority* implicit in the tendency of historians of criticism to conceive their material in terms of intellectual constructs, and the seeming impossibility of thinking of this material in any other way. The historian locates the work of an earlier critic at a conceptually more primitive stage in the development of the logical subject of the history than his own. Hence the explanatory value accorded to the defects of Johnson the Man - as when Saintsbury (like Macaulay before him) constructs a caricature based on Johnson's variously alleged physical and temperamental eccentricities and ailments. Johnson, according to Saintsbury, approached the task of criticism with his mind made up, with a natural Toryism and a 'transcendental scepticism'. Being near-sighted, he was 'entirely insensible of the beauties of nature', and 'liked human society in its most artificial form - that provided by towns, clubs, parties'. Predictably enough, Johnson has no ear for poetry except for 'an extremely regular and almost mathematical beat of verse'.[29]

Saintsbury's tale of cheerful inconsistency and dogmatism in Johnson creates a trivially comic persona (where Toryism and visual or aural impairment are logically linked). Wellek's account some half a century later is darker in tone. Johnson is here a transitional mind in turmoil, suspended at mid-point between the fixed statutes of neoclassical theory and the freedoms of a romantic aesthetic; his consciousness is the site of a cultural schizophrenia in which the field of conflict is his mentality and the inner narrative a tragedy of psychic incoherence. The historian can accordingly stand in a position of superior modernity to Johnson that makes even his praise seem faint:

> Johnson's concept of poetic justice is not always so obtusely literal minded.... it is impossible to dismiss him as a mere moralist or expounder of a realistic view which confounds art and life.... He recognizes that realism is not enough.... Johnson correctly grasps what modern aestheticians would call 'aesthetic distance'.[30]

Wellek stresses the difficulty Johnson found in reconciling concepts that there is no evidence he actually used as critical terms: so, 'realism', 'moralism' and 'abstractionism' are dealt with by Johnson 'apparently without a clear consciousness that these criteria lead to very different conclusions about the nature of art and the value of particular works of art'.[31]

As an important adjunct to the radical historiography of Collingwood and Ricoeur, Isaiah Berlin has rightly insisted that just as we convict historians for their bias and distortions, so the notion of bare facts untainted by interpretation or arrangement is equally mythological. Indeed, the alternative to a history biased only by being incomplete is the past itself. But there comes a point where the historical patterning of Wellek's account of Johnson's significance offends too deeply against the canons of verification which we ordinarily apply to what does not change whoever is looking at it, and where what is left out of the account seems too elementary. Instances tackled in the present study include Wellek's writing that 'Johnson frequently required poetical justice', but without revealing that Johnson rarely uses this term; that Johnson complained of 'Shakespeare's lack of morality', but without mentioning the extraordinary praise of Shakespeare's moral power in the *Preface* and his sensitivity to questions of right and wrong in his notes; that Johnson's conception of genius has 'none of the romantic connotations' without recalling Johnson's most telling elaboration of the term 'genius' in his 'Life of Pope'; that 'Johnson cannot show any interest in the new theory of creative imagination', while neglecting Johnson's enthusiasm for 'the current of the poet's imagination' in *King Lear*; that in versification and diction Pope is 'the summit of perfection' for Johnson, without reference to the many qualifying judgments of Pope in the 'Life' (not least Johnson's passage on the luxurious language of the translation of Homer).[32]

There is, once more however, no *essential* difference between the certainties of Wellek's history (now nearly half a century old), with its unsubstantiated image of Johnson, and what can be confidently said of Johnson's criticism in the 1997 *Cambridge History*. Again the deviation from what is ascertainable through the canons of verification seems too gross; but the provisionality and incompleteness of this work is not mitigated by the scholarly conditions prevailing when a mid-twentieth-century history was conceived, and was unable to avail itself of the vast expansion in historical knowledge about Johnson since the Second World War.[33] In contrast to the 'Histories' of Saintsbury and Wellek the editors of this latest volume opt not to devote a separate chapter or section to Johnson's critical oeuvre, but point out that 'criticism remained an ancillary, or at least a secondary activity' in the eighteenth century, and that 'The Arnoldian idea of the function of criticism, and its attendant sense of the importance of the critic's calling, seldom appear'[34] - a generalization which may seem oddly unconscious historically in the light of the contents and influence of the *Essay on Criticism* of Pope, its central passage in praise of the literary critic's moral and religious vocation and the extraordinary tribute to the poem, in his 'Life of Pope', that Johnson accorded him:

> One of his greatest earliest works is the *Essay on Criticism*, which if he had written nothing else would have placed him among the first critics and the first

poets, as it exhibits every mode of excellence that can embellish or dignify didactick composition, selection of matter, novelty of arrangement, justness of precept, splendour of illustration, and propriety of digression. I know not whether it be pleasing to consider that he produced this piece at twenty, and never afterwards excelled it: he that delights himself with observing that such powers may be so soon attained, cannot but grieve to think that life was ever after at a stand. (*Lives*, 3: 228-29)

Once again, statements by Johnson are taken out of the context of Johnson's individual achievement by the *Cambridge History* (as that of a critical life worthy of historical treatment on its own terms) to be re-absorbed into the fabric of eighteenth-century critical theory. Thus the possibilities of Johnson's contribution to criticism are shrunken by history.[35] But what seems most crucially missing, I would suggest, is a sense of the historical significance of moments in the criticism of the seventeenth and eighteenth centuries where subjectivities are invaded, where critical testimony cannot be reduced to historicizable doctrines or classifying generalizations, to epistemes or the products of a prevailing *Geist* or gestalt, and where the criticism is nothing more, and nothing less, than an act of personal witness, moral, aesthetic, emotional or religious. History which fails to take such moments into account will, I argue, convey too narrow a present experience of the past of criticism to refute the view that Johnson's criticism is 'not for direct instruction in critical thinking', or that 'His mind, whatever else it may have been, was not a modern mind'.[36] It will thus fail to be sufficiently critical as history.

In seeking to expose to criticism the most pervasive images of Johnson and of judgment, we will therefore need to look more closely at the inferences to be drawn from Johnson's major critical statements (or more often his evocations of poetry and his emotional response to literary works) when they are of this kind, and at the texts of criticism on which the supposition of his representative role in the history of criticism is most often based. Initially, we will want to consider how far historians are correct to insist that both the Shakespearean criticism of the 1760s and the later *Lives of the Poets* were rooted in principles that Johnson had acquired in the earliest part of his literary career. In this connection, we will need to consider not only the principles of criticism in their alleged coherence with the changing cultural totalities of 'classic to romantic', but the more holistic 'idea of criticism' from which Johnson's critical practice arose.

Here the immediate task is to put back a sense of the integrity, intellectual *and* emotional personality of the critic - the conception of internal biography and immediate aesthetic experience, immediately apprehended, the textual detail and distinction that cultural historicization tends to take out. Before therefore moving on to the later criticism of the *Preface* and the *Lives* on which Johnson's claims to historical value must ultimately be based, I will begin by surveying the essays on criticism in the *Rambler* and the *Idler*. These essays are predictive of the mature criticism of Johnson in more subtle and more positive ways than could be achieved by the construction of intellectual context, a theoretical system or Johnson's integration within a narrative of theory. In what they leave out, they point to the tentativeness that is necessary to generalization about Johnson and about his critical origins, his contexts, and the kinds of relations these contexts have to the critical texts. In what they include they point to the movement away from the abstraction of theory, and towards concrete judgment, within Johnson's critical practice. Moreover, in inviting a transition of attention from the intellectual or theoretical content of critical history to matters of tone, and to other aesthetic characteristics of criticism, they enable us to determine what choice in the matter of principle Johnson had, and, above all, how *seriously* he took 'criticism'.

Notes

---

[1] Michel de Certeau, *The Writing of History*, trans. Tom Conley (New York: Columbia University Press, 1988), 3.

[2] *Cambridge History*, 4: 365.

[3] Pat Rogers, writing in vol. 4 of the *Cambridge History* of 1997, remarks for instance on 'the relative conventionality of ... [Pope's] *Essay on Criticism*' (371).

[4] F.R. Leavis, 'Johnson as Critic', 187.

[5] John Wain, Introduction, *Johnson as Critic* (London: Routledge and Kegan Paul, 1973), 55.

[6] William Edinger, *Johnson and Detailed Representation: The Significance of the Classical Sources* (English Literary Studies Monograph Series, no. 72. Victoria, B.C.: University of Victoria, 1997), 8; 75. Though 'few ... will be disposed to deny that his [Johnson's] was one of the most powerful and experienced minds ever to operate upon literary data', yet 'many will surely feel', writes Jean Hagstrum - in what is still the standard book-length study of Johnson's criticism - 'that his example is not one to be followed in our day'. See *Samuel Johnson's Literary Criticism* (1952; rpt. Chicago: University of Chicago Press, 1967), xvii.

[7] *The Idea of History* (1946), ed. Jan van der Dussen (Oxford: Oxford University Press, 1994), 205-31, esp. 215-28.

[8] See Hans Robert Jauss, 'Literary History as a Challenge to Literary Theory', *Toward an Aesthetic of Reception*, trans. Timothy Bahti (Minneapolis: University of Minnesota Press, 1982), 3-45.

[9] Johnson's notes to Shakespeare's *Hamlet*, iii.ii.124.

[10] David Perkins, *Is Literary History Possible?* (Baltimore and London: Johns Hopkins University Press, 1992), 19.

[11] Paul Ricoeur, *Time and Narrative*, trans. Kathleen Blamey and David Pellauer, 3 vols. (Chicago and London: University of Chicago Press, 1988), 3: 142.

[12] *The Idea of History*, 215.

[13] Ricoeur, 3: 144.

[14] Ricoeur, 3: 147.

[15] Ricoeur, 3: 149.

[16] Wellek, 1: 7.

[17] F.R. Leavis, 'Criticism and Philosophy', *The Common Pursuit* (London: Chatto and Windus, 1952), 213.

[18] D.H. Lawrence, 'John Galsworthy', in *Phoenix: The Posthumous Papers of D.H. Lawrence*, ed. Edward D. McDonald (London: Heinemann, 1936), 539.

[19] See Isaiah Berlin, 'Historical Inevitability' (1954), *Four Essays on Liberty* (Oxford: Oxford University Press, 1969), 45. Historians' reduction of the history of eighteenth-century criticism to a sequence of empty abstractions was trenchantly criticized as an

institutionalized misconception by R.S. Crane in his 'On Writing the History of Criticism in England 1650-1800' (1953), *The Idea of the Humanities and other essays Critical and Historical*, 2 vols. (Chicago and London: University of Chicago Press, 1967), 2: 157-75.

[20] See John Dryden, 'A Discourse Concerning Satire', *Of Dramatic Poesy and Other Critical Essays*, ed. George Watson, 2 vols. (London: Everyman, 1962), 2: 130; Alexander Pope, 'Preface to the *Iliad*', *Homer*, 7: 4; Samuel Johnson, *Shakespeare*, 8: 704.

[21] *Phoenix*, 539.

[22] Hans-Georg Gadamer, *Truth and Method*, 2nd rev. ed., trans. Joel Weinsheimer and Donald G. Marshall (London: Sheed and Ward, 1989), 289-90. Readers may be reminded at this point of the admirable study by Leopold Damrosch Jr., *The Uses of Johnson's Criticism* (Charlottesville: University of Virginia Press, 1976). While I share the general assumptions about Johnson's critical pertinence held by Damrosch, I do not always accept the reasons he maintains them, nor always his particular readings and judgments of Johnson.

[23] 'Unlike novels', writes Paul Ricoeur, 'historians' constructions do not aim at being *re*constructions of the past. Through documents and their critical examination of documents, historians are subject to what once was. They owe a debt to the past, a debt of recognition to the dead, that makes them insolvent debtors'. See Ricoeur, 3: 142-43.

[24] They thus overlook the representation of the single quality that criticism capable of making history would seem to require - radical independence of judgment and individual freedom of choice. Isaiah Berlin explains how all deterministic theories of history have one common characteristic - 'the implication that the individual's freedom of choice ... is ultimately an illusion, that the notion that human beings could have chosen otherwise than they did usually rests upon ignorance of facts'. See 'Historical Inevitability' (1954), *Four Essays on Liberty*, 58.

[25] Saintsbury, *A History of Criticism*, 2: 479-80.

[26] Wellek, 1: 90. For Leopold Damrosch Jr. Wellek's chapter on Johnson in *A History of Modern Criticism* is 'The most serious modern attack on Johnson's qualifications as a critic'. See *Samuel Johnson and the Tragic Sense* (Princeton: Princeton University Press, 1972), 208. From the point of view of the present argument, it is significant that this 'most serious modern attack' should occur within an historical account of Johnson's value.

[27] Wellek, 1: 92-93.

[28] *Cambridge History*, 4: 206.

[29] *History*, 2: 478-79.

[30] Wellek, 1: 83, 84, 85, 89.

[31] Wellek, 1: 87.

[32] Wellek, 1: 83, 84, 96, 103. 'Johnson's defence of Pope's translation of Homer' (*Lives*, 3: 239) is for Wellek an instance only of 'the historical argument' (103).

[33] For a recent survey of this expansion see Greg Clingham, 'Resisting Johnson' in *Johnson Re-Visioned: Looking Before and After*, ed. Philip Smallwood (Lewisburg: Bucknell University Press, 2001), 19-36.

[34] *Cambridge History*, 4: xvi-xvii.

[35] And in even its most recent and sophisticated of forms. Here the history of criticism echoes the fragmentations of authorial integrity in the postmodern *literary* history; see, for example, Perkins's chapter on 'The Postmodern Encyclopedia', *Is Literary History Possible?*, 53-60.

[36] Wain, *Johnson as Critic*, 55. Amongst recent scholars G.F. Parker has written of the need for 'Taking Johnson Seriously'. Parker's 'historicization' of Johnson involves a subtle interplay between past and present perspectives, and his study largely succeeds in its endeavours 'to grasp Johnson's meaning sympathetically enough to begin to see Shakespeare through Johnson's eyes, and to reflect on the implications of his appreciation for our own ways of reading'. See *Johnson's Shakespeare* (Oxford: Clarendon Press, 1989), 1.

On the basis of the historical methodologies employed more generally by critics and historians of criticism, the value of Johnson's criticism is one domain where T.S. Eliot's doctrine seems (exceptionally) *not* much regarded. In 'Johnson as Critic and Poet' (1944), *On Poetry and Poets* (London: Faber and Faber, 1957), Eliot had written of the *Lives of the Poets* that: 'Their first value is a value which all study of the past should have for us: that it should make us more conscious of what we are, and of our own limitations, and give us more understanding of the world in which we live'. 'Their secondary value', Eliot continued, 'is, that by studying them, and in so doing attempting to put ourselves at their author's point of view, we may recover some of the criteria of judgment which have been disappearing from the criticism of poetry' (192).

Chapter 2

'Only Designing to Live': Personal History and the Non-Reductive Context of Johnsonian Criticism

In Praise of Critical Folly: *The Rambler* **and** *The Idler*

Johnson's belief in the humility necessary to the literary critic, here mixed in the final paper of the *Rambler* (no. 208) with a paradoxical pride in his own achievement, and with the necessary confidence and certainty that make critical judgment possible at all, points to a conceptualization of critical performance that is both heroic and deflationary:

> Next to the excursions of fancy are the disquisitions of criticism, which, in my opinion, is only to be ranked among the subordinate and instrumental arts. Arbitrary decision and general exclamation I have carefully avoided, by asserting nothing without reason, and establishing all my principles of judgment on unalterable and evident truth. (*Rambler*, 5: 319)

It is clear that Johnson had from the first a deep fascination with the critical role, its morality, situational relations and its methods. Johnson had explored the task of the critic in the essays of the *Rambler* with increasing confidence, first allegorically and then comically and satirically. In the 'Allegory on Criticism' of *Rambler* 3, for example, the critic is depicted through the medium of a mystical vision. Criticism is seen here to have sprung from exalted sources as the 'eldest daughter of Labour and of Truth' who was at her birth 'committed to the care of Justice, and brought up by her in the palace of Wisdom'. But having evoked his high ideal of literary criticism in this paper, Johnson's aim is also to reveal its degenerate current state. The critic is now become the professional obstacle to literary merit, one of 'a certain race of men, that either imagine it their duty, or make it their amusement, to hinder the reception of every work of learning or genius, who stand as sentinels in the avenues of fame, and value themselves upon giving Ignorance and Envy the first notice of a prey'. Modern critics are like Cerberus at the gates of hell; however their bark is often worse than their bite: they can be bribed: 'I have heard how some have been pacified with claret and a supper, and others laid asleep by the soft notes of flattery' (*Rambler*, 3: 15-16).

In *Rambler* 23, 'The contrariety of criticism. The variety of objections', Johnson ridicules the critics' vulgar retreat into formulas that have long lost their meaning and force. Johnson here casts himself more emphatically in the guise of the 'Rambler', an embattled persona who speaks for the experience of all authors ill-served by literary critics. He remarks how little is to be gained by submitting one's writings to the critical scrutiny of even the friendliest reader, and then draws a contrast between the standing of a literary work - in the eyes of its critics - before and after its publication (*Rambler*, 3: 125-30). The critic of a text in manuscript form, claims Johnson, produces the kinds of 'petty cavils' that Johnson is later to scorn in defence of the practice of Shakespeare (*Shakespeare*, 7: 66), and his account appears to reflect his sympathy with the heroic solitude of the 'young enthusiast' from his second Juvenal imitation (*Poems*, 97, lines 135-75). According to the *Idler* Dick Minim is to pursue his career by listening 'very diligently day, after day, to those who talked of language and sentiments, and unities and catastrophes, till by slow degrees he began to think that he understood something of the stage' (*Idler*, 185-86). The critic of *Rambler* 23 is less innocently parasitic, less cheerfully gullible. He:

> brings an imagination heated with objections to passages, which he has yet never heard; he invokes all the powers of criticism, and stores his memory with Taste and Grace, Purity and Delicacy, Manners and Unities, sounds which, having been once uttered by those that understood them, have been since re-echoed without meaning, and kept up to the disturbance of the world, by a constant repercussion from one coxcomb to another. He considers himself as obliged to shew, by some proof of his abilities, that he is not consulted to no purpose, and, therefore, watches every opening for objection, and looks round for every opportunity to propose some specious alteration. Such opportunities a very small degree of sagacity will enable him to find. (*Rambler*, 3: 127)

Johnson goes on to argue that the critic is not the ultimate arbiter in matters of literary taste, and he comments that there is always 'an appeal from domestick criticism to a higher judicature': 'the publick, which is never corrupted, nor often deceived, is to pass the last sentence upon literary claims' (*Rambler*, 3: 128) - a statement that looks forward to the rather differently conceived, as it is indicatively more broadly imagined, 'appeal open from criticism to nature', which in the *Preface to Shakespeare* condones Shakespearean practices contrary to 'the rules of criticism' (*Shakespeare*, 7: 67).

Anticipations and Expectations: the Endurance of Critical Comedy

But how far, in more general terms, do the periodical papers establish clear expectations of what is to come in Johnson's criticism in later years and the extent of its doctrinal commitments, and how far is the criticism of these papers consistent with Johnson's acquiring his central theories and principles of judgment unshakably in early life? Traditional historicizations, I suggest, appear not to do justice to the unheralded and often surprizing nature of Johnsonian judgments, the relationship of these judgments to the literary works Johnson contemplates at the time, nor the broad traditional affinities and contexts of creative inspiration through which he addressed himself to his future. But nor do they seem to recognize the promise of the early papers as part of Johnson's conception of criticism, as not primarily verbal and theoretical anticipations, but more crucially I would suggest, in terms of the satire on critics that we find everywhere in them. Such comedy both belongs to the *oeuvre* of Johnson's criticism and is at the same time a reflective context of its critical maturity.

Not that Johnson does not often have many serious observations to make about critics and criticism in the periodical papers. In *Rambler* 93 on 'The prejudices and caprices of criticism' (and in the midst of a sequence of papers on the theme of Milton's poetry), we learn that:

> In trusting ... to the sentence of a critick, we are in danger not only from that vanity which exalts writers too often to the dignity of teaching what they are yet to learn, from that negligence which sometimes steals upon the most vigilant caution, and that fallibility to which the condition of nature has subjected every human understanding; but from a thousand extrinsick and accidental causes, from every thing which can excite kindness or malevolence, veneration or contempt.
>
> Many of those who have determined with great boldness, upon the various degrees of literary merit, may be justly suspected of having passed sentence, as Seneca remarks of Claudius ... without much knowledge of the cause before them
> ....
> Criticks, like all the rest of mankind, are very frequently misled by interest. (*Rambler*, 4: 131-32)

Johnson concludes this paper without any trace of the irony that is to accompany his characteristic thought about critics. The 'duty of criticism', he writes at this point, 'is neither to depreciate, nor dignify by partial representations, but to hold out the light of reason, whatever it may discover; and to promulgate the determinations of truth, whatever she shall dictate' (4: 134).

Johnson's sense of the 'duty of criticism' (as he defines it in this *Rambler* paper) is by the same token solemnly to expose the 'accidental causes' that have given rise to dubious or corrupt received ideas. Much of the theory of the *Rambler*, like the theoretical digressions of the *Preface* and the *Lives*, is consistent with this aim. Thus in *Rambler* 4 (on 'romance'), Johnson distinguishes the old definition of romances whose moral inefficacy is to remove the reader from the world, from modern novels whose morality is their approximation to life.[1] The proximity to real experience of works of fiction 'such as exhibit life in its true state' (*Rambler*, 3: 19) imposes a responsibility upon writers, claims Johnson, because where fictions 'are diversified only by accidents that daily happen in the world, and influenced by passions and qualities which are really to be found in conversing with mankind', the standards of practical conduct are destined to decline:

> when an adventurer is levelled with the rest of the world, and acts in such scenes of the universal drama, as may be the lot of any other man; young spectators fix their eyes upon him with closer attention, and hope by observing his behaviour and success to regulate their own practices. (3: 19, 21)

The method that Johnson adopts in *Rambler* 60 (on biographical writing) is again to question the historical status quo and to engage in more subtle terms with the 'reality' of literature. Johnson distinguishes bad biographers who assemble 'a chronological series of actions or preferments' (3: 322), or confine themselves to the 'most prominent and observable particularities, and the grosser features of ... mind' (3: 323) from those who approximate to what he is later to call 'general nature' (*Shakespeare* 7: 61):

> All joy or sorrow for the happiness or calamities of others is produced by an act of the imagination, that realises the event however fictitious, or approximates it however remote, by placing us, for a time, in the condition of him whose fortune we contemplate; so that we feel, while the deception lasts, whatever motions would be excited by the same good or evil happening to ourselves.
>
> Our passions are therefore more strongly moved, in proportion as we can more readily adopt the pains or pleasures proposed to our minds, by recognising them as our own, or considering them as naturally incident to our state of life. (*Rambler*, 3: 318-19)

Johnson is here sowing the seeds of 'general nature' (a central conception of his mature criticism): 'We are all prompted by the same motives, all deceived by the same fallacies, all animated by hope, obstructed by danger, entangled by desire, and seduced by pleasure' (3: 320). In the *Preface to Shakespeare* of 1765 no 'deception', as such, is required: the spectators are 'always in their senses'. Indeed, Shakespearean dialogue, as Johnson was later to conceive this in the *Preface*, seems 'scarcely to claim the merit of fiction, but to have been gleaned by diligent selection out of common conversation, and common occurrences' (*Shakespeare*, 7: 77; 63).[2] We see that even as early as *Rambler* 4 Johnson could write that: 'It is justly considered as the greatest excellency of art, to imitate nature' adding that: 'it is necessary to distinguish those parts of nature, which are most proper for imitation' (*Rambler*, 3: 22).

Many other papers show how far and how often, in isolated theoretical or transiently verbal terms, Johnson had anticipated his later criticism. *Rambler* 60 is devoted to the narratives of historical writing, and its principles underlie the histories of the various individual lives that Johnson was later to write.[3] Other essays discuss the relation of sound to sense in poetry eventually addressed in the 'Life of Pope', and the question of the epistle (*Rambler* 152), where the 'duty of the critic', as performed by Johnson, is to uncover the misguided assumptions of conventional doctrines. It is this procedure that Johnson himself adopts in two contiguous papers on pastoral poetry (*Ramblers* 36 and 37). Pastoral's literary history prompts Johnson's largest claims for a poetry which: 'cannot dwell upon the minuter distinctions, by which one species differs from another, without departing from that simplicity of grandeur which fills the imagination' (3: 197). Clearly, once again, such critical language evokes the terms of Johnson's critical maturity - as in his essay on the metaphysical poets in the 'Life of Cowley', for example, and in his definition of the 'sublime' in the same 'Life' as 'that comprehension and expanse of thought which at once fills the whole mind' (*Lives*,

1: 20-21). The mentalization of literary experience - fifteen years in advance of the *Lives* - is further expressed in Johnson's final note on Shakespeare's *King Lear*, a play which 'fill[s] the mind with a perpetual tumult of indignation, pity, and hope' (*Shakespeare*, 8: 703).

It is however on the humbler topic of pastoral - in a periodical essay designed to expose the absurdity of 'piscatory eclogues' - that Johnson mingles the tones that look forward in the most important ways to the detachment of his comic and ultimately more comprehensive view of the critic. Johnson's mockery of the lyrical here recalls the extempore skits he recited at the expense of the ballad,[4] but also draws on the kind of poetical parody of poetry (this time in prose) that appears in Pope:

> The sea, though in hot countries it is considered by those who live, like Sannazarius, upon the coast, as a place of pleasure and diversion, has notwithstanding much less variety than the land, and therefore will be sooner exhausted by a descriptive writer. When he has once shewn the sun rising or setting upon it, curled its waters with the vernal breeze, rolled the waves in gentle succession to the shore, and enumerated the fish sporting in the shallows, he has nothing remaining but what is common to all other poetry, the complaint of a nymph for a drowned lover, or the indignation of a fisher that his oysters are refused, and Mycon's accepted. (*Rambler*, 3: 199)

Johnson recalls the papers on pastoral later in *Rambler* 121, where he applies the same gentle art of sinking used here of the pastoral poem more widely to the *history* of poetry:

> At one time all truth was conveyed in allegory; at another, nothing was seen but in a vision; at one period, all the poets followed sheep, and every event produced a pastoral; at another they busied themselves wholly in giving directions to a painter. (4: 284)

Johnson's satirical eye is here levelled at poetry; but criticism is not for long to evade the deflationary mode.

The consciously self-parodic mode of the 'Rambler' offers a succession of satirical portraits in which a professional commitment to criticism is viewed as a characteristically urban pose. Johnson adopts the persona of Ruricola in *Rambler* 61 and has the ludicrous Mr. Frolick brag to his old acquaintance in the country of his celebrity as an arbiter of taste 'at' London. Frolick is prophetic of the '*cultural critic*' from our perspective. He makes no distinction between élite and popular culture, between - as we would call them - the privileged and the marginal. His judgment ranges unimpeded over various kinds of social and textual practice:

> But yet greater is the fame of his understanding than his bravery; for he informs us, that he is, at London, the established arbitrator of all points of honour, and the decisive judge of all performances of genius; that no musical performer is in reputation till the opinion of Frolick has ratified his pretensions; that the theatres suspend their sentence till he begins the clap or hiss, in which all are proud to

concur; that no publick entertainment has failed or succeeded, but because he
opposed or favoured it; that all controversies at the gaming-table are referred to
his determination; that he adjusts the ceremonial at every assembly, and prescribes
every fashion of pleasure or of dress. (*Rambler*, 3: 328)

Frolick recalls the milieu of eighteenth-century stage comedy. He reflects at the
same time the pictorial world of the satirical caricature, its ridicule of smug
connoisseurs, of antiquarians and of all the varieties of critical posturing and
bourgeois pretension in the society of the time. But Frolick also overlaps with
Misocapelus, the apprentice haberdasher whose fate is the subject of *Rambler* 116.
As his professional training advanced and his ambitions to politeness were fired,
Misocapelus has become by *Rambler* 123 'a critick in small wares' (4: 255). He
reflects the falling arc of illusions, the realization of the 'vanity of human wishes'
that points the moral of Johnsonian biography. Excluded from the wider social
scene, Misocapelus writes a despairing letter to the 'Rambler' and describes his
visits to a coffee house 'frequented by wits':

> among whom I learned in a short time the cant of criticism, and talked so loudly
> and volubly of nature, and manners, and sentiment, and diction, and similes, and
> contrasts, and action, and pronunciation, that I was often desired to lead the hiss
> and clap, and was feared and hated by the players and poets. Many a sentence
> have I hissed, which I did not understand, and many a groan have I uttered, when
> the ladies were weeping in the boxes. At last a malignant author, whose
> performance I had persecuted through nine nights, wrote an epigram upon Tape
> the critick, which drove me from the pit for ever.
> My desire to be a fine gentleman still continued.... (4: 294)

Less excusable, in this satirical vein, are the wits of *Rambler* 128 who fret over
the rise and fall of their reputations, and, 'if they happen to inherit wealth, often
exhaust their patrimonies in treating those who will hear them talk' (4: 318).
Another contrast is with the pretenders to criticism of *Rambler* 121 (on 'The
dangers of imitation'). These, 'instead of endeavouring by books and meditation to
form their own opinions, content themselves with the secondary knowledge, which
a convenient bench in the coffee-house can supply; and, without any examination
or distinction, adopt the criticisms and remarks, which happen to drop from those,
who have risen, by merit or fortune, to reputation and authority' (4: 281). Johnson
later touches in *Rambler* 144 on the various critical misdemeanours of 'the
envious, the idle, the peevish, and the thoughtless' (5: 7), and the irresistible
attraction of the critical life to them. The first of these is the 'Roarer' who, 'if a
new performance of genius happens to be celebrated, he pronounces the writer a
hopeless ideot, without knowledge of books or life, and without the understanding
by which it must be acquired' (5: 5). The 'Whisperer' inspires Johnson's mockery
of the eighteenth-century critical character assassin:

> Of the writer he affirms with great certainty, that though the excellence of the
> work be incontestable, he can claim but a small part of the reputation; that he
> owed most of the images and sentiments to a secret friend; and that the accuracy

and equality of the stile was produced by the successive correction of the chief criticks of the age. (5: 6)

Finally, there is the 'most pernicious enemy' of all - 'the Man of Moderation':

> Without interest in the question, or any motive but honest curiosity, this impartial and zealous enquirer after truth, is ready to hear either side, and always disposed to kind interpretations and favourable opinions.... The author he knows to be a man of diligence, who perhaps does not sparkle with the fire of Homer, but has the judgment to discover his own deficiencies, and to supply them by the help of others; and in his opinion modesty is a quality so amiable and rare, that it ought to find a patron wherever it appears, and may justly be preferred by the publick suffrage to petulant wit and ostentatious literature.
>
> He who discovers failings with unwillingness, and extenuates the faults which cannot be denied, puts an end at once to doubt or vindication; his hearers repose upon his candour and veracity, and admit the charge without allowing the excuse. (5: 6-7)

In the honing of irony at such points, and in the intermixture of social comedy, sorrow, satire and outbursts across a range of essays of unambiguous moral disdain, Johnson's early writing on criticism suggests a sceptical spirit that is carried forward into the judgments of his later work. Such a spirit suggests a further dimension to the kind of historical contextualism we apply to his work (that of tone), and how we might view the context in its relation to the text.

Critical Evolutions: From Theory to Judgment

This comedy - in being a matter of tone as the expression of content - resists historicization of Johnson's criticism entirely as a body of 'thought', and Johnson's status as a figure amenable to generalization, and to systematization by critical history, is by the same token questioned. In other aspects there is, however, much in Johnson's mature criticism that the periodical papers do not prepare for,[5] where their material can suggest only the *contrast* between the orientations of earlier and later critical work, and where the early essays supply a *deflective* context. Miscellaneous allusions to Dryden[6] and to Pope occur at many points in the *Rambler* (in *Rambler* 37 on pastoral poetry Johnson, for example, had complained that Pope imitated Dryden's version of Virgil's Eclogues in 'Autumn' and 'was carried to still greater impropriety' (3: 203), an evaluation self-borrowed in his critique of Pope's poetical diction in the 'Life').[7] But the most exhaustive treatment of any author is found in the papers on Milton (*Ramblers* 86, 88, 90, 94, 139, 140), and only two English poets, Shakespeare and Milton, receive more than intermittent attention in the essays. Attention in the periodical papers seems as frequently to fall on classical literature, or English literature's Greek and Roman roots, as on such major English writers as Dryden or Pope.

As part of this development, the significant emphasis on 'theory' in the periodical papers gives way to comprehensive assessments, acts of making up one's mind on a whole poet or poem, in all the relevant aspects, duly weighed, to be found in the *Preface* and the *Lives*. These acts of judgment subsume and displace Johnson's passing and provisional focus in the periodical papers on the details of literary forms and conventions - tragedy, comedy, heroes (such as are later rejected as concepts by Johnson[8]), or generic types - romance, pastoral, biography, imitation,[9] history, the essay, the epistle,[10] the art of translation and criticism itself (such as require to be re-defined). Key critical and stylistic ideas such as 'easy poetry', 'low' or 'hard' words or 'terrifick diction' are dealt with in specific discussions, as are such perennial problems as an author's writings in relation to his life, or the conditions of authorship. It is thus that Johnson's periodical papers suggest Johnson's unresolved struggles at this stage of his life - his ambidextrous dictionary-making in the attention to criticism's fluid technical terminology; his own frustrated editorial plans in his allusions to Shakespeare; his mixed success as a dramatist in the papers on the Greek tragedy of Milton; the relation of his past authorial preoccupations to literary history. Johnson discourses in *Rambler* 125 on the doubtful progress of tragic composition through the last one hundred years:

> There is scarce a tragedy of the last century which has not debased its most important incidents, and polluted its most serious interlocutions with buffoonery and meanness.... The later tragedies indeed have faults of another kind, perhaps more destructive to delight, though less open to censure. That perpetual tumour of phrase with which every thought is now expressed by every personage, the paucity of adventures which regularity admits, and the unvaried equality of flowing dialogue, has taken away from our present writers almost all that dominion over the passions which was the boast of their predecessors. (4: 305)

Could Johnson already be implicating his own *Irene* in these remarks?

Thus it is that a satire *upon* contemporary critical manners (rather than a tendency to carry them forward into later criticism *ahead* of judgment) should prevail in the periodical papers, and that it is at the same time more skilfully mocking of the present scene than any novel by David Lodge or any parody of modern critics by Frederick Crews. At a point in Boswell's biographical record of Johnson's various literary 'schemes', Johnson reveals that he had at one time planned a history of literary criticism from Aristotle to the present day.[11] What this projected history would have been like had it entered the canon of Johnson's published works it is interesting to speculate. Would the story of the 'rise and improvements' of criticism in Johnson's hands have in fact related a tragic tale of cultural and critical decline - much like the story that Pope tells of the descending spiral towards the present of criticism in the passage from the *Essay* (lines 631-80)? Or would it have been a 'tragi-comedy' or 'mingled drama', a chaos of coincident or conflicting positions in which Johnson is able to situate the serio-comic figure of himself? Answers to these questions (as they impact on the idea of criticism we derive from Johnson) can again be grasped by Johnson's developing and, I would argue, substantially *comic* conception of criticism in the *Rambler* or (more especially as we shall now see) the *Idler*.

Johnson, Dick Minim and Critical Self-Parody

Question: What is 'criticism'? Answer:

> Criticism is a study by which men grow important and formidable at very small expence. The power of invention has been conferred by nature upon few, and the labour of learning those sciences which may, by mere labour, be obtained, is too great to be willingly endured; but every man can exert such judgment as he has upon the works of others; and he whom nature has made weak, and idleness keeps ignorant, may yet support his vanity by the name of a critick. (*Idler*, 184)

So commence Johnson's *Idlers* 60 and 61 on Dick Minim the critic. One need make no comparison in detail between what Johnson says in these papers with today's systems of authority in literary criticism. There is the critical celebrity of Minim, his plans for an 'academy of criticism', his establishment 'of a critical society selected by himself', the opinions on literary subjects he dispenses from the 'chair of criticism' (*Idler*, 190), and his mindless mouthing of the contemporary jargon of Critical Theory.[12] All suggest the unsettling proximity of modern and minimal critical worlds, and the papers on Minim in the *Idler* fall in this respect timelessly outside the generalizations normalized by critical history. The link between the present of textual analysis and the neoclassical manners of Minim, the apprentice brewer who 'resolved to be a man of wit and humour' (*Idler*, 185), proves to be Practical Criticism of a kind that is still taught to students in schools but that Johnson regales as cliché in the 1750s.[13] The sense that we derive of the permanent follies and failings of critics here overrides any 'historical' sense that there ever was a rise or decline. The comedy cuts through the cultural divide.

To achieve his ambition, Minim could not mimic the eloquence of an armchair Marx, or an eminence of Parisian intellectual circles, but apes the pundits of the coffee-house set, with their own, earlier debt to the fashionable critics of France. Their caffeinated chat was music to his ears. Having listened to their talk, he 'hoped in time to talk himself' (186). Johnson relates how Minim soon became 'an acknowledged critick' and 'the great investigator of hidden beauties'. We are told that he was 'particularly delighted when he ... [found] "the sound an echo to the sense"' (188). Minim reflects sagely in this vein on the reasons why Butler's 'wonderful lines upon honour and a bubble have hitherto passed without notice':

> Honour is like the glassy bubble,
> Which costs philosophers such trouble,
> Where one part crack'd the whole does fly,
> And wits are crack'd to find out why.
> (189)

Johnson confides to us with exceptional solemnity at this point the extraordinary wisdom and insight of Minim's textual analysis of Butler's lines:

> In these verses, says Minim, we have two striking accommodations of the sound to the sense. It is impossible to utter the two lines emphatically without an act like

that which they describe; 'bubble' and 'trouble' causing a momentary inflation of the cheeks by the retention of the breath, which is afterwards forcibly emitted, as in the practice of 'blowing bubbles'. But the greatest excellence is in the third line, which is 'crack'd' in the middle to express a crack, and then shivers into monosyllables. Yet has this diamond lain neglected with common stones, and among the innumerable admirers of *Hudibras* the observation of this superlative passage has been reserved for the sagacity of Minim. (189)

Such exquisitely genial irony is quite different in approach from the 'Allegory on Criticism' of *Rambler* 3, and shows how far Johnson has come in his role as 'the critic as artist' whose art is to criticize the critic. The ponderous abstractions of the former paper recall the awkward gravity and strained levity of the *Vanity of Human Wishes*. The later papers from the *Rambler* and the *Idler* seem to belong more closely with the ambiguously comic and serious moment in *Rasselas*, Chapters 10-11, where Johnson's fluency is double-tongued, and Imlac's enthusiasm for his own poetic vocation is expressed in terms equally sacred to Johnson, but sceptically received by the Prince of Abyssinia: 'Enough!', cries Rasselas at Imlac's rhapsodic 'dissertation upon poetry', 'Thou hast convinced me, that no human being can ever be a poet. Proceed with thy narration' (*Rasselas*, 46). In using Minim to transfer the same kind of mingled comic and serious attention to *critics* of poetry, Johnson clears the air of all that is bogus in the critical and scholarly life, and stands on the brink of an intensified self-dedication to the work of the practising critic in the *Preface* and the *Lives*. In this the papers on Minim prepare the way for the most significant single stage in Johnson's development as a critic - the criticism of Shakespeare.

Creativity, Temporality and the Presence of Shakespeare

Here, too, the change evident within Johnson's perspective resists historical homogenization and reductive contextualism. There is both a development, where the early elements of Johnson's response are drawn together by later criticism in the *Preface*, are sifted, combined and transcended, while the elements in question do not themselves give incontrovertible cause for depressed expectations of critical success, as anticipations of *inescapable* failure with Shakespeare. Johnson's first acquaintance with Shakespeare gave him a shock. As a boy in Lichfield, and reading Shakespeare's *Hamlet* in the basement of his father's shop, he was frightened by the scene with the ghost and rushed upstairs 'that he might see people about him'.[14] Later, in the relatively unsuperstitious maturity of early middle age, Johnson published some sample notes for a planned edition of Shakespeare. In these, the *Miscellaneous Observations on the Tragedy of Macbeth* (1745),[15] he lights on a passage that arouses but also scares him. Johnson here compares the passage from Shakespeare with some famous lines from Dryden's *Indian Emperour* (1667):

Night is described by two great poets, but one describes a night of quiet, the other of perturbation. In the night of Dryden, all the disturbers of the world are laid asleep; in that of Shakespeare, nothing but sorcery, lust, and murder is awake. He that reads Dryden, finds himself lull'd with serenity, and disposed to solitude and contemplation. He that peruses Shakespeare, looks round alarmed, and starts to find himself alone. One is the night of a lover, the other that of a murderer. (*Shakespeare*, 7: 19-20)[16]

Johnson seems in these comments to be registering the naked energy and fearful power in moments from the plays of Shakespeare which make their impact without mediation. Johnson could not always feel unmixed pleasure in alarming experiences of this kind, and we have seen that there are times in Johnson's mature career where he found in Shakespeare scenes so deeply shocking that he could only face them with great reluctance and acute pain: 'if my sensations could add any thing to the general suffrage, I might relate, that I was many years ago so shocked by Cordelia's death, that I know not whether I ever endured to read again the last scenes of the play till I undertook to revise them as an editor' (*Shakespeare*, 8: 704).

But the most convenient *historical* description for these remarks will invariably suggest the negative valuation implicit in the narrative of 'classic to romantic' - a valuation most often expressive of emotions hemmed in by a fixed critical structure, reflective context, or cultural generalization, by correspondingly conservative tastes, and by an historical situation that places the restrained 'neoclassic' Johnson at a critical and cultural remove from the wild genius of Shakespeare. Thus it is that historicization can explain the critical notions of Johnson in terms of earlier writers whose work was inspired by the Greek and Roman classics (such as Dryden and Pope), and that these notions were rigid, rule-bound and unavoidable - a body of opinion that later (more enlightened) critics sympathetic to Shakespeare would have to reject. In this view, Johnson came to Shakespeare with the wrong expectations and was *inevitably* disappointed. But the coherence of this explanation of Johnson's approach to Shakespeare has always been open to question on fairly elementary grounds. Johnson's commitment to the poetry and principles of Dryden and Pope seems for example not unqualified. Johnson does not subordinate Shakespeare to Dryden; nor does he suggest that the standards he is using for valuing the one are the only standards fit to apply to the other. No single standard is unambiguously present. When Johnson brings Shakespeare and Dryden together (and the passage I have quoted is one of the rare occasions when he does), he does not take Dryden as the sole measure of Shakespeare. Indeed, in Johnson's main statements on Dryden and main statements on Shakespeare, the latter *precedes* the former by approximately fifteen years: (*Preface to Shakespeare*, 1765; *Lives of the Poets*, 1779-81).

There is, moreover, too little concrete evidence within any part of the early criticism - one way or the other - to be sure what context of interpretive background, or what preparatory contextual strands it is appropriate to apply - contrastively, symbolically, reflectively or deflectively - to the critical text. A few hints (and that is all there are) of how Johnson conceived of *any* English or European drama in advance of the *Preface* appear, as we have observed, in the *Rambler*. Thus Johnson begins the discussion of *Samson Agonistes* in *Rambler* 139 by appealing to the Aristotelian rules of tragedy and asks whether:

> a performance thus illuminated with genius, and enriched with learning, is composed
> according to the indispensable laws of Aristotelian criticism; and omitting at present
> all other considerations, whether it exhibits a beginning, a middle and an end.
> (*Rambler*, 4: 371-72)

He concludes that *Samson:*

> has a beginning and an end which Aristotle himself could not have disapproved; but it
> must be allowed to want a middle, since nothing passes between the first act and the
> last, that either hastens or delays the death of Sampson. (*Rambler*, 4: 376)

Johnson returns to the Aristotelian definition of tragedy in *Rambler* 156, arguing for
the observation of unity of action and the need for a hero. Recalling Shakespearean
'mingled drama', he pays an eloquent tribute in this paper to:

> that transcendent and unbounded genius that could preside over the passions in sport;
> who, to actuate the affections, needed not the slow gradation of common means, but
> could fill the heart with instantaneous jollity or sorrow, and vary our disposition as he
> changed his scenes.

But he also expresses critical reservations at this point:

> Perhaps the effects even of Shakespeare's poetry might have been yet greater, had he
> not counter-acted himself; and we might have been more interested in the distresses of
> his heroes had we not been so frequently diverted by the jokes of his buffoons.
> (*Rambler*, 5: 69)

Other occasions where Johnson seems to have valued 'serious' tragedy are his 1756
review of Joseph Warton's *Essay on the Genius and Writings of Pope*, where he
complained that Warton 'justly censures *Cato* for want of action and of characters; but
scarcely does justice to the sublimity of some speeches, and the philosophical
exactness in the sentiments'.[17] Three years later in *Idler* 77, Johnson praised the
soliloquy from *Cato* as 'at once easy and sublime' (*Idler*, 241).

But these, once again, are comparative details of the critical oeuvre of Johnson,
speculative and perfunctory in their theoretical purpose, and open to different
interpretations. Probably the most notorious example of this early experimentation in
criticism (judged by the number of critics who have called upon this context to
dispraise Johnson), is the comment on Shakespeare in *Rambler* 168 (26 October 1751,
5: 125-29). Here, Johnson had taken the case of another tragic set piece, again a
speech from *Macbeth*,[18] and queried Shakespeare's use of the words 'dun', 'knife' and
'blanket' as diction that is unacceptably 'low':

> When Mackbeth [sic] is confirming himself in the horrid purpose of stabbing his
> king, he breaks out amidst his emotions into a wish natural to a murderer,
>   Come, thick night!
> And pall thee in the dunnest smoke of hell,
> That my keen knife see not the wound it makes;

> Nor heav'n peep through the blanket of the dark,
> To cry, hold, hold! ---------- (*Rambler*, 5: 127)

In Shakespeare's reference to everyday domestic objects, contextually and historically-minded critics have often supposed that Johnson regarded the words 'dun', 'knife' and 'blanket' as too low for this sublimely horrific moment of Shakespearean tragedy. 'If Johnson', writes Leavis, 'can scarcely contain his "risibility" when he hears of the "avengers of guilt *peeping through a blanket*," that is because he doesn't respond fully to Shakespeare's poetry'. 'He cannot', Leavis continues, 'because his training opposes';[19] and if Johnson intends a serious negative criticism of Shakespeare here, the case would doubtless be made for concluding that he approached the task of judgment with a kind of mental block, and with fixed, culturally inappropriate rules, unchanged by any proper appreciation of Shakespearean language. And yet it seems difficult to accord an *overwhelming* importance to this isolated periodical essay. We see the topic of 'low words' does not arise again in the later criticism of Shakespeare in the *Preface*, and while there may have been a rule in Johnson's mind against low diction at the time of *The Rambler*, it is not *applied* in 1765.[20] Moreover - as even Leavis must concede[21] - if Johnson has reservations about the language of Shakespeare in this particular paper, he also writes in the same place with great warmth of Shakespeare's genius in language:

> In this passage is exerted all the force of poetry, that force which calls new powers into being, which embodies sentiment, and animates matter.... (5: 127)

Johnson was to assert categorically in *Rambler* 168 that:

> No word is naturally or intrinsically meaner than another; and our opinion therefore of words, as of other things arbitrarily and capriciously established, depends wholly upon accident and custom. (126)

It is this appreciation of the 'force of poetry' (and not after all his age's addiction to an exalted decorum of language) that in fact seems most fully to anticipate the mature criticism of Shakespeare of 1765, and is more characteristic of it at every level than any doubt about the lowness of words. There is, therefore, an altogether different kind of relation linking earlier and later criticism of Johnson, and Johnson with earlier critics, than current modes of historical contextualism (and the prefix 'neo') normally allow. Here, once again, it is possible to interpret the proximate context of the criticism non-reductively. Thus, for example, 'the force of poetry' is recalled when in the *Preface* of 1765 Johnson writes in general terms of Shakespeare that 'The effusions of passion which exigence forces out are for the most part striking and energetick' (*Shakespeare*, 7: 73), and he included examples of this power in his notes. A speech by Posthumus in Act v of *Cymbeline* is 'a soliloquy of nature, uttered when the effervescence of a mind agitated and perturbed spontaneously and inadvertently discharges itself in words. The speech, throughout all its tenour ... seems to issue warm from the heart' (*Shakespeare*, 8: 902). Johnson marked out a speech from *King John* in his notes where 'These reproaches vented against Hubert are not the words of art or policy, but the eruptions of a mind swelling with consciousness of a crime, and desirous of discharging its misery on another' (*Shakespeare*, 7: 425). More significantly, Hamlet's 'celebrated soliloquy' beginning 'To be, or not to be?' is claimed by Johnson to be 'bursting from a man distracted with contrariety of desires, and overwhelmed with the magnitude of his own purposes' and 'connected rather in the speaker's *mind*, than on his *tongue*' (my emphases, *Shakespeare*, 8: 981).

How essential to drama this transparency of poetic language actually is can be inferred from the note that Johnson first composed to *Macbeth* for the *Observations* of 1745 and then went on to include in the edition of 1765. Johnson drew attention at this point to an interpolation which 'weakened the author's sense by the intrusion of a remote and useless image into a speech bursting from a man wholly possess'd with his own present condition, and therefore not at leisure to explain his own allusions to himself' (*Shakespeare*, 7: 24-25). In the 1756 *Proposals* for the edition of Shakespeare, Johnson had recalled as characteristic of Shakespeare 'a forcible eruption of effervescent passion' (*Shakespeare*, 7: 57), and his sensitivity to Shakespeare's emotional directness appears to owe much to principles of judging, enjoying and creating established by the critical past. Pope had himself written of a speech in Homer's *Iliad* in language very similar to Johnson's utterance on Shakespeare: 'That hasty manner of Expression', he on one occasion suggests, is 'extreamly natural to a Man in Anger, who thinks he can never vent himself too soon' (*Homer*, 7: 192).

But as this last example will imply - as it is typical of many of Pope's Homeric notes - Johnson did not take his standards unselectively either from Dryden or from Pope and then apply them *to* Shakespeare, as a twenty-first-century critic might apply 'theory' to a literary text in order to expose its meaning.[22] Even the most basic chronological facts of Johnson's career will suggest this, and criteria in the *Rambler* or the *Proposals* cannot be simply *exchanged* with the criteria of the *Preface*. We shall see that the standards that matter in the construction of Johnsonian judgment emerge as part of his comprehensive estimate of Shakespeare. Whether these still seem the right standards for considering the plays is something we can go on to examine.

Rasselas, Dryden, Shakespeare and Montaigne

Johnson seems actually to have had more time for Shakespeare in his early years than for any other dramatist or poet with the possible exception of Milton. His *Miscellaneous Observations on the Tragedy of Macbeth* of 1745 was followed in 1753 by the Dedication to the *Shakespear Illustrated* of Charlotte Lennox, and in 1756 by the *Proposals* for his edition, delayed by the publication of Warburton's edition. The first edition of the *Dictionary* of 1755 contains numerous Shakespearean quotations. But Johnson was also a writer of imaginative prose, a dramatist, and a poet, and at the time when he was spending long hours with Shakespeare's plays, and deep in the midst of these labours, a re-direction of Johnson's creative energies seems to have occurred. This was the time when Johnson virtually gave up his career as a serious, public poet, and after the limited stage success of the poetic tragedy *Irene* (1749) he completely abandoned drama. The consequence or corollary of this evolution seems to be that Johnson's experience of Shakespeare comes together with a new prospect of human experience that finds its focus in the wisdom of *Rasselas* (1759), in its ease, its humanity and its comedy. Johnson discovers in *Rasselas* a relationship with the disappointments of life that is neither tragic (in the manner of Johnson's own play *Irene*), nor merely satiric (like his imitations of Juvenal). It is a view less rooted in the turbulent irritations of Johnson's personal history, or external biography, than either the somewhat abrasive *London* (1738) or the pessimistic *Vanity of Human Wishes* (1749). It implies as the latter poem cannot an unregretful comprehension of the inevitable failure of human beings to live in the present.

Written during Johnson's most intensive period of editorial work on the plays, *Rasselas* is thus the most suggestive context for comprehending Johnson's criticism of Shakespeare. In evoking at every stage and in every state of life the irony of time, and a creative relationship with this irony, *Rasselas* pre-empts the tension of Johnson's later criticism between the literary-historical past and the unchangingly human and reveals the falseness of the dichotomy between classical and Shakespearean ways of apprehending human experience. Here the interdependence of past, present and future is suggested by the cadence of Johnson's prose, by the artistry which brings studied philosophical language close to the language of poetry, and by the intimations of mutability - of the flux of human experience - that pervade the philosophy of *Rasselas*, its fictional analysis of elusive human happiness and of the 'choice of life'. In this *Rasselas* is heir to a legacy of poems which are themselves re-creations, and re-animations, of classical originals.[23] The loss of Nekayah, the Princess's maid, seems for example to produce in *Rasselas* that characteristically consolatory wisdom that runs through so much of Johnson's writings. The episode re-shapes for the Johnsonian present (as for our present as readers of a Johnsonian past) the language of Dryden's poetry as he translates the *Metamorphoses* of Ovid on Time's destructive and re-creative nature:

> 'The state of mind oppressed with a sudden calamity', said Imlac, 'is like that of the fabulous inhabitants of the new created earth, who, when the first night came upon them, supposed that day never would return. When the clouds of sorrow gather over us, we see nothing beyond them, nor can imagine how they will be dispelled: yet a new day succeeded to the night, and sorrow is never long without a dawn of ease. But they who restrain themselves from receiving comfort, do as the savages would have done, had they put out their eyes when it was dark. Our minds, like our bodies, are in continual flux; something is hourly lost and something acquired. To lose much at once is inconvenient to either, but while the vital powers remain uninjured, nature will find the means of reparation. Distance has the same effect on the mind as on the eye, and while we glide along the stream of time, whatever we leave behind us is always lessening, and that which we approach increasing in magnitude. Do not suffer life to stagnate; it will grow muddy for want of motion: commit yourself again to the current of the world'. (*Rasselas*, 126-27)

The historical foundation of this passage, Dryden's corresponding figuration of time as a stream (in the poem from, *Fables Ancient and Modern* he entitled 'Of the Pythagorean Philosophy'), leads outwards from his translation of Ovid's 'cuncta fluunt' in Book 15 of the *Metamorphoses* to a tradition of European thought in its widest and most unspecific historical range:

> Nature knows
> No stedfast Station, but, or Ebbs, or Flows:
> Ever in motion; she destroys her old,
> And casts new Figures in another Mold.
> Ev'n Times are in perpetual Flux; and run
> Like Rivers from their Fountain rowling on;
> For Time no more than Streams, is at a stay:
> The flying Hour is ever on her way;
> And as the Fountain still supplies her store,
> The Wave behind impels the Wave before;
> Thus in successive Course the Minutes run,
> And urge their Predecessor Minutes on,
> Still moving, ever new: For former Things
> Are set aside, like abdicated Kings:
> And every moment alters what is done,
> And innovates some Act till then unknown.
> (lines 260-77)[24]

In his 'Preface to *Fables*' of 1700 Dryden had written of the former part of the fifteenth book as 'the masterpiece of the whole *Metamorphoses*'.[25] Recent scholarship on Dryden's translations, sensitive to this estimate, has suggested that Dryden may have been thinking here of Francis Bacon's essay 'Of Vicissitude of Things', the book of Revelation, and the 'flying hour' of Rochester's 'Song'. There may be a play on the word 'Act' in the final line of this passage that incorporates both Dryden's personal awareness of the fundamental political and parliamentary change he had lived through in the long span of his life as a poet, and an engagement with the day-to-day technicalities of stage performances.[26] But when towards the conclusion of *Rasselas* the Egyptian catacombs recall Imlac's attention to the shortness of human life, Johnson returns to the theme of Time (with Dryden's passage behind him) to explore the folly of allowing life to glide by without choice or commitment: 'Those that lie here stretched before us, the wise and the powerful of antient times, warn us to remember the shortness of our present state: they were, perhaps, snatched away while they were busy, like us, in the choice of life' (*Rasselas*, 174). The corresponding admonition at this point is, of course, Shakespeare's:

> She should have dy'd hereafter;
> There would have been a time for such a word.
> To-morrow, and to-morrow, and to-morrow,
> Creeps in this petty pace from day to day,
> To the last syllable of recorded time;
> And all our yesterdays have lighted fools
> The way to dusty death. Out, out, brief candle!
> Life's but a walking shadow; a poor player,
> That struts and frets his hour upon the stage,
> And then is heard no more: it is a tale

Told by an idiot, full of sound and fury,
Signifying nothing.[27]

In the 1745 notes to *Macbeth*, Johnson begins annotating this passage in the matter-of-fact tone of an editor: 'It is a broken speech, in which only part of the thought is expressed'. He then offers a paraphrase: '"The Queen is dead". Macbeth. "Her death should have been deferred to some more peaceful hour; had she lived longer, *there would at length have been a time for* the honours due to her as a queen, and that respect which I owe her for her fidelity and love"'. But at this intermediate point in his note on the play, Johnson's 'official' voice opens out to the accents of the timeless commonplace, and transforms into a moving general statement of what it is like to be human and to live and die within Time:

> Such is the *world* - such is the condition of human life, that we always think *to-morrow* will be happier than to-day, but to-morrow and to-morrow steals over us unenjoyed and unregarded, and we still linger in the same expectation to the moment appointed for our end. All these days, which have thus passed away, have sent multitudes of fools to the grave, who were engrossed by the same dream of future felicity, and, when life was departing from them, were like me reckoning on to-morrow. (*Shakespeare*, 7: 41-42)

This evocation of the irony of time, which Johnson reprinted without change in his notes of 1765 (*Shakespeare*, 8: 793), links the Shakespearean text intimately with the creative classicism of Dryden. This includes such moments as Dryden's version of Horace's 9th Ode of the 1st Book:

To morrow and her works defie,
Lay hold upon the present hour
(lines 19-20)[28]

but also thoughts against the fear of death from Dryden's 1685 translation of the latter part of the third book of Lucretius. It further suggests the reverberation between this outer world of literary tradition and literary history and the inner life of a literary critic who was later to record his fear of death in his *Diary* (24 September 1773):

> But when I consider my age, and the broken state of my body, I have great reason to fear lest Death should lay hold on me, while I am yet only designing to live. (160)

'The truth is', writes Johnson via Imlac in *Rasselas*, 'no mind is much employed upon the present: recollection and anticipation fill up almost all our moments' (112). Such sentiments are accordingly reflected in the edition of Shakespeare. On Shakespeare's 'that function / Is smother'd in surmise; and nothing is, / But what is not' (also from *Macbeth*), Johnson commented:

> All powers of action are oppressed and crushed by one overwhelming image in the mind, and nothing is present to me, but that which is really future. Of things now about me I have no perception, being intent wholly on that which has yet no existence. (*Shakespeare*, 8: 760)

In a similar vein is Johnson's note to a speech from Shakespeare's *Measure for Measure* (III.i.32):

> DUKE. Thou hast nor youth, nor age;
> But as it were an after-dinner's sleep,
> Dreaming on both
> This is exquisitely imagined. When we are young we busy ourselves in forming schemes for succeeding time, and miss the gratifications that are before us. (*Shakespeare*, 7: 193)

The irony of time's sleight of hand was a theme doubtless made more urgently present to Johnson by texts such as Cowley's essay 'The Danger of Procrastination',[29] and this, too, may have sharpened his awareness of the kinds of 'axiomatic' wisdom to be drawn from Shakespeare. But in the celebrated passage from *Macbeth*, as in his note on the lines, Johnson also moves beyond the immediacy of 'Augustan' literary history (and like Dryden any narrow interpretation of his 'classical' source material) to a peculiar reminiscence of Montaigne: 'all human Nature is always in the midst, betwixt being Born and Dying, giving but an obscure appearance and a shadow'.[30] Matthew Arnold was later to write of *Hamlet* that Shakespeare had 'conceived this play with his mind running on Montaigne, and placed its action and its hero in Montaigne's atmosphere and world'. 'What is this world?', asked Arnold: 'It is the world of man viewed as a being *ondoyant et divers*, balancing and indeterminate, the plaything of cross motives and shifting impulses, swayed by a thousand subtle influences, physiological and pathological'.[31] But it is also through the language of *Rasselas* that Johnson recalls Montaigne's evocation of the fragility and instability of human Reason in ways that clearly suggest a Johnsonian openness to the Shakespearean view of the world and a sense of the boundary beyond which detachment of judgment cannot go. 'Disorders of intellect', Johnson had Imlac propose in Chapter 44 of *Rasselas*, 'happen much more often than superficial observers will easily believe':

> Perhaps, if we speak with rigorous exactness, no human mind is in its right state. There is no man whose imagination does not sometimes predominate over his reason, who can regulate his attention wholly by his will, and whose ideas will come and go at his command. No man will be found in whose mind airy notions do not sometimes tyrannise, and force him to hope or fear beyond the limits of sober probability. All power of fancy over reason is a degree of insanity; but while this power is such as we can control and repress, it is not visible to others, nor considered as any depravation of the mental faculties: it is not pronounced madness but when it becomes ungovernable, and apparently influences speech or action. (*Rasselas*, 150-51)

Here now (in Charles Cotton's 'Augustan' translation) is Montaigne:

> 'Tis not only Fevers, Debauches and great Accidents that overthrow our Judgments; the least things in the World will do it. We are not to doubt, though we are not sensible of it, but that if a continued Fever can overwhelm the Soul, a *Tertian* will in

some proportionate measure alter it. If an *Apoplexy* can stupifie, and totally extinguish the sight of our Understanding, we are not to doubt but that a great Cold will dazle it. And consequently there is hardly one single hour in a Man's whole Life, wherein our Judgment is in its due place and right condition.... As to what remains, this Malady does not very easily discover it self, unless it be extream and past remedy.[32]

At that moment in his critical career when he was preparing his edition of Shakespeare, composing editorial notes and ultimately his *Preface*, Johnson was also in the process of conceiving the activity of criticism afresh. In this he looks beyond formalist laws (and inherited *theories* of all kinds), and rises, prospectively on account of Shakespeare, to a performance of judgment that no critical element in his early career, practical or theoretical, could wholly predict.[33] In this his criticism transcends the fragmentation, experimentation, and theorization of the periodical essays, the brief suggestions of his notes to *Macbeth* and his early *Proposals*, to engage a context outside the 'history of ideas'. Here the translated poetry that Dryden wrote towards the end of his life and the prose of *Rasselas* and of Montaigne combine in an historical continuum with Johnson's evolving account of Shakespeare's plays and replace formalist sources with a creativity whose content is the notion of flux, the irony of time and the instability of reason. Such texts enrich and elevate our conception of the milieu in which Johnson was 'trained',[34] dismantle the programmatic image of his criticism in favour of receptivity and flexibility, and modify and complicate the kind of historical story that can be told about criticism. The example of Johnson, here in response to Shakespeare, suggests the kinds of factors that must be taken into account if we are to re-chart the history of criticism where literature is part of the context of critical history, and if the critic's sensitivities to literature are to make alternative plots, more complex plots, and alternative contexts available. (Johnson was himself later to organize a history of poetry as a sequence of *Lives*.)

Finally, the great breadth of the reflective context most often used narrowly by historians and critics to interpret Johnson's criticism is also apparent from the comedy and self-parody of the 'Ramblers' and 'Idlers'. At the time when he was 'only designing to live', Johnson's critical authority is defined historically in the knowledge of a human judgment - like human life - at its most uncertain, its most pitiful, and its most sympathetic and forgivably absurd. One of the nearest equivalents in the following century, in her essay 'Silly Novels by Lady Novelists', might here be George Eliot's satire: her description from another essay on the satires of Young of the poet who 'owns loving fellowship with the poor human nature ... [he] laughs at'[35] uncannily reflects the attitude of Johnson to Minim. Thus does Johnson through the image of the harmless and amiable Minim join with George Eliot in the great past Erasmian tradition of Praising Folly, and a timeless celebration of the pure, uncontaminated joy of the critically self-deceived, the true Sophoclean bliss where 'To know nothing is the sweetest life'. Such reflective contexts, past and future, internal and external, together enable us to re-imagine Johnsonian judgment as the material of history and to recover Johnson's responses to Shakespeare from the kinds of contextualism that tend to reduce them. By giving concerted attention to Johnson's judgment of Shakespeare, and the words that he uses, the next chapter looks at the detail of how this recovery can take place, and turns from matters of context to matters of text.

Notes

---

[1] Jonathan Brody Kramnick has recently cited this early paper to suggest Johnson's innate hostility to prose fiction, his distaste for the moral ambiguity of Fielding and his approval of Richardson's 'virtuous' characters and plots. See Kramnick, 'Reading Shakespeare's Novels: Literary History and Cultural Politics in the Lennox-Johnson Debate', *Eighteenth-Century Literary History: An MLQ Reader*, ed. Marshall Brown (Durham and London: Duke University Press, 1999), 43-67. Kramnick draws attention to the contrast between Charlotte Lennox's literary history and Samuel Johnson's to show that where Lennox had located the novel amongst Shakespeare's sources and thus prior to his achievement in the plays, Johnson had canonized Shakespeare, seeing the novel as a revival of pre-Shakespearean romance and defending élite culture and masculine values. For Kramnick, citing Patricia Meyer Spacks, Johnson's commitment to Shakespeare can be traced to an anxiety about women: 'he pitches Shakespeare against the novel as a masculinized high-cultural form' (63). But Kramnick's reading conveys an overly secure sense of the obsolescence of Johnson's historical role in that it seems to ignore facts we have in our hands about Johnson's attitude to Shakespearean heroines, such as Cordelia. It also seems to overlook the texture of Johnson's literary relations with women in life. See, variously, on this issue, recent work by Isobel Grundy, James G. Basker, Kathleen Nulton Kemmerer, Norma Clarke and Jaclyn Geller.

[2] In the very passage from the *Preface* that is quoted by Wellek to suggest that Johnson had confused art and life, Johnson had clearly insisted on art's responsibility to select from experience and, equally clearly, Johnson conceives art only in a specialized sense as the 'mirror of life'. Cf. Wellek, 1: 79: 'Dr Johnson ... is ... one of the first great critics who has almost ceased to understand the nature of art, and who, in central passages, treats art as life'.

[3] In *Rambler* 122, a sympathetic account of English historical narrative that is not recorded amongst the Yale editors' 'critical' papers, Johnson defends contemporary historians against the charge that their work is of easy attainment. Much of what passes for the writing of history, he observes, is no more than 'chronological memorials' which 'fright away curiosity and disgust delicacy' (4: 288). Exceptions to this rule include Raleigh, Clarendon and Knolles in his history of the Turks, this last a major source of Johnson's tragedy of *Irene*.

[4] See, for example, his parody of Thomas Warton, *Poems*, 294-95.

[5] In *The Rambler*, writes Robert DeMaria, 'Johnson found a distinctive voice and created a literary persona that he enjoyed being'. *The Life of Samuel Johnson: A Critical Biography* (Oxford: Blackwell, 1993), 144. For Lawrence Lipking, it was also in *The Rambler* that 'the essential Johnson came of age'. *Samuel Johnson: the Life of an Author* (Cambridge MA: Harvard University Press, 1998), 145. Steven Lynn has meanwhile elaborated the notion that Johnson was engaged in the process of '(Mis)Reading *The Spectator*' and converted a 'looker-on' to a 'Rambler'. See *Samuel Johnson after Deconstruction: Rhetoric and The Rambler* (Carbondale: Southern Illinois University Press, 1992), Chapter 2. It seems moreover clear that the *Rambler* and the *Idler* mark a stage in Johnson's critical development by the impression they left on the rhetorical structures of Johnson's later critical work. There are the embedded essays within essays on the unities of action, time and place in the *Preface* (*Shakespeare*, 7: 74-80), the account of metaphysical wit in the 'Life of Cowley', of religious poetry in the 'Life of Waller', or the extended comparison of Dryden

and Pope (*Lives*, 1: 18-22, 291-93; *Lives*, 3: 220-23). Robert D. Spector has argued that 'Johnson's very approach to literature is that of an essayist, not simply in any narrow generic sense ... but, rather, in the qualities of mind that lead naturally enough to the creation of what are commonly regarded as essays'. See *Samuel Johnson and the Essay* (Westport, Conn.: Greenwood Press, 1997), 2.

[6] In *Rambler* 31, 'The defence of a known mistake highly culpable', for example, Johnson touched on Dryden's attempts to refute criticism of the *Indian Emperor*, where he remarked that there is not 'a single reader of this poet, who would not have paid him greater veneration, had he shewn consciousness enough of his own superiority to set such cavils at defiance, and owned that he sometimes slipped into errors by the tumult of his imagination, and the multitude of his ideas' (3: 171) - an assessment characteristic of the later Johnson in tracing the effects of a writer's work to its temperamental and pre-textual roots, and it seems in this respect to foreshadow the later judgment of Dryden's majestic mixture of energy and error in the 'Life': 'With the simple and elemental passions, as they spring separate in the mind, he seems not much acquainted, and seldom describes them but as they are complicated by the various relations of society and confused in the tumults and agitations of life' (*Lives*, 1: 457).

[7] Johnson wrote of Pope's *Iliad* in his 'Life of Pope' that 'The chief help in this arduous undertaking was drawn from the versions of Dryden.... He cultivated our language with so much diligence and art that he has left in his *Homer* a treasure of poetical elegances to posterity.... [B]ut repletion generates fastidiousness, a saturated intellect soon becomes luxurious....' (*Lives*, 3: 237-39).

[8] So, for example: 'Shakespeare's plays', wrote Johnson in his *Preface* of 1765, 'are not in the rigorous and critical sense either tragedies or comedies, but compositions of a distinct kind' (*Shakespeare*, 7: 66).

[9] In *Rambler* 121, Johnson discusses Virgil's borrowings from the epics of Homer. (*Rambler*, 4: 280-86).

[10] In *Rambler* 152, Johnson makes reference to the epistles of Seneca, Pliny and Horace.

[11] *Boswell's Life of Johnson*, ed. George Birkbeck Hill and L.F. Powell, 6 vols. (Oxford: Clarendon Press, 1934-50), 1: 381.

[12] 'He has several favourite epithets, of which he has never settled the meaning, but which are very commodiously applied to books which he has not read, or cannot understand' (*Idler*, 192).

[13] See Alan Brown, 'On the Subject of Practical Criticism', *CQ* 28, no. 4 (1999): 293-327. Howard Mills has wittily linked Dick Minim's methods to C.B. Cox and A.E. Dyson's *The Practical Criticism of Poetry: A Textbook*. See '"Wonderfully alert word usage"', *CQ* 1, no. 3 (Summer 1966): 298-306.

[14] See Hester Lynch Piozzi, 'Anecdotes of the Late Samuel Johnson, LLD.', *Johnsonian Miscellanies*, ed. George Birkbeck Hill, 2 vols. (London: Clarendon Press, 1897), 1: 158.

[15] Even at this stage in his budding critical career, Johnson's distinction was evidently marked out. In his 1747 'Preface to "The Works of Shakespear"', William Warburton praised the *Observations* as 'written, as appears, by a Man of Parts and Genius' while condemning the work of other commentators as 'absolutely below a serious notice'. See D. Nichol Smith, ed., *Eighteenth Century Essays on Shakespeare*, 2nd ed. (Oxford: Clarendon Press, 1963), 93.

[16] The passage had been subjected to detailed practical criticism by Thomas Rymer in his 'Preface to Rapin' (1674). See *The Critical Works of Thomas Rymer*, ed. Curt A. Zimansky (New Haven: Yale University Press, 1956), 15.

[17] *The Works of Samuel Johnson LL.D.* Ed. Arthur Murphy. 12 vols. (London: T. Longman, 1792), 2: 357.

[18] This paper was selected for special attention by Leavis in his efforts to suggest how 'his

[Johnson's] training gets more radically in the way of appreciation than where Milton is concerned' and that despite 'the strong positiveness of the criteria', 'Nothing could be more unlike the Shakespearean use of English than that in which Johnson's mind and sensibility have been formed'. See 'Johnson as Critic', 192-93.

[19] F.R. Leavis, 'Dr. Johnson', 650.

[20] I owe this observation to a series of unpublished lectures by Mr. John Newton, formerly Fellow of Clare College, Cambridge. W.J. Bate has hinted appropriately at the status one needs to accord to the periodical criticism in general, writing that while a few of the *Rambler* essays try to explain to readers who are not critics why the stylized poetic diction of the period takes the form it does, 'these can be cited, *if one wishes to forget his other criticism*, as a final expression of ... [Johnson's] taste' (my emphasis). *The Achievement of Samuel Johnson* (New York: Oxford University Press, 1955), 191.

[21] Leavis writes of the 'paradoxical way in which he [Johnson] shows appreciation while giving the irresistible reasons for "disgust"' ('Dr. Johnson', 650).

[22] It is notable how often Johnson pointedly *refuses* to echo the criticisms of Pope's *Preface to Shakespeare*. Pope had attributed the majority of Shakespeare's faults to his writing down 'to please the *Populace*' (*Eighteenth Century Essays on Shakespeare*, 46); but Johnson makes no mention of this in *his* section on the faults, and elsewhere in the *Preface* he seems to have regarded Shakespeare's responsiveness to his audience as a reason for his permanent *strength* as a dramatist: 'His plots, whether historical or fabulous, are always crouded with incidents, by which the attention of a rude people was more easily caught than by sentiment or argumentation; and such is the power of the marvellous even over those who despise it, that every man finds his mind more strongly seized by the tragedies of Shakespeare than of any other writer' (*Shakespeare*, 7: 83). This is less like Pope's criticism of Shakespeare than Pope's *praise* in the 'Preface to the *Iliad*' of Homer: 'Yet this [subject] he has supplied with a vaster Variety of Incidents and Events, and crowded with a greater Number of Councils, Speeches, Battles, and Episodes of all kinds, than are to be found even in those Poems whose Schemes are of the utmost Latitude and Irregularity' (*Homer*, 7: 5).

[23] For a treatment of *Rasselas* particularly sensitive to Johnsonian prose imagery, and to Johnson's limpid simplicity of language, see Ian White, 'On Rasselas', *CQ* 6, no. 1 (July 1972): 6-31.

[24] *The Poems of John Dryden*, ed. James Kinsley, 4 vols. (Oxford: Clarendon Press, 1958), 4: 1724-25.

[25] *Essays*, 2: 270.

[26] See, for example, David Hopkins, *John Dryden* (Cambridge: Cambridge University Press, 1986), 194-95, and the discussion of this passage in the unpublished Ph.D. dissertation by Tom Mason, University of Cambridge, 1981. James A. Winn notes of this passage that 'Dryden is indulging in a wry comment on the Revolution of 1688, reminding his readers that the succession of monarchs, the burning political issue of the century just closing, is finally another example of "perpetual flux"'. See 'Past and Present in Dryden's *Fables*', *HLQ* 63 (2000): 163.

[27] Quoted from the Johnson-Steevens edition of *The Plays of William Shakespeare*, 2nd ed., 10 vols. (London: C. Bathurst, 1778), 4: 600-602.

[28] *Poems*, 1: 433.

[29] See 'The Danger of Procrastination: A Letter to Mr. S.L.' in A.R. Waller, ed., *The English Writings of Abraham Cowley*, 2 vols. (Cambridge: Cambridge University Press, 1905-06), 2:452-55.

[30] From the 'Apology for Raimond de Sebonde', *Essays of Michael, Seigneur de Montaigne*, trans. Charles Cotton, 3nd ed., 3 vols. (London, 1700), 2: 446.

[31] 'Hamlet Once More', *Pall Mall Gazette* (23 October 1884), rpt. *Selected Criticism of Matthew Arnold*, ed. Christopher Ricks (London: New English Library, 1972), 309.

[32] Montaigne, 2: 385. Cf. William Richardson, *A Philosophical Analysis of some of Shakespeare's Remarkable Characters*, 3nd ed. (London, 1784): 'We are not always in the same state of mind; we are more susceptible at one time than another: even the same appearance shall at different moments affect us differently; and we shall be capable of relishing at one time, what, in a less happy mood, would have given us no sort of pleasure.... Thus it is manifest, that trusting to feeling alone, our judgements may be capricious, unsteady, and inconsistent' (123).

[33] Martin Maner has observed suggestively of the 'Life of Pope' that 'Questions involving the judgment of opposed probabilities tended to activate a set of powerful, well-integrated, habitual responses in Johnson's writing, and these were more than just mannerisms; they were logical, rhetorical, stylistic, and characterological embodiments of a dialectical mode of thought'. *The Philosophical Biographer: Doubt and Dialectic in Johnson's Lives of the Poets* (Athens and London: University of Georgia Press, 1988), 122-23.

[34] I intend here something more substantial than the 'familiarity' with Montaigne noted by Spector, 131.

[35] George Eliot, 'Worldliness and Other-Worldliness: The Poet Young' (1857), *Essays of George Eliot*, ed. Thomas Pinney (London: Routledge and Kegan Paul, 1963), 362.

Chapter 3

Historicization and the Judgment of Shakespeare

Nature and the Manners

To assess the value of context to historical explanations of Johnson, and to clear a space for thinking about his historical relation in a different or better way, it will be necessary at this point to shift the focus, here and in the following chapter, from the patterns of critical history to the structures of critical judgment. The aim will be to test as far as possible the low expectations of Johnsonian judgment against the reality that derives from Johnson's own choice of terms. We will need - in this chapter that is - to start with the critical text which is context to itself, and is thus unencumbered by cultural generalizations or narrative archetypes. Though they are frequently presented as settled long ago, the topics from Johnson's Shakespearean criticism it seems best to take up have long been controversial: the meaning of 'Nature' and of 'Manners', what Johnson understood by 'Tragedy' and 'Comedy' and how he weighed them, and, finally, the question of 'moral purpose', including the conception of 'poetical justice' through which Wellek and other critical historians have explained their sense of the reality of the 'neoclassical' past.

The shift in Johnson's creative viewpoint to the position creatively defined through Johnson's *Rasselas*, and in sympathy with the spirit of Montaigne, inevitably affects how we understand the central critical term of the Shakespeare criticism - 'general nature'. The ramifications of this term can be directly appreciated from an early and famous passage in the *Preface*:

> Nothing can please many, and please long, but just representations of general nature. Particular manners can be known to few, and therefore few only can judge how nearly they are copied. The irregular combinations of fanciful invention may delight a-while, by that novelty which the common satiety of life sends us all in quest; but the pleasures of sudden wonder are soon exhausted, and the mind can only repose on the stability of truth.
>
> Shakespeare is above all writers, at least above all modern writers, the poet of nature; the poet that holds up to his readers a faithful mirrour of manners and of life. (*Shakespeare*, 7: 61-62).[1]

Johnson used the phrase 'general nature' for the first time in the *Preface*, and though the term can seem very empty of meaning for readers today, it is the crux of an historical understanding of Johnson's criticism, and one important source of an alternative structure of historical narration. In this, critical continuity is implicitly pitched against the historical periodization of Johnson, and the allegation of Johnson's role in promoting the 'eternal verities'[2] - a topic I reserve for the final chapter. But that it has been perfectly possible within and without 'radical' circles to misapprehend the term 'general nature', and to interpret its content loosely, is apparent, even at first glance, from the number of occasions when it is said that in appealing to 'general nature' Johnson means, simply, the platitudes of 'human nature'.[3] Before a history of criticism including Johnson can be written, it is therefore necessary to deduce the most plausible interpretation of this critical term. Johnson does indeed at one point say that Shakespeare has 'human sentiments in human language' and that his plays contain the language 'of men' (*Shakespeare*, 7: 65; 84). But Johnson also praised Shakespeare as 'an exact surveyor of the inanimate world', and he is clearly including inanimate alongside human nature in his epithet 'general' (*Shakespeare*, 7: 89). As the above passage will help to suggest, a sense of the complex which is 'general nature' emerges in the relations between 'nature' and what Johnson called in the *Preface* 'particular manners'. For Johnson, in the criticism of Shakespeare we find first hand in the *Preface to Shakespeare*, there is *both* an apartness of 'manners' and 'nature' and a necessary link.

The 'apartness' first. Modern and eighteenth-century critics alike have associated the power of Shakespeare with the features of an Elizabethan world picture, or the qualities inhering in the spirit of Renaissance England. So Shakespeare's language, for example, draws with exceptional range and variety - as critics generally have acknowledged - on the linguistic fabric of his time. For Johnson (who had a detailed - a lexicographer's and textual editor's - awareness of the relations between Shakespeare and the contemporary resources of the English language) the important things in Shakespeare owe little to his time. He stands, finally, independent of the mass of contemporary ideas, fashionable humour and his political and personal situation. As we see from the above, the central paragraphs of the *Preface* drive this distinction home with the full weight of Johnson's prose cadences.

We can understand the 'manners' Johnson refers to in these paragraphs first in their contrast with nature - as free-floating, independent entities. The 'manners', in this conception, consist of socially determined and personally cultivated habits, gestures, mannerisms, speech-features, eccentricities, nervous tics and so on. These mark particular people out and make them 'of their time' or 'of their place' or just make them the people they are. Johnson was later to write of Cowley's poems, the *Anacreontiques*, that 'Men have been wise in very different modes; but they have always laughed the same way', and he compared Dryden and Pope in the 'Life of Pope' on the grounds that 'Dryden knew more of man in his general nature, and Pope in his local manners' (*Lives*, 1: 40; 3: 222). Johnson established the groundwork for many of these future critical distinctions when he contrasted 'manners' and 'nature' in the *Preface*. The divide that he marks out there has several aspects to it. It is in part a distinction between surface and depths - how things and people appear to us and how they really are when we look deeper: (the 'manners' reflect how they appear). But it is also a division between things temporary and things permanent. Johnson seems to be thinking how law, language, customs, society all alter with the passage of time and belong to the 'manners' in that sense. Finally, Johnson has in mind the extensive scope of the plays, and the proportion of human experience they embrace - the sense of 'God's plenty' that Dryden derived from Chaucer.[4] But here he seems to be pointing to how the achievement of Shakespeare is analytic as well as inclusive or collective. Johnson finds Shakespeare working in an exploratory or experimental way to uncover a principle concealed behind all the mere everyday 'manners' which makes them 'particular' to their time and place, or to the individual exhibiting them.

There is however a sense in which the 'manners' also express 'nature'. Shakespeare may be the 'poet of nature' but the 'nature' in question is revealed in and through the 'manners', that is, by means of an unmediated experience of the actual life and society of the world around us and a knowledge of the people we find there. When Johnson writes of the 'manners', he seems to be saying that a poet cannot represent 'nature' without this immediate contact with life. The 'manners' (as this would suggest) do not therefore have to be specific to Shakespeare's own society (brutish uncouth Elizabethans in contrast to cultivated, polished, Augustans - Shakespeare has the complete range). They are rather the habits, details of behaviour, gesture and speech found in the dead and gone society which remain atemporally human and therefore visible today. They are accessible now. These 'manners' are spread out across time and are not culturally specific. In the words Johnson was later to use in the 'Life of Butler', they are 'co-extended with the race of man' (*Lives*, 1: 214).[5] In copying 'nature', Johnson thought Shakespeare made a selection from the 'manners' in this specialized sense. Little contextual scholarship of the 'age' was necessary to bring the characters of Shakespeare alive to the contemporary reader because such a reader could know them from life.

But to understand more fully Johnson's position on how the characters of drama ought to be drawn (and to see this in the light of the Johnsonian principle of 'general nature'), we must again turn to Johnson's development away from *The Rambler*. Johnson wrote in *Rambler* 156 that plays must have 'heroes' in order to qualify as tragedies; and by the 1750s, the 'hero' of a tragedy was only a 'hero' if the author of the play had constructed a character of appropriate dignity for him. But the Johnson of the *Preface to Shakespeare* was not only in no doubt that the ennobling of heroes was at odds with Shakespeare's practice. He shows no inclination to suggest that obeying the rule would have made the plays better than they are: 'Shakespeare has no heroes.... His story requires Romans or kings, but he thinks only on men' (*Shakespeare*, 7: 64-65).[6] Johnson is here renouncing a standard formula for the creation of character in order to centralize the humanity of his internalized *experience* of Shakespeare. In traditional terms, authors of tragedies were obliged to portray their heroes in line with a code of social decorum (a doctrine of verisimilitude based on the illusion of universal 'good manners'). Such 'good manners' required Romans to be noble and kings to act and be treated in a kingly fashion.[7] Johnson thus answers once and for all the criticisms of Shakespearean character-drawing made by Voltaire among the French and by Rymer and Dennis among the English critics.[8] Johnson noted in his *Preface* that Rymer had thought Shakespeare's heroes 'not sufficiently Roman' and in his detailed notes to *Julius Caesar*, which is the occasion for Rymer's criticism, he took a diametrically contrary view. He stands the criticism of Rymer on its head: it is precisely the Roman qualities, Johnson complains, which obstruct nature:

'[Shakespeare's] adherence to the real story, and to Roman manners, seems to have impeded the natural vigour of his genius' (*Shakespeare*, 8: 836).

In comments of this kind, Johnson is affirming the importance of Shakespeare's characters according to the temporal principle of 'general nature'.[9] It does not matter if kings or Romans are dramatically represented by Shakespeare with the imperfections common in the rest of the human race; if they are, say, weak or indecisive. If Shakespeare is the 'poet of nature', they have to appear in this way. The characters, ultimately, for all their individual vitality, are 'a species'. They are that which remains when individuals or whole societies die or fade. In this, Johnson rejects the demand that plays incorporate the incidentals of profession or rank as they appear from one historical and social perspective. But he does not wish to jettison particularity of character in all of its forms; nor is his attachment to generality the fatuous or naïve embracing of Shakespeare's characters as 'morality play' types, or empty ciphers for an explicit authorial message. If Shakespeare's characters are not merely exceptional 'heroic' beings, they do not lack the precise definition we expect in a poet of Shakespeare's extraordinary powers of human analysis. Johnson states clearly that 'perhaps no poet ever kept his personages more distinct from one another'. Such a comment conflates the notes to several plays where Johnson explicitly praises the distinctness of character - in *The Tempest*, for example:

> But whatever might be Shakespeare's intention in forming or adopting the plot, he has made it instrumental to the production of many characters, diversified with boundless invention, and preserved with profound skill in nature, extensive knowledge of opinions, and accurate observation of life. In a single drama are here exhibited princes, courtiers, and sailors, all speaking in their real characters. (*Shakespeare*, 7: 135)[10]

In the end-note on *Troilus and Cressida*, it is again strong individual character-drawing which comes to mind:

> As the story abounded with materials, he has exerted little invention; but he has diversified his characters with great variety, and preserved them with great exactness. His vicious characters sometimes disgust, but cannot corrupt, for both Cressida and Pandarus are detested and contemned. The comick characters seem to have been the favourites of the writer, they are of the superficial kind, and exhibit more of manners than nature, but they are copiously filled and powerfully impressed. (*Shakespeare*, 8: 938)

- while Johnson also notices distinctness of character in one or another form in notes to *King Lear* ('the striking opposition of contrary characters') and *Henry IV Part 2* ('characters diversified with the utmost nicety of discernment'). In long notes on Polonius and Falstaff meanwhile, Johnson praises Shakespeare for creating some of the most dramatically realized, unheroic individuals in English literature (*Shakespeare*, 8: 703; 7: 523; 8: 973-74; 7: 523).[11] This is not to say that Johnson thought Shakespeare *always* individualized his characters to this extent: Polonius is described as 'a mixed character of nature and of manners'. Most of the characters are less fully drawn.

Tragedy and Comedy

It follows from Johnson's defence of the Shakespearean pursuit of 'life' at the level of 'nature' rather than 'manners' that he should be duly sceptical - in the *Preface* of 1765 if not in *The Rambler* of 1751 - about the modes of dramatic representation specific to the concept of 'tragedy'. We have seen how sceptically Johnson defended Shakespeare's treatment of character against hostile critics; but his degree of detachment from seventeenth and eighteenth-century literary thought also has a bearing on two further (connected) aspects of Johnson's criticism of Shakespeare which we can now explore: how to apply the concept of 'tragedy' validly to Shakespeare (and whether we can), and, finally, how to do justice to the sense in which Shakespearean drama is 'moral'. Both are areas in which Johnsonian criticism of Shakespeare has seemed too remote from our own view to affect it, and this is one of the reasons why Johnson's voice has often seemed to go unheard as a critic and his judgments have appeared of little direct *use*. It is one of the reasons why, on the subject of Shakespeare, Johnson is 'not for direct instruction in critical thinking'.

How then does Johnson, by the time of the *Preface*, regard the concept of 'tragedy' as relevant to Shakespeare? (We have already observed the shift in Johnson's work as a creator from *Irene* and the *Vanity of Human Wishes* to *Rasselas*). The answer seems to be that just as Johnson could set aside the concept of tragic 'heroes' by that date, so he could abandon 'tragedy' whenever he needed to do justice to the *whole* of Shakespeare, or the appeal of *whole* plays. We have seen that the *Preface* contains the following famous statement:

> Shakespeare's plays are not in the rigorous and critical sense either tragedies or comedies, but compositions of a distinct kind; exhibiting the real state of sublunary nature, which partakes of good and evil, joy and sorrow, mingled with endless variety of proportion and innumerable modes of combination; and expressing the course of the world.... (*Shakespeare*, 7: 66)[12]

Johnson does not develop a theory for the notion that Shakespeare's plays are 'compositions of a distinct kind' and neither tragedies nor (their opposite) comedies. And yet our own *experience* of reading Shakespeare's plays may suggest quite adequately what Johnson means by 'mingled drama' and how this is more important than the plays being tragedies or comedies. Neither Johnson's earlier comments on drama, nor the earlier creative works of 'tragic' import such as the *Vanity of Human Wishes* or *Irene* (Johnson's one experiment in noble and correct tragedy) anticipate the collapse in formalistic concepts of 'tragedy' and 'comedy' that takes place here. There is however in *Rasselas* an example derived from Johnson's creative oeuvre where 'nature' includes the stability of both optimistic and pessimistic positions but inclines finally toward neither. Many passages in this work reflect the conception of 'nature' that appears in the *Preface* and from which the particular judgments flow. In this they are part of Johnson's 'training' as a critic of Shakespeare as *Irene*, the *Vanity of Human Wishes* and the essays of *The Rambler* and *Idler* are not. One such passage is this representative statement of the central philosophy of *Rasselas*:

'The causes of good and evil' ... [said Imlac] 'are so various and uncertain, so often entangled with each other, so diversified by various relations, and so much subject to accidents which cannot be foreseen, that he who would fix his condition upon incontestable reasons of preference, must live and die enquiring and deliberating'. (*Rasselas*, 67)

We have seen that Johnson's critical affinities have evolved markedly in the direction of this conception of 'general nature' by the time of the *Preface*. And the extent to which Johnson's mind was opening and unfolding to terminology of different kinds in tandem with his attention to Shakespeare is again reflected in the subtle but important differences between the *Preface* and the *Rambler*.

Once more, it seems, little in the earlier criticism is firm or fixed enough to constitute a determining context of origin for Johnson's criticism, nor does it allow the historian of criticism to merge or simplify his work in this way, or to found reliable expectations upon it. In *Rambler* 156, Johnson had defended the concept of 'tragicomedy'; but at this stage he had maintained a sense of the generic distinctness of 'tragedy' and 'comedy' along with a commitment to both of these forms. Thus the arguments of *Rambler* 156 and the *Preface* are only superficially similar: Johnson did not 'defend' 'tragicomedy' in the *Preface*, nor, apparently, are 'tragicomedy' and 'mingled drama' there employed - as they seem to be in the *Rambler* - as synonymous terms. If 'tragicomedy' is an alternation of serious and comic *scenes*, 'mingled drama' is a mixing *within* any scene - comic speeches, lines and nuances in desperate, bitter, wretched or terrible contexts, and cruel or solemn ones in otherwise comic plays or those having 'happy' endings. In identifying Shakespeare's plays as 'mingled drama', Johnson opens himself to more of Shakespeare as Shakespeare seems in reality to affect his readers, and as he might affect us (regardless of the particular critical affinities or theories of *our* time). Johnson has now broadened his standard from one adequate to describe alternating settings of courtly propriety and tavern jocularity such as we find in *Henry IV*, to one able to account for the mix of elements in a play like *Hamlet*, where gravediggers joke over skulls and where 'tragedy' and 'comedy' are not defined by the limits of scenes.

But facing this fact about the direction of Johnson's personal development as a critic also entails abandoning the idea common from the earliest eighteenth-century reviews that Johnson preferred Shakespeare's comedies (in the generically defined sense of the term) to his tragedies (similarly defined), and that his criticism of Shakespeare is thereby perverse (a consequence of the odd personality emphasized in the wake of Macaulay's criticism and by such historians as Saintsbury).[13] Johnson says of Shakespeare in the *Preface* that 'In his tragick scenes there is always something wanting, but his comedy often surpasses expectation or desire'. He also writes that Shakespeare's 'tragedy seems to be skill, his comedy to be instinct' (*Shakespeare*, 7: 69).[14] But in the former of these two statements Johnson is writing about 'scenes' rather than whole plays. This does not conflict with the relatively full attention that Johnson gives to *King Lear*, *Macbeth*, *Hamlet* and *Othello* in his notes to those plays. Nor is this a preference for comed*ies* since Johnson has just that minute praised (and we have just discussed) the Shakespearean 'mingled drama'. To understand the second statement we need to know what Johnson meant by 'skill'. The information we want is in the notes to the plays: *Othello* shows 'such proofs of Shakespeare's skill in human nature, as ... it is vain to seek in any modern writer' (*Shakespeare*, 8: 1047).[15] 'Skill', for Johnson, meant something closer to 'knowledge' than our modern restricted significance of 'technical expertise'. The term describes the means used by Shakespeare to produce tragedy, and in its gesture toward the human knowledge of the plays as distinct from their rhetorical craft, it cannot be taken to reflect adversely on Shakespearean trage*dies*.

But the key statement, that Shakespeare's 'disposition ... led him to comedy', suggests that Johnson may not *in the main* be weighing Shakespeare's types of drama, comedies on the one hand *versus* tragedies on the other.[16] Johnson is rather analysing the source of all that Shakespeare wrote (tragedies, comedies, histories etc.), and diagnosing the effect of Shakespeare working at times *pro* and at times *con* the natural disposition which led him to 'repose, or to luxuriate' in comedy. One of Johnson's most important services to the modern reader, whenever he is writing about tragedy and comedy, is to suggest how hard Shakespeare found it to hold back from the comic, and how he delighted in comedy up to and beyond the point where it warranted praise - hence the indulgence in quibbles, or 'fatal Cleopatra[s] for which he lost the world, and was content to lose it' (*Shakespeare*, 7: 74).

Johnson praises comedy, and he criticizes tragedy. But the scene, not the play, is the unit of evaluation in which he thinks. Accordingly, the main difference between Johnson and most of the Shakespearean criticism in the world not written by him (and in this sense the origin of his real 'perversity', recalcitrance and consequent historical alienation as a critic) is the very high value that Johnson accords to Shakespeare's comic *scenes*. As the plays as wholes are in any case 'mingled dramas', it does not matter whether such scenes come in plays officially designated as comedies or as tragedies. But the praise of the comic scenes in the *Preface* is exceptionally full. Plays of all kinds are covered by it:

> The force of his comick scenes has suffered little diminution from the changes made by a century and a half, in manners or in words. As his personages act upon principles arising from genuine passion, very little modified by particular forms, their pleasures and vexations are communicable to all times and to all places; they are natural, and therefore durable; the adventitious peculiarities of personal habits, are only superficial dies, bright and pleasing for a little while, yet soon fading to a dim tinct, without any remains of former lustre; but the discriminations of true passion are the colours of nature; they pervade the whole mass, and can only perish with the body that exhibits them. (*Shakespeare*, 7: 69-70)[17]

As this tends to reinforce, it is in his comic *scenes* that Shakespeare approaches nearest to 'general nature'. It is in comedy that Johnson thought Shakespeare had most fully transcended the 'manners'.

The faults of the tragedy, the declamatory speeches and the swollen language, are correspondingly faults in the work of much more ordinary dramatists than Shakespeare; and they resemble what Johnson in the *Lives of the Poets* was later to criticize in the tragedies of Thomson or of Young.[18] Shakespeare's disposition led him to comedy. From this it follows that his tragedy is flawed according to the visible effort (the non-instinctual labour) Shakespeare seems to have expended upon it. In tragedy, Shakespeare works against the grain of his natural disposition, and it is then that 'his performance seems constantly to be worse, as his labour is more' (*Shakespeare*, 7: 72-73). But again the point is made by reference to how an ordinary reader of the tragic scenes and passages would be likely to experience them, and how, in the present day, we might experience them ourselves. Johnson is not engaged in marking down Shakespeare against some historically validated standard of 'Augustan' or neoclassical purity in the tragic. Nor is he deploying some personal theory of tragedy to the terms of which Shakespeare does not correspond. In fact, where Johnson praises the tragedy of Shakespeare, as he does in a later passage of the *Preface*, it is because Shakespeare is in general profoundly *unlike* the kind of tragedy that he (Johnson) had once tried to write. The important point is that Johnson had *abandoned* all ambitions as a tragedian by the time of his major criticism of Shakespeare. In the *Preface* Johnson can momentarily switch the commentary into the first person plural and appear to include himself in the criticism: 'we still find that on our stage something must be done as well as said, and inactive declamation is very coldly heard, however musical or elegant, passionate or sublime' (*Shakespeare*, 7: 84).

Moral Purpose

This difference between the failed author of *Irene* and the disinterested critic of Shakespeare is finally defined in Johnson's account of how Shakespeare's drama is moral. We have seen that Johnson had stressed the 'mingled drama' of Shakespeare, and Shakespeare's 'disposition' to comedy. He had lavished an exceptional praise on the comic scenes. But a taste of this kind must also raise the question of whether Shakespearean drama can, for Johnson, comprehend the 'seriousness' of tragedy. The power of tragedy to improve or to teach its audience was a considerable part of the value attached to this form by critics of Johnson's immediate age - as the many contemporary theorists of tragedy can suggest. Yet Johnson himself regards the dramas as neither deadened by an over-emphatic moral didacticism (like *Irene*) nor wanting in morals. What he says (somewhat controversially) is that Shakespeare 'sacrifices virtue to convenience and is so much more careful to please than to instruct, that he seems to write without any moral purpose' (*Shakespeare*, 7: 71).[19] 'Seems' is the operative word in this sentence: there are many occasions in the notes where Johnson shows that Shakespeare points an extremely purposeful moral. In *Macbeth*, for example, 'The passions are directed to their true end. Lady Macbeth is merely detested; and though the courage of Macbeth preserves some esteem, yet every reader rejoices at his fall' (*Shakespeare*, 8: 795). The difference here between what Johnson says and what might be said of *Macbeth* by enthusiastic readers of the present day is not that Johnson does not feel or see moral purpose. It is that he makes so much of it. (We do not normally say we 'rejoice' at Macbeth's fall).

Johnson is thus sharply alive to the variety of ways in which Shakespeare incorporates in vividly dramatic form the content of a moral proposition. And whatever the spirit of his negative criticisms, Johnson does not proceed to assert that Shakespeare, in order to make these points, adheres only to stated morals.[20] Here, doubtless, confusion has arisen through a fallacious argument from Johnson's *exclusive* commitment to stated truths, this presupposed on the basis of historical generalizations about neoclassical criticism. It is true that Johnson appreciates the quantity and importance of Shakespearean moral statement whenever it occurs: 'From his writings indeed a system of social duty may be selected, for he that thinks reasonably must think morally' (*Shakespeare*, 7: 71). Johnson's point is however that Shakespeare does not *always* think morally. Because Shakespeare is 'so much more careful to please than to instruct', 'his precepts and axioms drop casually from him'. And rather than aim his criticism at one kind of morality, Johnson's suggestion is that Shakespeare is not *consistent* in his moral concerns. Johnson highlights in the notes times when it suited Shakespeare to leave moral questions aside - because it was convenient to do so:

> I do not see why Falstaff is carried to the Fleet. We have never lost sight of him since his dismission from the king; he has committed no new fault, and therefore incurred no punishment; but the different agitations of fear, anger, and surprise in him and his company, made a good scene to the eye; and our authour, who wanted them no longer on the stage, was glad to find this method of sweeping them away. (*Shakespeare*, 7: 522)

Shakespeare 'seems' to write without any moral purpose here because he is being more careful to please than to instruct. That is a fault, and it is the first and most serious that Johnson lists in his 'faults and defects' section of the *Preface*. But Johnson qualifies the criticism quite severely in two ways. First, it is not, and cannot be, a criticism that damns Shakespeare outright: 'Nothing can please many, and please long, but just representations of general nature' (*Shakespeare*, 7: 61). We have seen from this earlier observation how enthusiastically Johnson celebrated the power of Shakespearean drama to please; and pleasure in the Johnsonian system has priority over instruction, as is appreciable whenever or wherever Johnson considers moral purpose in the *Lives*, as in his essay on Pope, say, or on Addison or Matthew Prior. In all such cases, Johnson always metes out the harshest treatment to work that tries to instruct without a sufficient regard to pleasure. Johnson was one of the most easily bored of literary critics, and an over-conscious morality bored him most.

The second qualification is that Johnson sees Shakespeare as determining for himself the standard by which he is judged. In his morally most powerful work, Shakespeare constitutes the ideal by which his seeming to sacrifice virtue to convenience is a fault, and Johnson strikes a balance on the issue of moral purpose that reflects the disposition of praise and blame in the *Preface*. This is at once an overall judgment of Shakespeare, and though the general verdict is overwhelmingly positive, Johnson - in judging Shakespeare - is holding the good and the bad in the scales. The more strained, declamatory passages, and the overt moralizing Johnson does not want (in tragedy or anywhere else) are hard for any reader to take because Shakespeare's 'real power', his dramatically realized hold over questions of right and wrong, lies quite elsewhere:

It is from this wide extension of design that so much instruction is derived. It is this which fills the plays of Shakespeare with practical axioms and domestick wisdom.... Yet his real power is not shewn in the splendour of particular passages, but by the progress of his fable, and the tenour of his dialogue.... (*Shakespeare*, 7: 62)

Nowhere, of course, in all this, does Johnson demand that '*poetical* justice' be done.

Particularity and Generality: 'Surveying the Whole'

To recapitulate: first, the *Preface to Shakespeare* of 1765 is the focus of Johnson's Shakespearean criticism, and is Johnson's earliest extended critical treatment of any writer. We have little unambiguous evidence of Johnson's critical commitments before 1765 and little solid evidence of the Johnsonian 'training' (other than the fact of striking developments in his creative grasp of 'nature' at around the time of his work on Shakespeare, his intimate knowledge of the plays and some enthusiastic thinking upon them). Histories which fail to register Johnson's development as a critic in consequence of his reading of Shakespeare will thus seem unwarrantably selective. Second, it is in the *Preface to Shakespeare* that Johnson's mature critical terminology emerges for the first time. 'Nature' and 'mingled drama' replace 'tragedy' and 'tragicomedy'. These and other concepts applicable to the criticism of drama (such as the concept of the tragic 'hero') are abandoned or critiqued by Johnson at this point, and again, the pattern of historical narrative must preserve a crucial distinction. Third, in the light of the non-reductive context of Johnson's criticism that I have proposed, Johnson is exceptionally *well* disposed to appreciate the moral power of Shakespearean drama and the source of this power in Shakespeare's human ambitiousness as writer, his 'wide extension of design'. For Johnson the sense of right and wrong in Shakespeare must always be dramatically realized. Johnson's appreciation does not stop short at approving the didactic *statement* of a pre-existing ethical code, and Johnson the critic of Shakespeare is not the author of *Irene*: the moral import of the plays must be an intrinsic part of their life. Only when Shakespeare deviates from a portrayal of life (as Shakespeare's own dramas have created it for him and as Johnson finds it created convincingly in them) do Johnson's negative criticisms tell.

Perhaps the most striking single feature of Johnson's criticism of Shakespeare, from the perspective of the modern reader, is not however connected with any positive or negative aspect of the content of the criticism, nor with any difficulty in critical language or controlling concepts. It rests with the developing Johnsonian 'idea of criticism' - Johnson's unusual confidence as a critic of the whole of Shakespeare and his judgment in the *Preface* of so much detailed and diverse material in exceptionally general terms. 'Great thoughts are always general', Johnson was later to write in his 'Life of Cowley', 'and consist in positions not limited by exceptions, and in descriptions not descending to minuteness' (*Lives*, 1: 21). Johnson explains with some precision in the *Preface* what it means to write criticism of this general kind:

> These observations are to be considered not as unexceptionably constant, but as containing general and predominant truth. Shakespeare's familiar dialogue is affirmed to be smooth and clear, yet not wholly without ruggedness or difficulty; as a country may be eminently fruitful, though it has spots unfit for cultivation: His characters are praised as natural, though their sentiments are sometimes forced, and their actions improbable; as the earth upon the whole is spherical, though its surface is varied with protuberances and cavities. (*Shakespeare*, 7: 70-71)

Johnson is here establishing the grounds for an evaluative estimate of the whole of Shakespeare. In so doing, the prefatory mode of utterance in which he shapes his most important propositions may seem somewhat remote and unbodied compared with the sort of expositional monograph on Shakespeare current today, or a modern ('Arden' style) introduction to individual plays; but it is one which makes his criticism's relation both to the modern reader and to the plays useful in different and perhaps more challenging ways. It has always been easy to exaggerate the shallowness of this method or to miss its purpose. The global statements of the *Preface to Shakespeare* do not pointlessly distance the reader or critic from the experience of the plays, nor do they suggest that Johnson lacked the resources of a modern and sophisticated apparatus of practical criticism, or textual, linguistic and structural analysis. Their function is to complete and to release the congregate mass of local, regional and subordinate judging, appreciating, interpreting, commenting, glossing, responding and so forth that go on all the time when editing and mediating Shakespeare for readers. The generalizations subsume several prior and inferior levels of the dramatic and critical text and are an act of 'comprehending' in the dual sense - they 'include' and they 'understand'.

Johnson's detailed reactions to Shakespeare, word by word, line by line, speech by speech, and play by play, arise as notes. There are notes at the foot of the page, and there are 'General Observations' drawing the notes on each play to a close. If some of the latter are brief in the extreme, others seem consciously developed as miniature essays. They record the mix of arguments, definitions, affirmations of taste, and the kind of personal testimony that we find in the concluding note on *King Lear*. As the foregoing commentary has tended to suggest, hardly a play escapes without criticism of some kind, and this is sometimes *surprisingly* harsh, cryptic, or liable to strike the reader from an unexpected angle, or with an unusual 'edge'. A throwaway brevity is occasionally adopted by Johnson, as if he, like Shakespeare before him when the end of a play drew near, had shortened the labour to snatch the profit. Praise takes every possible form, and no two 'General Observations' are exactly alike. There is no standard pattern or critical template.

As indicated above, the 'General Observations' most likely to interest readers today are those on the conventionally regarded 'great tragedies' - on *Othello* for example, where Johnson writes with unrestrained enthusiasm that 'The beauties of this play impress themselves so strongly upon the attention of the reader, that they can draw no aid from critical illustration' and remarks on 'The fiery openness of Othello ... the cool malignity of Iago' and 'the soft simplicity of Desdemona' (*Shakespeare*, 8: 1047). On *Hamlet*, which inspires a fairly structured account of merits and flaws (echoing, as do other local judgments, the rhetorical equipoise of the general *Preface*),

Johnson writes that the 'particular excellence' is 'the praise of variety'. At this level - one stage removed from the detailed glosses and explanatory comments of the incidental notes - Johnson's approach is judicial rather than interpretive:

> The incidents are so numerous, that the argument of the play would make a long tale. The scenes are interchangeably diversified with merriment and solemnity....
>
> The conduct is perhaps not wholly secure against objections. The action is indeed for the most part in continual progression, but there are some scenes which neither forward nor retard it. (*Shakespeare*, 8: 1010-11)

But interesting and extended commentary of an evaluative or interpretive nature can also appear at any point in the run of notes to a play - on important individuals such as Polonius or Falstaff, for example, whose character sketches I have touched on above. Comments in response to the dramatic significance of a scene, a habit of language or moment of acute tension, humour, pity or delight are too various to tie down to particular examples.

It would be wrong, however, to overstate the importance that Johnson attaches to weighing the merits, or fixing the defects of whole individual plays (whether in 'General Observations' or by inferences drawn together from different notes). In valuing Shakespeare's achievement as one, Johnson is appreciating a larger unit than that of the play. This is a focus that blurs the success or failure of achievements within the Shakespearean oeuvre at levels which include the unitary 'work' and any *particular* 'mingled drama', so that compared with most modern critics of Shakespeare, Johnson's sense of the quintessence of the play as 'the thing' is secondary to his apprehension of the sustained commitment of an active and varied total dramatic career. The best of plays and the worst of plays, great tragedies or run-of-the-mill comedies, are almost all accorded a comment; but their boundaries are ultimately dissolved in this larger view. Johnson's criticism has the holistic completeness that only distance from the object allows. And that, of course, is the key to the visibility - to Johnson's eyes - of the Shakespearean 'general nature'. This is the combining quality of the manifold that is all the plays. For 'The Works of Shakespeare' Johnson might have substituted the singular concept 'Work': his 'poet of nature' is in one sense the author of a single 'poem'.

Shakespearean Standards and the *Lives of the Poets*

That the judgment of Shakespeare is for such reasons at the centre of Johnson's achievement and development as a critic will surprise no one used to finding affinities between the *Preface* and the *Lives of the Poets*.[21] What may be surprising, after the relatively scattered, experimental and unconnected criticism of Johnson's periodical essays, and the inferences drawn by historians about Johnson's early influences, is how wonderfully Shakespeare had concentrated Johnson's mind. We have seen that in reading and responding to Shakespeare, Johnson enjoyed above all the 'progress of his fable and the tenour of his dialogue'. This sense of the 'dramatic' quality to be found when good drama alerts the attention with its reality and life, when it 'seizes' or 'fills' the mind, or even when it shocks, became part of the whole body of thinking, responding, ordering, juxtaposing, experiencing pleasure and enduring pain, that distinguishes Johnson's criticism. Johnson ultimately appreciates Shakespearean drama as drama *rather than* as poetry. In this connection Shakespeare imposed a demand that Johnson wanted satisfied, but mostly found unsatisfied, in almost every kind of poet or dramatist he later went on to discuss. We have seen that Johnson had admired at an earlier date the formal model of tragic perfection he found in Addison's *Cato* (*Idler*, 241). But when he compares Addison directly with Shakespeare in the *Preface*, his judgment on *Cato* is unmistakably cool:

> Voltaire expresses his wonder, that our authour's extravagances are endured by a nation, which has seen the tragedy of *Cato*. Let him be answered, that Addison speaks the language of poets, and Shakespeare, of men. We find in *Cato* innumerable beauties which enamour us of its authour, but we see nothing that acquaints us with human sentiments or human actions; we place it with the fairest and noblest progeny which judgment propagates by conjunction with learning, but *Othello* is the vigorous and vivacious offspring of observation impregnated by genius. *Cato* affords a splendid exhibition of artificial and fictitious manners, and delivers just and noble sentiments, in diction easy, elevated and harmonious, but its hopes and fears communicate no vibration to the heart; the composition refers us only to the writer; we pronounce the name of *Cato*, but we think on Addison. (*Shakespeare*, 7: 84)

Johnson is not any more enthusiastic about *Cato* when he comes to discuss the play in his 'Life of Addison' fifteen years later as 'rather a poem in dialogue than a drama, rather a succession of just sentiments in elegant language than a representation of natural affections, or of any state probable or possible in human life' (*Lives*, 2: 132). The lines from Cato's soliloquy had been praised as sublime in the *Idler*; but the play as a whole is now dismissed as frigid: 'its success has introduced amongst us the use of dialogue too declamatory, of unaffecting elegance, and chill philosophy' (*Lives*, 2: 133).

The significance of this metamorphosis in Johnson's critical outlook is suggested by Boswell, who may almost have been thinking of the comparison between *Cato* and *Othello* in the *Preface* when he touched on the failings of *Irene* in his *Life of Johnson*:

> IRENE, considered as a poem, is intitled to the praise of superiour excellence. Analysed into parts, it will furnish a rich store of noble sentiments, fine imagery, and beautiful language; but it is deficient in pathos, in that delicate power of touching the human feelings, which is the principle end of drama.[22]

Johnson conveys his disillusion with *Cato* by his comments on the characters of the play: 'Of the agents we have no care: we consider not what they are doing, or what they are suffering; we wish only to know what they have to say' (*Lives*, 2: 132).

Johnson's account of a second, similarly respected, drama on the classical model, Milton's *Samson Agonistes*, seems equally radicalized by the experience of Shakespeare. We have seen that Johnson had discussed the play in fairly neutral terms in the *Rambler*; but by the time of the *Lives* both its formal deficiencies and the linguistic beauties he had noted at the periodical stage had become less important than its weakness *as* a play:

> It could only be by long prejudice and the bigotry of learning that Milton could prefer the ancient tragedies with their encumbrance of a chorus to the exhibitions of the French and English stages; and it is only by a blind confidence in the reputation of Milton that a drama can be praised in which the intermediate parts have neither cause nor consequence, neither hasten nor retard the catastrophe.

And while continuing to praise the tragedy for its many 'particular beauties, many just sentiments and striking lines', Johnson nevertheless felt that 'it wants that power of attracting attention which a well-connected plan produces'. He wrote that Milton: 'would not have excelled in dramatick writing' and explained this remark in terms closely related to those developed in the *Preface*. Milton:

> knew human nature only in the gross, and had never studied the shades of character, nor the combinations of concurring or the perplexity of contending passions. He had read much and knew what books could teach; but had mingled little in the world, and was deficient in the knowledge which experience must confer. (*Lives*, 1: 188-89)

Still more striking, perhaps, is the way that the appeal of the Shakespearean 'dramatic', with its requirement for the progress of the fable and the reality of a dialogue that seems to be drawn from the experience of life, remains a presence even when Johnson is not talking about the drama necessary to plays, but has turned to narrative poetry: Butler's *Hudibras* is less interesting than it might have been, according to the 'Life of Butler', because it requires 'a nearer approach to dramatick spriteliness without which fictitious speeches will always tire, however sparkling with sentences and however variegated with allusions' (*Lives*, 1: 212).

In all of these ways Shakespeare's impact on Johnson was something more than a temporary shock from which it was possible to recover one's Augustan composure and then read on, unchanged by the experience. Shakespeare contributed to the sum of the criteria that formed the amalgam of literary and personal understanding present in the critical thinking and feeling of the *Lives*; he re-formulated the existing language of Johnson's criticism as this is defined and re-shaped by unification, intensification and transformation of the Johnsonian 'idea of criticism'.[23] His value to Johnson thus lies behind many of the negative as well as the positive judgments in the *Lives*. The effect of this Shakespearean presence may be to diminish somewhat the sense in which the poets treated within the *Lives* are significant in defining the critical ideas and ideals of Johnson, how he formed his taste or experienced a 'training'. This includes the place of the poetry of Dryden and Pope in that training, and more broadly the 'Augustan' dramatic and poetical model. But that is one way that Johnson's criticism of Shakespeare (and his criticism more generally perhaps) secures its continuity with the future. Or, to apply T.S. Eliot's words on the life of dead poets to the life of a dead critic, it is one way that Johnson 'asserts[s] ... [his] immortality most vigorously'.[24]

History and Emotion: Poetical Justice, Natural Justice and the Death of Cordelia

Before moving on from the text of the criticism of Shakespeare and its significance to the historicization of Johnson, some fuller account must however be given of one of the most suggestive and historically intractable moments of Johnson's Shakespearean criticism, his judgment on the tragic scene of Cordelia's death from which we began. The passage commences at the point where Johnson has been defending Shakespeare against Joseph Warton's charge, in *Adventurer* 122,[25] that the character of 'Edmund destroys the simplicity of the story':

> The injury done by Edmund to the simplicity of the action is abundantly recompensed by the addition of variety, by the art with which he is made to co-operate with the chief design, and the opportunity which he gives the poet of combining perfidy with perfidy, and connecting the wicked son with the wicked daughters, to impress this important moral, that villainy is never at a stop, that crimes lead to crimes, and at last terminate in ruin. (*Shakespeare*, 8: 703-704)

Johnson continues:

> But though this moral be incidentally enforced, Shakespeare has suffered the virtue of Cordelia to perish in a just cause, contrary to the natural ideas of justice, to the hope of the reader, and, what is yet more strange, to the faith of chronicles. Yet this conduct is justified by the Spectator, who blames Tate for giving Cordelia success and happiness in his alteration, and declares, that, in his opinion, 'the tragedy has lost half its beauty'. Dennis has remarked, whether justly or not, that, to secure the favourable reception of *Cato*, 'the town was poisoned with much false and abominable criticism', and that endeavours had been used to discredit and decry poetical justice. A play in which the wicked prosper, and the virtuous miscarry, may doubtless be good, because it is a just representation of the common events of human life: but since all reasonable beings naturally love justice, I cannot easily be persuaded, that the observation of justice makes a play worse; or, if other excellencies are equal, the audience will not always rise better pleased from the final triumph of persecuted virtue.
>
> In the present case the publick has decided. Cordelia, from the time of Tate, has always retired with victory and felicity. And if my sensations could add any thing to the general suffrage, I might relate, that I was many years ago so shocked by Cordelia's death, that I know not whether I ever endured to read again the last scenes of the play till I undertook to revise them as an editor. (*Shakespeare*, 8: 704)

The distance between the present of criticism and the Johnsonian critical past must ultimately be seen as shaped by the present's perception of the past, the narrative archetypes that can be extracted from it, and the past's determination of what the present will be. But in responses to Johnson's note to the final scene of *Lear*, the conviction that Johnson, as the age's chief representative figure, instinctively requires 'poetical justice', reinforces the sense of a succession of systems, and validates in turn the inexorable rise, or 'progress', from 'classic to romantic'. In allowing Cordelia to survive unscathed and Lear to live on, Tate's adaptation of Shakespeare was the popular dramatic success of 1681, and Johnson's sympathies with its audience-appeal are expressed in this note. But the difficult poise of Johnson's judgment that is captured here has failed to modify the historical 'plot' of criticism in substantial terms. Cast within the historical mode, Johnson's criticism has seemed unable to relay the collaborative tension, the flux and reflux that unites at any historical moment the author, the audience, the world, the text and the critic, and establishes communication between Johnson, Shakespeare and ourselves. My suggestion is that Johnson's pain at the death of Cordelia stands in a different kind of historical continuity; and while itself literature, it rests on a different order of testimony from any narrative of purely *literary* rules. We see, to begin with, the moral disturbance of *Lear* which makes editing the play so difficult for Johnson and explains its compelling and justifiable success, the fact that it is 'deservedly celebrated among the dramas of Shakespeare'. 'There is perhaps', as Johnson had written earlier in his note, 'no play which keeps the attention so strongly fixed; which so much agitates our passions and interests our curiosity':

> The artful involutions of distinct interests, the striking opposition of contrary characters, the sudden changes of fortune, and the quick succession of events, fill the mind with a perpetual tumult of indignation, pity, and hope. There is no scene which does not contribute to the aggravation of the distress or conduct of the action, and scarce a line which does not conduce to the progress of the scene. So powerful is the current of the poet's imagination, that the mind, which once ventures within it, is hurried irresistibly along. (*Shakespeare*, 8: 702-703)

The emotional drive of this passionate and dispassionate passage, going as it does with Johnson's rhetorically managed cadence, suggests that like much criticism that has endured it offers to the modern reader a present aesthetic (a poetic) as well as an historical experience. It both constitutes a feeling and communicates one. There is a combination of the inward and the disinterested. We see that Johnson is not applying a concept of any kind derived simply from outside the experience - from what Peter Lamarque in his discussion of Cordelia's death in the terms of aesthetic philosophy calls the 'external perspective'.[26] Johnson's mind is filled by the feelings he has; but Johnson remains at the same time removed from the 'perpetual tumult'. He speaks of 'the' mind, not 'my' mind, and the unhistrionic weight of his generalizing abstractions conveys a restrained emotional response to the emotions - 'passions', 'curiosity', 'opposition', 'succession', 'indignation, pity and hope'. Johnson thus seems to combine his critical subjectivity with a community of feeling that is not culturally specific and he recommends the response he records as available to all normally sensitive readers. The passage in this way rhetorically prepares the ground for the sudden transition to the intimate and confessional insight into 'my sensations' some two paragraphs later - to the *description* of shock whose only recommendation is the sincerity with which it is felt, and the common ground of the experience on which we commonly see that it rests. Johnson thus provides a setting for the entry of the first person singular in 'I cannot easily be persuaded'; 'I might relate'; 'I know not whether I ever endured'.

Filled though the mind seems to be, when Johnson recalls his experience of the play, he adopts a delicately tactful, an almost apologetic tone at this point.[27]

But Johnson's resistance to the tragedy of Cordelia's death is specifically *not* an apologia for any *particular* rule of drama independent *of* the experience. It is not a *consequence* of Johnson 'preferring the comedies to the tragedies' (because he did not prefer them). It is not the *result* of a neoclassic prejudice against linguistic and dramatic indecorum in Shakespeare (because he did not unequivocally possess one). What he says, rather, exists within a conception of justice and history attuned to the emotional content of its logical subject, and its radicalism emanates from the depths of Johnson's own psychological history of pain and self-resistance and from the play's distinction as drama. Johnson draws attention to what ought to be a critical shortcoming - not being robust enough to face the last scenes of the play again until he had to - to evoke the critical sense of being out on a limb where, as a condition of judgment, one's company is only the play and what is only human about it. So expressive is Johnson's statement on *Lear*'s distressing consequence as a drama - and the difficult pleasure which is also pain that derives from this - that we can see how Johnson's reaction may be held together with, and distinguished from, the best known of his paragraphs on Shakespeare's 'faults' from the *Preface*:

> His first defect is that to which may be imputed most of the evil in books or in men. He sacrifices virtue to convenience, and is so much more careful to please than to instruct, that he seems to write without any moral purpose. From his writings indeed a system of social duty may be selected, for he that thinks reasonably must think morally; but his precepts and axioms drop casually from him; he makes no just distribution of good or evil, nor is always careful to shew in the virtuous a disapprobation of the wicked; he carries his persons indifferently through right and wrong, and at the close dismisses them without further care, and leaves their examples to operate by chance. This fault the barbarity of his age cannot extenuate; for it is always a writer's duty to make the world better, and justice is a virtue independant on time or place. (*Shakespeare*, 7: 71)[28]

Culminating in an appeal to 'justice', this passage from the *Preface* applies to all or most of Shakespeare's plays. It is a considered judgment - an answer in part to Pope[29] - which brings together many experiences of many plays, and it is part of the larger estimate - which includes the praise - of the whole of Shakespeare. The passage on *Lear* is by contrast merely a note, a beautiful fragment itself composed of fragments, and an evocation of much that is exposed of the Johnsonian self and much that is withheld. Coleridgean and modern critics of Shakespearean tragedy (and even Johnson's contemporary Warton when he writes on *Lear*)[30] have explained the parts of a Shakespearean play in terms of its unity of imaginative structure. But Johnson never provides a total account of any play that aspires to completeness. His criticism comes occasionally and pragmatically to mind at a temporary pause in the editorial flow. His note is 'traditional' in conforming to Pope's principle of criticism as a 'short excursion', a brief intervention which leaves many things unsaid.

As with the 'Observation' on *Lear*, commentators and historians of criticism exposed to the notorious passage in the *Preface* have also made 'poetical [or poetic] justice' an organizing theme of historical knowledge about Johnson - as if *that* - and not the state of mind of which it is a figment - were the context of primary relevance and explanatory value. The illusory independence of 'poetical justice' provides in this way an escape clause whereby commentators and critical historians do not need to regard their object through Johnson's eyes: 'Shakespeare's first fault', writes Arthur Sherbo, 'is his failure to write with a moral purpose and to observe poetic justice. This is the combined weight of the eighteenth century speaking'.[31] Yet Johnson's emphasis falls here on Shakespeare's *pervasive* laxity of moral vision, and there is in common with the note no normalizing rule of thumb that Johnson stands to accept or reject. The paragraph moreover must of necessity apply (as any true generalization) to some plays more than to others. But the distinctive thing about the end of *King Lear*, as Johnson's note confirms, is that Shakespeare by contrast clearly *intended* the tragedy he produced. Johnson's account of the current of Shakespeare's imagination suggests the control he extended to this particular work (compared with *Hamlet* for example). His design is carried to its conclusion in the dead Cordelia in the arms of her howling father. And it is this *willed* descent into incoherence, the studied deliberation with which the tragedy unrolls, that has caused the Johnsonian 'shock'. The past tense here ('*was* many years ago so shocked') brings the history of Johnson, the inner biography we considered in the previous chapter, vividly into play.[32]

In her book on *Tragic Plots*, Felicity Rosslyn has called on the evidence of Shakespeare's source, where Cordelia won the war and lived to be queen, to suggest that 'we cannot doubt that he is deliberately twisting the knife'. '[T]here may', she concludes, 'be impulses of love and creativity in the world ... [Shakespeare] describes, but mad disorder is what finally prevails'.[33] But if this modern critic when placed alongside Johnson also regrets the collapse into madness, would she or Johnson actually be right - ethically *or* aesthetically - not to want to repel the insane world of the play? The historian of criticism does not attempt to answer this question as an enquiry directed at us, but responds to a narrative of observed or discarded rules systematically remote from the emotional life of the present and external to the experience of the play. My reservation, first, is that such a paradigm is of all explanatory generalizations the worst, and that, once imposed at such a crucial point, the whole teleology of critical history comes under general suspicion.

Second, and with reference to what Johnson says *in his own words* in the *Preface*, Shakespeare '*seems* to write without any moral purpose'. I have already argued that Shakespeare's moral purpose is for Johnson immense: 'he that thinks reasonably must think morally' (*Shakespeare*, 7: 71). And to think reasonably implies a unity with those same 'reasonable beings' who 'naturally love justice' mentioned in the note on *King Lear*. But here the audience enters into a moral universe of 'indignation, pity and hope'. And it is through the experience of pathos, inspiring pity but not hope at the close, that the reader's or spectator's 'naturally' felt awareness of right and of wrong is so fundamentally outraged. Indeed the equanimity reasonable people require to make moral decisions and ethical calculations at all is radically deranged by *Lear*. So, ultimately, are Cordelia's own 'untenderly' spoken affections for her impossible father, the love dispensed arithmetically according to her bond, no more, no less, at the start of the play. Finally, in protesting in his *Preface* on behalf of the rational part of the human race against Shakespeare, Johnson appeals in a broader, moralist's spirit to the writer's 'duty to make the world better'.

Consonant with the timeless 'justice' required by the *Preface* is the value, a presence within the Johnsonian tone, conveyed in his note on *King Lear*. This has the poetical composure of poetry, but its referent is not uniquely 'poetical' in the specialized, time-touched eighteenth-century sense. It belongs to Johnson's governing conviction that the natural always exceeds the aesthetic; to the view that there 'is always an appeal open from criticism [and critical theory] to nature' (*Shakespeare*, 7: 67). But because Shakespeare had constructed a play in its moral aspect beyond what 'reasonable beings' are able to *think* natural, or therefore coherent in its treatment of evil and good, Johnson's role is to reclaim the paradox of tragedy by asserting the remedial, therapeutic, saner, sense-making organizations of art. Readers of *Lear* project themselves into the world of the drama and feel *along with* the characters. They adopt the 'internal perspective' that Lamarque has referred to as that of the 'fictive stance, namely, direct imaginative involvement with the subject of a work'.[34] Yet as Johnson had written in his *Preface*, 'the spectators are always in their senses' (*Shakespeare*, 7: 77), and when he says in his note on *Lear* that an audience will at the close 'always rise better pleased from the final triumph of persecuted virtue', he does not suggest the need to *delude* oneself about life. One does not forget that Cordelia is a character in a play:

> The reflection that strikes the heart is not, that the evils before us are real evils, but that they are evils to which we ourselves may be exposed .... The delight of tragedy proceeds from our consciousness of fiction; if we thought murders and treasons real, they would please no more. (*Shakespeare*, 7: 78)

Thus once again does the death of Cordelia appeal to a 'justice' (requiring a 'judgment') not mutually reducible to, or co-extensional with, 'poetical justice', and there is in Johnson's protest against the tragedy no *ultimate* relief from pain in the stilted, ethically formulaic drama where nothing is brought to justice because nothing has moral or fictive life, either in Tate, where 'poetical justice' is done, or in Addison's *Cato*, where it is not. Rather, being 'better pleased' by 'the broken heart and limp body of death' (in Wilson Knight's phrase)[35] arises from the 'consciousness of fiction' that permits a transcendental perspective upon the play's terrible events, and gives coherence to its imitation of life. The events we see are possible in the world even though it is not *in* the world that we know them. Johnson confronts the events with reluctance, and his emotional past is exposed temporarily in the fractured marginality of his editorial note. But Johnson transmutes his raw and personal emotions of past pain into the whole completed and completing experience of a present and permanent art in his 'Observation' on *King Lear*. The aesthetic effect of his critical language (its pulse, beat, form, tone, rhythm) is not essentially different from any poetical expression in verse or in prose, and it exists to balance and shape and close the tortured experience of the play in Johnson's edition. Thus does Cordelia's death, in Johnson's account of it, define the exceptional conditions that give tragedy its power. Its 'general nature' lifts us from daily reality onto what H.A. Mason once called the 'tragic plane'.[36] G.F. Parker has observed that 'There is ... [for Johnson] nothing which *mediates* the shockingness of the action to us in a form that we can not only endure but even, in however complex a sense of the word, take pleasure in'.[37] My contention is that Johnson's transmutation of the experience of Shakespeare into a critical statement that collapses art and criticism, that joins the dull duty of an editor to the expressive powers of the poet, demonstrates that there is.

To return from this example of criticism's literary and aesthetic description to the idea of history in which Johnson's criticism of Shakespeare (and idea of criticism) is itself enclosed. In his essay 'On Writing the History of Criticism in England 1650-1800', R.S. Crane drew on the example of J.W.H. Atkins' *History* to expose 'an inadequate and mainly external conception of what a history of criticism in this or indeed any other period should be'. 'You begin', wrote Crane:

> by assuming that the literary criticism of any age is a body of pronouncements about something, called literature or poetry, which is thought to have a fixed and determinable nature (however elusive or hard to state) in much the same sense as any concrete event in human affairs; and you assume, similarly, that criticism itself is a single discipline, which can be judged to be better or worse, more or less adequate in its methods, according to its fitness for making clear the real or full truth about its supposed common objects and for appreciating their proper values.... You therefore concentrate, in your reading of texts, on their doctrinal content....[38]

When historians predicate 'doctrinal content' without adequate reference to the beauty and composure of the critical text, its context of literary origin, status or occasion relative to other non-reductively contextualizing utterances by the same critic, its verbal particularity, moral consciousness and emotional depth of field or the quantity of 'passionate intelligence'[39] that lies behind it, this is, I conclude, a mythologizing approach to the history of criticism that goes beyond the selectivity and incompleteness of history. And it is for the reasons advanced here by Crane that twentieth-century histories of criticism of the eighteenth century have tended to construct monuments to criticism, such as Johnson's, that are not *expected* to enlighten, and can *only* be thought eccentric or odd, or 'not for direct instruction in critical thinking'. But except in response to questions that are real questions for us - not whether Johnson adheres to, or is free from 'poetical justice', but how *we* respond to Cordelia's death and what resources of sympathy *we* bring to bear - history cannot make sense of the past through its critical texts.[40] The emotional life of the dead critics in which the modern reader might yearn to participate becomes simply a casualty of a lingeringly 'neo-positive' history. It is an image of Johnson that the most intelligent historical theory of the twentieth century has left largely unchanged to this point.

Notes

---

[1] Cf. Imlac's celebrated dissertation on poetry in *Rasselas*, Chapter 10, where he says that a poet must not 'number the streaks of the tulip, or describe the different shades in the verdure of the forest' (*Rasselas*, 43). Johnson's pejorative use of 'general' as a critical term has been less commonly appreciated. In the 'Life of Dryden', he could write that Dryden's *Eleonora*, 'being ... general fixes no impression on the reader' (*Lives*, 1: 441-42). For an in-depth discussion of the philosophical and theological context of Johnson's use of the term 'nature' see Scott D. Evans, *Samuel Johnson's 'General Nature': Traditionand Transition in Eighteenth-Century Discourse* (Newark: University of Delaware Press, 1999).

[2] See, for example, Terry Eagleton, who blames a commitment to timeless values for literary theory's 'obstinate, perverse, endlessly resourceful refusal to countenance social and historical realities'. *Literary Theory: An Introduction* (Oxford: Blackwell, 1983), 196.

[3] For example John Wain, Introduction to *Johnson as Critic*: 'Johnson's Shakespearean criticism is close to neo-classical norms. And the gist of his praise of Shakespeare, the reasons he gives for elevating Shakespeare to his throne among poets, is the same. Shakespeare is "the poet of nature" - that is, of human nature' (36).

[4] Dryden, Preface to *Fables Ancient and Modern* (1700), *Essays*, 2: 284.

[5] Johnson's use of the term 'manners' is very much in continuity with the spirit of the definitions assigned to 'les moeurs' by Boileau in *l'Art Poétique* and by Rapin in his *Réflexions* (both 1674). The latter, in Rymer's influential and passionate translation, had declared that: 'The sovereign Rule for treating of *Manners*, is to copy them after *Nature*, and above all to study well the *heart* of Man, to know how to distinguish all its *motions.* 'Tis this which none are acquainted with: the *heart* of man is an *abyss*, where none can sound the bottom: it is a *mystery*, which the most quick-sighted cannot pierce into, and in which the most cunning are mistaken'. See *Reflections on Aristotle's Treatise of Poesie*, trans. Thomas Rymer (London, 1674), 38.

[6] For an indication that Johnson is looking not only before, but after, in this claim, cf. William Hazlitt on *Richard II*, *The Characters of Shakespear's Plays* (1817), *The Complete Works of William Hazlitt*, ed. P.P. Howe, 21 vols. (London and Toronto: Dent, 1930), 4: 273: 'He [Richard] is ... human in his distresses; for to feel pain, and sorrow, weakness, disappointment, remorse and anguish, is the lot of humanity, and we sympathise with him accordingly. The sufferings of the man make us forget that he ever was a king'.

[7] In the words of the (text-book) treatise on drama translated from the Abbé d'Aubignac: 'When a King speaks upon the Stage, he must speak like a King, and that is the Circumstance of his Dignity, against which nothing ought to be done with Decency'. See *The Whole Art of the Stage made English* (London, 1684), 76. Johnson seems to have transcended this extremely narrow sense of the 'manners' in his *Preface to Shakespeare*; yet he could also write in *The Rambler* (4: 302) that 'the heroes and queens of tragedy should never descend to trifle, but in the hours of ease, and intermissions of danger'. Johnson's artistic intuition that regal decorum was sometimes dramatically necessary, though sometimes overlooked by Shakespeare, is moreover intermittently a presence in the notes to the plays, where he mentions in passing the occasional deviation from, or adherence to, the 'manners' of royalty. See, for example, *Shakespeare*, 7: 444 (*Richard II*); 8: 529, 553 (*Henry V*); 8: 602 (*Henry VI*).

[8] Cf. John Dennis, *On the Genius and Writings of Shakespear* (1711), *The Critical*

Works of John Dennis, ed. Edward Niles Hooker, 2 vols. (Baltimore: Johns Hopkins University Press, 1939-43), 2: 5; Rymer, *Short View of Tragedy*, Chapter 8, 'Reflections on the *Julius Caesar*', *Critical Works*: 'In the former play [*Othello*], our Poet might be bolder, the persons being all his own Creatures, and meer fiction. But here he sins not against Nature and Philosophy only, but against the most known History, and the memory of the Noblest Romans, that ought to be sacred to all Posterity' (165).

The Yale edition of *Johnson on Shakespeare* notes that Johnson also seems to be replying to various remarks in Voltaire's *Appel à toutes les nations de l'Europe* (1761), and a criticism of *Hamlet* forms a substantial section of the *Appel*. See *Oeuvres Complètes de Voltaire*, 52 toms. (Paris: Garnier, 1877-85), 24, *Mélanges*, 3: 191-221. Voltaire was not in the event silenced by Johnson. He responded satirically to Johnson's defence of Shakespearean buffoonery in his *Art Dramatique* (1770), *Oeuvres*, 17, *Dictionnaire Philosophique*, 1: 393-428.

[9] There is much common ground between Johnson's eighteenth-century reviewers and the criticisms of the major romantic critics of Shakespeare (which I examine in Chapter 6). Thus the author of *The Critical Review* 20 (November 1765) could brusquely protest that Johnson's paragraph on the Shakespearean 'species' was 'by no means descriptive of Shakespeare, *since* Shakespeare has succeeded better in representing the oddities of human nature than her general properties' (323).

[10] When in the *Preface* Johnson describes Shakespeare's characters as 'discriminated and preserved' (*Shakespeare*, 7: 64), he means quite uncontroversially that they are properly distinguished and consistently maintained throughout a play. Johnson commented elsewhere in the notes on Shakespeare's success or failure in preserving character: Jacques, in *As You Like It*, was 'natural and well preserved' (*Shakespeare*, 7: 264).

[11] Warburton had in practice criticized Polonius in his notes on *Hamlet* as a character only of 'manners', while in his *Reflections on Aristotle* (1674), Rapin (in Rymer's translation) had asserted in the broadest theoretical terms the weakness of the particular: 'Truth is well nigh alwayes *defective*, by the mixture of particular conditions that compose it. Nothing is brought into the world that is not remote from the *perfection* of its *Idea* from the very birth. Originals and Models are to be search'd for in *probability*, and in the *universal principles* of things, where nothing that is *material* and *singular* enters to corrupt them' (34-35). My point, however, would be that Johnson is here incorporating into his *Preface* a continuity that is also a value via the channels of Augustan *poetry*. In his play between the general and the particular, Johnson transfuses into the critical text the thought (and the serenity of feeling about the thought) that Dryden had recreated from Chaucer in his version of 'The Knight's Tale' (1700):

> Parts of the Whole are we; but God the Whole;
> Who gives us Life, and animating Soul.
> For Nature cannot from a Part derive
> That Being, which the Whole can only give:
> He perfect, stable; but imperfect We,
> Subject to Change, and diff'rent in Degree.
> Plants, Beasts, and Man; and as our Organs are,
> We more or less of his Perfection share.
> But by a long Descent, th'Etherial Fire
> Corrupts; and Forms, the mortal Part, expire:
> As he withdraws his Vertue, so they pass,
> And the same Matter makes another Mass:

> This Law th'Omniscient Pow'r was pleas'd to give,
> That ev'ry Kind should by Succession live;
> That Individuals die, his Will ordains;
> The propagated Species still remains. (lines 1042-57)

See *The Poems of John Dryden*, ed. James Kinsley, 4 vols. (Oxford: Clarendon Press, 1958), 4: 1526-27.

[12] The Yale edition (*Shakespeare*, 7: 66) omits to note that the terms 'tragedy' and 'comedy' were placed in italics in the 1778 text of Johnson's edition, perhaps to signify Johnson's detachment from them, or his implicit criticism of their value. See *The Plays of William Shakespeare*, 2nd ed. 10 vols. (London: C. Bathhurst, 1778), 1: 9.

[13] The approach adopted by the major romantic critics was in this connection only to *strengthen* the initial eighteenth-century reading of Johnson's remarks. William Hazlitt was to presume that 'DR JOHNSON thought Shakespeare's comedies better than his tragedies' and that - therefore - Johnson was indisposed to sympathy with 'works of high-wrought passion or imagination' ('On Shakespeare and Ben Jonson', *Works*, 6: 30). A.W. Schlegel believed similarly that Johnson's 'paradoxical assertion ... that "Shakspeare had a greater talent for comedy than tragedy"' pointed to his being insensitive to Shakespeare's tragic superiority: 'For its refutation, it is unnecessary to appeal to the great tragical compositions of the poet, which, for over-powering effect, leave far behind them almost everything that the stage has seen besides'. See *A Course of Lectures on Dramatic Art and Literature*, trans. John Black, rev. ed. 1809 (London: Bohn's Standard Library, 1846), 365-66. The major twentieth-century critic to argue from this contestable premise about Johnson is Leavis: 'The critic who can in this way exalt the comedy above the tragedy exhibits a failure in the appreciation of Shakespeare that no one today, surely, would hold to be anything but major'. 'Doctor Johnson', 649-50.

[14] The *Critical Review* 20 (November 1765) assumed a pejorative use of 'skill', while William Kenrick in the *Monthly Review* 33 (October 1765) concluded that 'Dr Johnson prefers Shakespeare's comic scenes to his tragic' (290). Johnson seems in fact to be answering Dennis: 'Tho' Shakespear succeeded very well in Comedy, yet his principal Talent and his chief Delight was Tragedy' (*Critical Works*, 2: 13). The dichotomy represented by this observation was to become an institution of pre-romantic criticism. Joseph Warton, for example, was later to complain of the critical trend seemingly represented by Johnson: 'the opinion, which I am sorry to perceive gains ground, that Shakespeare's chief and predominant talent lay in comedy, tends to lessen the unrivalled excellence of our divine bard'. See Warton's note to Edmond Malone, ed., Preface to *The Plays and Poems of William Shakespeare*, 21 vols. (London: Rivington, 1821), 1: 71.

[15] Johnson wrote that the characters of *Henry IV Part 2* are 'diversified with the utmost nicety of discernment, and the profoundest skill in the nature of man' (*Shakespeare*, 7: 523), and in the Dedication to Charlotte Lennox's *Shakespeare Illustrated* he had earlier claimed that Shakespeare 'had looked with great attention on the scenes of nature; but his chief skill was in human actions, passions, and habits' (*Shakespeare*, 7: 49).

[16] Commentators have noted that Johnson is probably thinking of Rymer's observation from the *Short View of Tragedy* that '*Shakespears genius* lay for Comedy and Humour. In Tragedy he appears quite out of his Element' (*Critical Works*, 169). But Johnson's sense of Shakespeare's disposition was also underpinned by his independent experience of the plays - as his notes will suggest. Parolles, in *All's Well that Ends Well*, seemed 'the character which Shakespeare delighted to draw' (*Shakespeare*, 7: 399); in *Troilus and Cressida*, 'The comick characters seem to have been the favourites of the writer'

(8: 938). The nurse, in *Romeo and Juliet*, was likewise 'one of the characters in which the authour delighted' (8: 957); in virtue of a stroke of wit from *The Comedy of Errors* Johnson noticed that Shakespeare 'only sports with an allusion, in which he takes too much delight' (7: 356).

[17] In his 'Life of Butler' Johnson was later to write of *Hudibras* that 'those modifications of life and peculiarities of practice which are the progeny of error and perverseness, or at best some accidental influence or transient persuasion, must perish with their parents' (*Lives*, 1: 214).

[18] In ways that are symptomatic of his sense of the failure of post-Shakespearean tragedy, Johnson was to write of Thomson's *Tancred and Sigismunda* that 'It may be doubted whether he was, either by the bent of nature or habits of study, much qualified for tragedy. It does not appear that he had much sense of the pathetick, and his diffusive and descriptive style produced declamation rather than dialogue' (*Lives*, 3: 293).

[19] But it would be another thing to say, as F.R. Leavis has done, that 'Johnson cannot understand that works of art *enact* their moral valuations' and that 'for Johnson a moral judgment that isn't *stated* isn't there' See 'Doctor Johnson', 652. Johnson did indeed write of Shakespeare's plays in the *Preface* as filled with 'practical axioms and domestick wisdom'; and that just as 'It was said of Euripides, that every verse was a precept', so 'it may be said of Shakespeare, that from his works may be collected a system of civil and oeconomical prudence' (*Shakespeare*, 7: 62). But such comments do not exclude Johnson's appreciation of other, inferred and enacted modes of moral communication. One of the most positive contemporary reactions to Johnson's criticism on ethical grounds is that of a female critic. Elizabeth Griffiths, Preface to *The Morality of Shakespeare's Drama Illustrated* (London, 1775), praised Johnson as the only editor 'who has considered Shakespeare's writings in a moral light' (viii-ix).

[20] There are numerous examples of moral inferences drawn by Johnson in the notes. In *Henry IV* 'The moral to be drawn from this representation is, that no man is more dangerous than he that with a will to corrupt, hath the power to please; and that neither wit nor honesty ought to think themselves safe with such a companion when they see Henry seduced by Falstaff' (*Shakespeare*, 7: 523-24). Among the notes on *Timon of Athens* Johnson wrote approvingly of the play's moral efficaciousness, and the catastrophe which 'affords a very powerful warning against that ostentatious liberality, which scatters bounty, but confers no benefits, and buys flattery, but not friendship' (*Shakespeare*, 8: 745). Rather than hunt out stated morals, or morality of any other *particular* kind, it is in general more common to find Johnson balancing the value of instruction against pleasure: 'Whatever professes to benefit by pleasing must pleased at once', he wrote in his 'Life of Cowley': 'The pleasures of the mind imply something sudden and unexpected; that which elevates must always surprise. What is perceived by slow degrees may gratify us with the consciousness of improvement, but will never strike with the sense of pleasure' (*Lives*, 1: 59). When Johnson actually experienced 'consciousness of improvement' his verdict was invariably negative. Thus Roscommon's translation of Horace's *Ars Poetica* was 'A poem frigidly didactick'; Johnson could remark of Dryden's 'Absalom and Achitophel' that 'A long poem of mere sentiments easily becomes tedious' (*Lives*, 1: 237, 437).

[21] I am therefore inclined to disagree with Leopold Damrosch Jr. who regards the *Preface to Shakespeare* as 'transitional rather than central in ... [Johnson's] critical writing'. *The Uses of Johnson's Criticism*, 104.

[22] *Life of Johnson*, 1: 198.

[23] It seems strange, on this account, that Paul Fussell should choose to omit the *Preface to Shakespeare*, and Johnson's notes to the plays, from his treatment of 'Johnson's

main writing enterprises'. See *Samuel Johnson and the Life of Writing* (London: Chatto and Windus, 1972), 143.

[24] 'Tradition and the Individual Talent' (1919), *Selected Essays* (London: Faber and Faber, 1932), 14.

[25] 5 January 1754. See *The Adventurer*, 4 vols. (London, 1778), 4: 148: 'I shall transiently observe ... that this drama is chargeable with considerable imperfections. The plot of Edmund against his brother ... distracts the attention, and destroys the unity of the fable....'

[26] Peter Lamarque, *Fictional Points of View* (Ithaca and London: Cornell University Press, 1996), 146. Lamarque writes of the death of Cordelia that 'internally and imaginatively, viewers are dismayed by so futile and tragic a loss. Yet, from the external perspective, few would welcome Nahum Tate's rewriting of the play where Cordelia is saved. Cordelia's death, as we come to see, is essential to the tragic structure of the play. From the internal perspective, we might wish her spared; from the external perspective, we want the play just as it is' (146). Such an insight (on philosophical-aesthetic grounds) implicitly acknowledges the *necessary* paradox of Johnson's response.

[27] Leopold Damrosch Jr. has drawn a distinction between present and past reactions to the scene by noting that 'The modern critic may take Cordelia's death as an authentication of what many men have come to believe, that no amount of penance and redemption may save us from an appalling fate'; for Johnson meanwhile, writes Damrosch, 'her death is an inexplicable violation of the direction in which the play seemed to be moving, a gratuitous outrage far more horrible than "the extrusion of Gloucester's eyes"'. See *Samuel Johnson and the Tragic Sense*, 250-51. My stress falls by comparison not on what Johnson finds to be 'inexplicable' here (in his contrast with a more knowing and sophisticated modern pessimism or nihilism), but on the remedial poise of Johnson's judgment, itself having the totality and completeness of an aesthetic experience.

[28] Echoing the climax of this paragraph, Johnson in his 'Life of Milton' was later to write that 'Prudence and Justice are virtues, and excellences of all times and of all places' (*Lives*, 1: 100).

[29] In his Preface to the *Works of Shakespear* (1725) Pope had written that 'We shall hereby extenuate many faults which are his, and clear him from the imputation of many which are not....' See *Eighteenth Century Essays on Shakespeare*, 44.

[30] Joseph Warton, essays on *King Lear* in *Adventurer* 113, 116, 122 (December 1753-Janunary 1754), 4: 58-67; 84-93; 140-48.

[31] Arthur Sherbo, *Samuel Johnson: Editor of Shakespeare with an essay on The Adventurer* (Urbana: University of Illinois Press, 1956), 57.

[32] The distance between Johnson's repulsion and the standard of contemporary sentimentalism over the ending of *Lear* can be judged from the passage that John Miller added to his translation of Batteux's *Course of the Belles Lettres or the Principles of Literature, translated from the French*, 4 vols. (London, 1761), 1: 349-50: 'The close of this tragedy is full of terror and compassion.... But ... after all the heart piercing sensations which we have before endured through the whole piece, it would be too much to see this actually performed on the stage; and it is beyond doubt that the play, as it is altered, will always be most agreeable to an audience, as the circumstances of Lear's restoration, and the virtuous Edgar's alliance with the aimiable Cordelia, must always call forth those gushing tears, which are swelled and ennobled by a virtuous joy'.

[33] Felicity Rosslyn, *Tragic Plots: A New Reading from Aeschylus to Lorca* (Aldershot: Ashgate, 2001), 132.

[34] *Fictional Points of View*, 146.

[35] G. Wilson Knight, *The Wheel of Fire: Interpretations of Shakespearean Tragedy* (London: Methuen, 1972), 175.

[36] H.A. Mason, *The Tragic Plane* (Oxford: Clarendon Press, 1985).

[37] G.F. Parker, *Johnson's Shakespeare*, 191.

[38] *The Idea of the Humanities*, 2: 159.

[39] I allude to Arieh Sachs, *Passionate Intelligence: Imagination and Reason in the Works of Samuel Johnson* (Baltimore: Johns Hopkins University Press, 1967).

[40] 'Nowhere is Johnson closer to the play's own spirit', writes Philip Davis suggestively of his note on *King Lear*, 'than when he pays it the tribute of his hatred, pain and fear'. *In Mind of Johnson: A Study of Johnson the Rambler* (London: Athlone Press, 1989), 286.

Chapter 4

Historicization and Literary Pleasure: Johnson Reads Cowley

The Significance of Johnson's Cowley

To return, now, from the Shakespearean criticism to the *Lives of the Poets*, and to their ramification of my case. Notwithstanding Milton's reported claim that the three greatest English poets were Spenser, Shakespeare and Cowley,[1] Cowley's poems have received by comparison very little concerted scholarly and critical comment.[2] Interpretation of Johnson's 'Life of Cowley' has tended correspondingly to focus on Johnson's theory of metaphysical poetry, his concept of poetical language and of 'wit'.[3] But the importance of the 'Life of Cowley' to the problem of critical history (beyond perhaps most other 'Lives') is that it again suggests constituents of criticism that fall outside 'theory' and includes the repertoire of Johnson's emotional range, from eloquent enthusiasm, through reluctant toleration, to a profound distaste for the habits ingrained within English poetry from Cowley's time. My commentary in this chapter will therefore draw further attention to dimensions of Johnsonian judgment *as distinct from* theory. This will include Johnson's assessment of whole collections of verses, such as Cowley's *Miscellanies*, his *Anacreontiques* and the *Mistress*; his appraisal of significant individual poems (such as 'The Chronicle'); but also pervasive characteristics not confined to any single collection or work. The example chosen here is what Johnson has to say about the 'diction' of Cowley. I assume throughout the detailed comparisons of this chapter that the poetry and the criticism are complementary experiences, and that they help to explain each other. I assume, that is, contra Wellek and other critical historians, and in common with the treatment of Johnson's Shakespearean criticism in the previous chapter, that poetry is an explanatory context of criticism that history must take into account.

To this purpose, I prioritize the fourth and final portion of the 'Life' - the least often discussed by critical historians or scholars of Johnson. The 'Life's' opening section is devoted to Cowley the Man; that which follows deals with Johnson's famous examination of the metaphysical school, and includes his meditation on the metaphysicals' 'heterogeneous ideas yoked by violence together'. In the initial biographical phase (paras. 1-48), Cowley's poetry is seen as the least important aspect of his career, insignificant beside his work as a secretary to Lord Jermin in Paris, where he was 'engaged in transacting things of real importance with real men and real women' (*Lives*, 1: 8). In the second section (paras. 49-63), Cowley is presented as mainly notable for what he shares with other metaphysical poets and their identity as a school. In the third section (paras. 64-101) Johnson supplies a rich variety of examples, sometimes from Donne, once from Cleveland, but mainly from Cowley. In the extended commentary which forms the long final quarter of the 'Life' (paras. 102-202), however, Johnson homes in on Cowley's poetry on its own terms, and it is here that he gives Cowley the attention he hoped would compensate for years of neglect. As he wrote to his publisher Nichols on 27 July 1778: 'You have now all *Cowley*. I have been drawn to a great length, but *Cowley* or *Waller* never had any critical examination before'.[4]

Defining Diversity: Cowley's *Miscellanies* and the Delights of Life

In this final section of the 'Life', where all but two of Cowley's collections are directly addressed, Johnson follows the poems in the order that they appear in the early Folio editions.[5] It is as if Johnson had his Cowley edition open before him as he wrote. This linearity of critical attention is nowhere more strongly in evidence than in the comments on Cowley's *Miscellanies*. Johnson seems here to be turning the leaves of his 'Cowley' as he moves from poem to poem, and his methods suggest a mixture of critical aims. In the first place, Johnson's object is to lead his reader through Cowley's *Miscellanies* by the hand. Of the collection's 23 poems Johnson mentions only ten by name, and the remarks upon them are usually kept brief. The first to be mentioned, 'The Motto', the 'Ode on Wit', the verses to Falkland, and the elegy on Sir Henry Wootton, are the first four in the series, in that order. Johnson then skips about half a dozen poems as he flicks through his edition (the 1680-81 Folio or others), moving directly to the next fairly considerable piece, 'On the Death of Mr William Hervey', to resume his commentary with 'The Chronicle', 'To Sir William D'avenant', 'An Answer to a Copy of Verses sent me from Jersey' and 'the two metrical disquisitions *for* and *against* Reason' (which Cowley had entitled 'The Tree of Knowledge' and 'Reason'). 'On the Death of Mr Crashaw', the last poem in the collection, is the last to be discussed.

Quite clearly, the poems that Johnson actually named, and then briefly examined, were ones that had caught his eye. But if Johnson's first ambition is to take his reader on a swift guided tour of Cowley's *Miscellanies* and give a comprehensive view of the whole collection, his second is to recommend Cowley's work at its best. There is perhaps nothing particularly significant in what Johnson lights upon, and what he passes over: 'To choose the best among many good is one of the most hazardous attempts of criticism' (*Lives*, 1: 35). We cannot conclude that Johnson had no time for the poems in Cowley's *Miscellanies* that are not named, and the poems he tables for comment seem somewhat selected at random. Johnson's paragraph of general praise clearly includes reference to both groups: 'His Miscellanies contain a collection of short compositions, written some as they were dictated by a mind at leisure, and some as they were called forth by different occasions; with great variety of style and sentiment, from burlesque levity to awful grandeur' (*Lives*, 1: 35). So, for example, among those exhibiting 'burlesque levity' may be Cowley's 'An Answer to a Copy of Verses sent me from Jersey', which Johnson cites by name: 'The lines from Jersey are a very curious and pleasing specimen of the familiar descending to the burlesque' (*Lives*, 1: 38). But, also, Cowley's 'Ode', which he does not:

> Here's to thee *Dick*; this whining *Love* despise;
> Pledge me, my *Friend*, and drink till thou be'st *wise*.
>> It sparkles brighter far than *she*:
>> 'Tis pure, and right without deceit;
>> And such no *woman* e're will be:
>> No; they are all *Sophisticate*.
> (*Miscellanies*, 10)

Those exhibiting 'awful grandeur' might include 'On his Majesties Return out of Scotland', which is not specifically chosen for comment:

> Welcome, Great Sir, with all the joy that's due
>> To the return of *Peace* and *You*.
> Two greatest *Blessings* which this Age can know,
> For *that* to *Thee*, for *Thee* to *Heav'en* we ow.
>> Others by *War* their *Conquests* gain,
>> You like a *God* ends obtain.
> Who when rude *Chaos* for his help did call,
> Spoke but the *Word*, and sweetly *Order'd* all.
> (*Miscellanies*, 7)

Johnson does not praise all the poems that he mentions, or all that is in those poems.[6] Sometimes, the fault is a small thing, a detail detracting only slightly from an otherwise successful poem: 'His elegy on Sir Henry Wotton [sic] is vigorous and happy, the series of thoughts is easy and natural, and the conclusion, though a little weakened by the intrusion of Alexander, is elegant and forcible' (*Lives*, 1: 36).

In Cowley's poem on the death of Hervey, the particulars are symptomatic of a more pervasive ethical and aesthetic flaw, and Johnson discerns this weakness in the poem's exemplification of the faults of 'metaphysical' verse as a whole. He writes that Cowley 'knew how to distinguish and how to commend the qualities of his companion', but that 'when he wishes to make us weep he forgets to weep himself, and diverts his sorrow by imagining how his crown of bays, if he had it, would *crackle* in the *fire*' (*Lives*, 1: 37). The reference here is to the ninth stanza of the poem:

> Had I a wreath of *Bays* about my brow,
> I should contemn that flouri'shing honour now,
> Condemn it to the *Fire*, and joy to hear
>> It rage and crackle there.
> (*Miscellanies*, 18)

It is not the detail itself which here offends Johnson, but the low opinion of his own compositions that Cowley's image reveals. Johnson had written in general of the *Miscellanies* that some 'were dictated by a mind at leisure' (*Lives*, 1: 35), as if to hint at the ease and delightfulness of many of the pieces. But his comment on Cowley's crackling bay-leaf suggests that, in the poem on Hervey, Johnson found 'leisure' improperly used:

> It is the odd fate of this thought to be worse for being true. The bay-leaf crackles remarkably as it burns; as therefore this property was not assigned it by chance, the mind must be thought sufficiently at ease that could attend to such minuteness of physiology. (*Lives*, 1: 37)

Johnson's selection, then, though 'the best among many good' (*Lives*, 1:35), has the value of a representative array; Johnson is attempting to capture something of the variety (in both kind and quality) in a collection he enjoyed *for* its variety: 'Such an assemblage of diversified excellence *no other poet* has hitherto afforded' (*Lives*, 1: 35; emphasis mine).

Johnson's praise of Cowley's *Miscellanies* seems therefore to suggest a critical diversity of approach at the same time that it strengthens our knowledge of Cowley's heterogeneity as a poet. Though small, the collection displays an answering diversity of poetical topics: the deaths of famous and less famous men; a painter, a schoolmaster, a diplomat, poet and college friend; military campaigns; the capriciousness of love; wit, heroic poetry, and poetic inspiration itself; drinking to forget; the pleasures of companionship and retirement. In treating these subjects, Cowley employs many different forms of verse, both original and translated. Some are stanzaic, some (especially those on 'serious' topics), use the heroic line, and are written in couplets. Sometimes Cowley varies his heroic line with lines of different numbers of syllables, as in 'The Motto'. Cowley can have as many as ten syllables to a line or as few as six; as few as six lines to a stanza or as many as eight.

But although he enjoyed the totality of this collection, certain poems had done more than others to intensify the personal pleasure in Cowley that Johnson wishes to share in the 'Life'. The pieces on poetry itself, for example - 'The Motto', 'Ode on Wit', 'To Sir William D'avenant', 'On the Death of Mr Crashaw' - explore themes where Cowley and Johnson - alike as critics and poets - come together as parts of critical history. In the stanza that Johnson quotes from the 'Ode on [or 'of'] Wit', Cowley exemplifies Johnson's own precepts from the general judgment of metaphysical poetry in the earlier part of the 'Life':

> Yet 'tis not to adorn, and gild each part;
> > That shows more *Cost* than *Art*.
> *Jewels* at *Nose* and *Lips* but ill appear;
> Rather than *all thing Wit*, let none be there.
> > Several *Lights* will not be seen,
> > If there be nothing else between.
> Men doubt, because they stand so thick i'th' skie,
> If those be *Stars* which paint the *Galaxie*.
> (*Miscellanies*, 3)

Johnson had followed Cowley in his paragraphs on the metaphysical school when he had defined True Wit by what it is not. Thus Cowley's 'Some things do through our Judgment pass / As through a *Multiplying Glass*' has its echo in Johnson's optical metaphor of poetical disintegration: 'Their attempts were always analytick: they broke every image into fragments, and could no more represent by their slender conceits and laboured particularities the prospects of nature or the scenes of life, than he who dissects a sun-beam with a prism can exhibit the wide effulgence of a summer noon' (*Lives*, 1: 21).

Cowley's 'To Sir William D'avenant', which Johnson thought 'vigorously begun', opens by celebrating the new heroic style of Davenant's *Gondibert*. In his contempt for the puerilities of 'mythology', and with his taste for the irresistible human interest of poetry, Johnson would clearly find much congenial to him in this poem.[7] And when Johnson says that the poem exhibits 'some hints of criticism very justly conceived and happily expressed' (*Lives*, 1: 38), he perhaps has in mind a distinction such as Cowley's 'So *God-like Poets* do past things rehearse, / Not *change*, but *heighten* Nature by their Verse', of which he would have approved. Again, Johnson saw Cowley (as he saw Dryden and Pope) as a significant *contributor* to the critical tradition in which he himself stood. In the same paragraphs as his praise of Cowley's 'D'avenant', Johnson included a tribute to the neglected critical talents of Cowley: 'Cowley's critical abilities have not been sufficiently observed'.

There was however substantially more in Cowley's *Miscellanies* than a number of readily shared criteria, congenial commonplaces to be located in many other poets and critics. While, undoubtedly, these conjunctions formed part of his appreciation, the central attraction was one which Johnson rarely found elsewhere in Cowley - single poems of an excellence unmatched, and, in certain instances unmatchable, by any other poet. With one exception - Cowley's 'The Tree of Knowledge' (26-27): 'The stanzas against knowledge produce little conviction' (*Lives*, 1: 38) - Johnson gives *some* praise to all the poems from the *Miscellanies*. But three clear personal favourites emerge: 'The Ode on Wit', 'The Chronicle', and 'On the Death of Mr Crashaw'. In his commentary on 'The Ode on Wit', Johnson seems to move into the lexicographical mode to explain Cowley's re-definition of 'Wit':

> The ode on Wit is almost without a rival. It was about the time of Cowley that *Wit*, which had been till then used for *Intellection* in contradistinction to *Will*, took the meaning whatever it be which it now bears. (*Lives*, 1: 36)

But if 'The Ode on Wit' is, in Johnson's opinion, an unequalled, or 'almost' unequalled poem, 'without a rival', it depends on a matchless, or 'almost' matchless moment to make it so: 'Of all the passages in which poets have exemplified their own precepts none will easily be found of greater excellence than that in which Cowley condemns exuberance of Wit' (*Lives*, 1: 36). Johnson has here in mind a tradition of criticism written in poetry - including the *Art Poétique* of Boileau, John Sheffield, the Earl of Mulgrave's *Essay on Poetry* and

Roscommon's translation of Horace of 1684 - which has Pope's *Essay on Criticism* as its most eminent example.

On Cowley's 'Crashaw', Johnson wrote that:

> Cowley seems to have had, what Milton is believed to have wanted, the skill to rate his own performances by their just value, and has therefore closed his *Miscellanies* with the verses upon Crashaw, which apparently excel all that have gone before them, and in which there are beauties which common authors may justly think not only above their attainment, but above their ambition. (*Lives*, 1: 39)

In what respects, precisely, the verses on Crashaw 'apparently' (not 'seemingly' but 'manifestly') excel all that have gone before them, Johnson does not say. He may not have strictly agreed with Cowley's exaltation of Crashaw's poetic merits; but Cowley's humility, and modest estimate of himself, concluding his *Miscellanies* by this tribute to a friend, were clearly an appealing sign of his having taken the measure of his own talents, and found them wanting.

Throughout the *Lives*, Johnson objects to the corruption of Christian poetry by imagery and deities drawn from pagan religion. One of his strongest objections is to Cowley's tendency - principally in *The Mistress* - to deify women. Cowley shows himself critically self-aware on both these topics in his poem on Crashaw:

> Ah wretched *We*, *Poets of Earth!* but *Thou*
> Wert *Living* the same *Poet* which thou'rt *Now*.
> ....
> Still the old *Heathen Gods* in *Numbers* dwell,
> The *Heav'enliest* thing on Earth still keeps up *Hell*.
> Nor have we yet quite purg'd the *Christian Land*;
> Still *Idols* here, like *Calves* at *Bethel* stand.
> And though *Pans Death* long since all *Or'acles* broke,
> Yet still in Rhyme the *Fiend Apollo* spoke:
> Nay with the worst of Heathen dotage We
> (Vain men!) the *Monster Woman Deifie*;
> Find *Stars*, and tye our *Fates* there in a *Face*,
> And *Paradise* in them by whom we *lost* it, place.
> What different faults corrupt our *Muses* thus?
> *Wanton* as *Girles*, as *old Wives, Fabulous!*
> (*Miscellanies*, 29)

The 'Unrivalled and Alone': The Excellence of Cowley's 'The Chronicle'

At the top of Johnson's 'shortlist' of poems chosen for special treatment from the *Miscellanies* is, however, 'The Chronicle'. Johnson's comments on this poem are quite unusual, and in my recollection, 'The Chronicle' is one of the *very* few individual poems in the entire *Lives of the Poets* on which Johnson lavishes unreserved praise. It is certainly one of the most enthusiastic passages on any single work - *anywhere* in Johnson's critical writings. Cowley is at his best in the poem, in Johnson's view, doing what he does better than anyone else: 'The *Chronicle* is a composition unrivalled and alone: such gaiety of fancy, such facility of expression, such varied similitude, such a succession of images, and such a dance of words, it is vain to expect except from Cowley' (*Lives*, 1: 37).

When Johnson writes of Cowley's 'gaiety of fancy', he seems here to be reacting to a tone pervasive throughout the poem, and in evidence from the very first stanza. Here the 'gaiety' of Cowley's 'fancy' is to compare his heart as a lover to a ball tossed wantonly around from player to player as part of a wild game of catch:

> Margarita first possest,
>   If I remember well, my brest,
>   *Margarita* first of all;
> But when a while the wanton Maid
> With my restless Heart had plaid,
>   *Martha* took the flying Ball.
> (*Miscellanies*, 22)

Later, in the eighth stanza, the eye of Isabella acts like gunfire of a victorious army on the competitors for the poet's affections. Her conquest of the poet is accomplished with the strutting pride of a victory parade:

> But when *Isabella* came
>   Arm'd with a resistless flame
>   And th'Artillery of her Eye,
> Whilst she proudly marcht about
> Greater Conquests to find out,
>   She beat out *Susan* by the By. (23)

This is, perhaps, what Johnson means by the 'varied similitude' of 'The Chronicle'; the diversified worlds of association which supply witty 'metaphysical' comparisons for the phasing in and the phasing out of the girls, from the game of ball to the military campaign. Perhaps, also, Johnson is thinking of the variety of political and military metaphors in the poem. In the second stanza, the players at ball become a succession of rival queens, each mightier and fiercer than the last, and the poet's heart (the ball of the first stanza), becomes the state. Martha catches the ball, but 'resigns' the throne:

> *Martha* soon did it resign
>   To the beauteous *Catharine*.
>   Beauteous *Catharine* gave place
> (Tho loth and angry she to part
> With the possession of my heart)
>   To *Elisa*'s conqu'ering face.

In the third stanza, the poet, or lover, becomes a neglected favourite at the court of the queen, casting off an unprincipled and ill-advised monarch's yoke of miss-rule:

> *Elisa* till this hour might reign,
>> Had she not *Evil Counsels* ta'ne.
>> *Fundamental Laws* she broke,
> And still new *Favorites* she chose,
> Till up in *Arms* my *Passions* rose,
>> And cast away her yoke.

In the fourth stanza, the courtier (or subject, perhaps), divides his loyalties between two contending queens. The crown is passed from head to head in accordance with the poet's changing fancies:

> *Mary* then and gentle *Ann*
>> Both to reign at once began.
>> Alternately they sway'd,
> And sometimes *Mary* was the *Fair*,
> And sometimes *Ann* the *Crown* did wear,
>> And sometimes *Both* I' obey'd.

In the fifth stanza, the poet falls victim to a tyranny:

> Another *Mary* then arose,
>> And did rigorous Laws impose.
>> A mighty *Tyrant* she!
> Long, alas! should I have been
> Under that *Iron-Scepter'd Queen*,
>> Had not *Rebecca* set me free.
> (*Miscellanies*, 22)

Rebecca's death brings another monarch to the throne. She in turn is deposed by the invading army - of Isabella's eyes! And then an interregnum ensues, and then an anarchy.

All this, it seems, Johnson may have brought together when he wrote of the *succession* of images in Cowley's 'The Chronicle'. It is also, perhaps, behind his praise of Cowley for his 'knowledge' in the poem, especially his knowledge of political affairs:

> His strength always appears in his agility; his volatility is not the flutter of a light, but the bound of an elastick mind. His levity never leaves his learning behind it; the moralist, the politician, and the critick, mingle their influence even in this airy frolick of genius. To such a performance Suckling could have brought the gaiety, but not the knowledge; Dryden could have supplied the knowledge, but not the gaiety. (*Lives*, 1: 37-38)

Cowley's mind, according to Johnson, does not flutter, it *bounds*. His agile leaps between different realms of association in the poem are confident and bold, not timid or nervous. Cowley recalls the 'warlike things' by which women prepare for the battle of winning men's hearts with the same single-minded ruthlessness as an army loading its weapons:

> But should I now to you relate
> > The strength and riches of their *state*;
> > The *Powder*, *Patches*, and the *Pins*,
> The *Ribbons*, *Jewels*, and the *Rings*,
> The *Lace*, the *Paint*, and *warlike things*
> > That make up all their *Magazins*.
> (*Miscellanies*, 23)

Or with the same scheming deviousness that typifies international politics:

> If I should tell the politick Arts
> > To take and keep men's hearts,
> > The Letters, Embassies, and Spies,
> The Frowns, and Smiles, and Flatteries,
> The Quarrels, Tears, and Perjuries,
> > Numberless, *Nameless Mysteries!*
> (*Miscellanies*, 24)

If, says Cowley, he were to list *all* these weapons of war, all these intrigues, tricks and devices, he would grow more voluminous 'Than *Holinshed* or *Stow*' - the serious historical and political chronicles against which Cowley's light-hearted poem is set. Cowley's 'levity', claims Johnson, 'never leaves his learning behind it'. To record all the changes in Cowley's affairs of the heart would require a volume as large as the old chroniclers' record of change in the political climate. Hence it is that Johnson can claim that 'the moralist, the politician, and *the critick*' mingle their influence in the poem (*Lives*, 1: 37; emphasis mine). Beside the political and military allusions is the literary one. Cowley's 'Chronicle' resembles Holinshed's and Stow's in that it is a record of change, but intrinsic to the wit of the poem is Cowley's light hint that alterations in the capricious weather of love are no different from changes in national affairs - no more a cause of happiness or misery to human beings, and no less!

Cowley's expression throughout, says Johnson, has facility and his words dance - a phrase suggestive of the opening lines of the 'Second Olympique Ode' of Cowley: '*Queen* of all Harmonious things, / *Dancing Words*, and *Speaking Strings*' (*Pindarique Odes*, 1). We can appreciate the aptness of Johnson's observation in all the stanzas of the poem; but how easily Cowley's words seem to come, and how he made them leap into a dance, can be particularly enjoyed in the final stanza of 'The Chronicle', from the throwaway lightness of: 'But I will briefer with them be, / Since few of them were long with Me', to the mock-solemn last lines where with considerable grace, wit, and balletic control of movement, Cowley weaves into his praise of his present passion, Heleonora, the conventional words of celebration lavished by the nation on its newly-crowned monarch. The girls' names, so important in the poem, are all, as it were, partners in the dance:

> An higher and a nobler strain
> My present *Emperess* does claim,
> *Heleonora, First o'th'Name*;

Whom *God grant long to reign.*
(*Miscellanies*, 24)

Tempered Enthusiasms: Cowley's *Anacreontiques*

In his critical commentary on Cowley's *Miscellanies*, Johnson had divided his
attention between the general quality of the collection and individual poems. The
Anacreontiques are given only a general criticism. What is said of the entire group
of twelve poems is true, more or less, of them all. Each poem has a different topic
('Love', 'Drinking', 'Beauty', 'Age', 'Gold', 'The Grasshopper', 'The Swallow').
All, however, exhibit a shared sense of the pleasures of life, a common spirit and a
similar 'voice'. Whether the voice of the poems was the voice of the obscure
Anacreon, or close to the originals, Johnson expresses some doubt.[8] Cowley had
called his poems 'Some Copies of Verses Translated Paraphrastically out of
Anacreon'. The *Anacreontiques*, or paraphrastical translations, Johnson said, 'pass,
however justly, under the name of Anacreon' (*Lives*, 1: 39). It was in fact the
morality of the poems that Johnson seemed least happy about. Johnson had praised
Cowley's 'gaiety of fancy' in 'The Chronicle', but his concern now is that these
poems, though 'pleasing', teach 'nothing but' the enjoyment of the present day.
One of the most outspoken and vigorous statements of this moral commonplace,
highly reminiscent of sentiments in the Horatian and Lucretian verse translations of
Dryden from the 1680s, is No. VIII, the poem entitled 'The Epicure':

> Fill the *Bowl* with rosie Wine,
> Around our temples *Roses* twine,
> And let us chearfully awhile,
> Like the *Wine* and *Roses* smile.
> Crown'd with Roses we contemn
> *Gyges* wealthy *Diadem.*
> *To day* is *Ours*; what do we fear?
> *To day* is *Ours*; we have it here.
> Let's treat it kindly, that it may
> *Wish*, at least, with us to stay.
> Let's banish *Business*, banish *Sorrow*;
> To the *Gods* belongs *To morrow.*
> (*Miscellanies*, 36)

The same injunction is present in implicit and explicit form again and again in the
collection. It is there, *implicitly*, in No. II, the verses on 'Drinking'. Why should I
not drink, asks the poet, since nothing else in nature refrains?

> The thirsty *Earth* soaks up the *Rain,*
> And drinks, and gapes for drink again.
> The *Plants* suck up the *Earth*, and are
> With constant drinking fresh and fair.
> The *Sea* it self, which one would think
> Should have but little need of *Drink,*

> Drinks ten thousand *Rivers* up,
> So fill'd that they o'reflow the *Cup*.
> ....
>
> Fill up the *Bowl* then, fill it high,
> Fill all the *Glasses* there for why
> Should every creature drink but *I*,
> Why, *Men* or *Morals*, tell me why?
> (*Miscellanies*, 32)

The thought is made explicit in the poem entitled 'Age', No. V in the *Anacreontiques* of Cowley:

> Oft am I by the Women told,
> Poor *Anacreon* thou grow'st old.
> Look how thy hairs are falling all;
> Poor *Anacreon* how they fall!
> Whether I grow old or no,
> By th'effects I do not know.
> This I know without being told,
> 'Tis time to *Live* if I grow *Old*,
> 'Tis Time short pleasures now to take,
> Of little *Life* the best to make,
> And manage *wisely* the *last stake*.
> (*Miscellanies*, 34)

In saying that the *Anacreontiques* teach 'nothing but' the enjoyment of the present day, the suggestion is perhaps that more, morally, might be done by poetry than Cowley does here. Perhaps Johnson felt that Cowley (like Anacreon before him) had been too swift to insist on the short-lived nature of human joy, and had done so without the struggle, or pain, that characterized Johnson's own efforts as a poetical moralist. But from unhappiness with the *matter* of the poems (in both original and paraphrastical forms), Johnson moves to dissatisfaction with the *manner* of Cowley's versions. In seeking to *please*, Johnson thought that Cowley had forfeited a quality of the original Greek: 'he has given … [them] rather a pleasing than a faithful representation, having retained their spriteliness, but lost their simplicity' (*Lives*, 1: 39). What Johnson means by the 'spriteliness' of Cowley can, I think, be illustrated from many of the lines, such as the opening of No. X, 'The Grasshopper':

> Happy *Insect*, what can be
> In happiness compar'd to Thee?
> Fed with nourishment divine,
> The dewy *Mornings* gentle *Wine*!
> (*Miscellanies*, 37)

All of the poems paraphrased by Cowley from Anacreon are substantial expansions of the Greek, and Cowley's versions do, observably, abound in what Johnson called 'modern graces'. In No. I, 'love' is 'melting' and 'desire' is 'soft', where the original has only the Greek word for 'loves'. In No. IV, '*Feet*' try 'their swiftness'; in No. VI lovers are 'flames'; in No. VIII, 'Wine' is 'rosie'; in No. IX, 'od'orous Oyls' flow over the poet's head; he is 'supinely laid' on 'flowry beds'. In the same piece, '*Fires*' are 'noble', '*Health*' is 'Vigorous', and '*Desires*' are 'gay'. In No. X, the grasshopper is a '*Prophet* of the ripened year'; in No. XI, the swallow is hailed as a 'Foolish *Prater*', the 'prattling swallow' of Anacreon.

'Spriteliness' in Cowley's *Anacreontiques*, even when treating 'serious' subjects, often takes the form of a certain tripping lightness of expression. This 'pleasing' example is from the 'Elegie upon Anacreon' (paraphrased from no particular Anacreontic, but drawing on several), the last piece in Cowley's collection:

> *Beauty* alone they should admire;
> Nor look at *Fortunes* vain attire,
> Nor ask what *Parents* it can shew;
> With *Dead* or *Old* t'has nought to do.
> They should not love yet *All*, or *Any*,
> But very *Much*, and very *Many*.
> All their Life should gilded be
> With Mirth, and Wit, and Gayety,
> Well remembring, and *Applying*
> The *Necessity* of *Dying*.

The gleeful irony of the poem is that Anacreon died by choking on the stone of the fruit to which he had dedicated his life: the grape! The thought clearly tickled Cowley, who, in sounding this note of mock discretion, is typically spritely:

> And whilst I do thus discover
> Th'ingredients of a happy *Lover*,
> 'Tis, my *Anacreon*, for thy sake
> I of the *Grape* no mention make.
> (*Miscellanies*, 40)

Johnson says that Cowley lost the simplicity of his originals. (How *very* spare, direct, brief and condensed are Anacreon's *Odes* can be readily grasped by glancing at the Greek). Simplicity, Johnson suggests, was replaced in Cowley's *Anacreontiques*, as in Pope's *Homer*, by 'the decoration of some modern graces, by which he is undoubtedly made more amiable to common readers, and perhaps, if they would honestly declare their own perceptions, to far the greater part of those whom courtesy and ignorance are content to style the Learned' (*Lives*, 1: 39).

Touches such as these are without doubt what Johnson had in view when he wrote of the *decoration* of some modern graces, as are the moments in the *Anacreontiques* where Cowley most self-consciously adds new English words, often adjectives, to adorn his thought. The latter part of Johnson's commentary on the *Anacreontiques* is devoted to bringing out the permanence of the poems' appeal, and to their exceptionally engaging polish, the kind of elegance that is not of the surface only, but allows the poems to permeate the barriers of culture and history:

> These little pieces will be found more finished in their kind than any other of
> Cowley's works. The diction shews nothing of the mould of time, and the
> sentiments are at no great distance from our present habitudes of thought. Real
> mirth must be always natural, and nature is uniform. Men have been wise in very
> different modes; but they have always laughed the same way'. (*Lives*, 1: 39-40)

What Johnson is saying here is that while the *Anacreontiques* are 'little pieces',
they satisfy nevertheless his highest poetical criterion, that same 'general nature'
he had ascribed to Shakespeare.[9] Cowley, like Shakespeare, comes closest to
'nature' - where nature is 'uniform' - in comedy; and he approaches the general by
finding expressions outside the learned or polite terms fashionable in one historical
period. As these comments on Cowley's *Anacreontiques* will suggest, neither
pomp nor grandeur are necessary qualities within the complex of Johnson's own
'Augustan' ideal, where the language of poetry draws similarly on common,
human, roots, achieving a universal vitality in the 'familiar'. Johnson's praise of
Shakespeare's 'comic dialogue' in his *Preface to Shakespeare* is specifically
echoed in his commentary on Cowley at this point:

> Levity of thought naturally produced familiarity of language, and the familiar part
> of language continues long the same: the dialogue of comedy, when it is
> transcribed from popular manners and real life, is read from age to age with equal
> pleasure. The artifice of inversion, by which the established order of words is
> changed, or of innovation, by which new words or new meanings of words are
> introduced, is practised, not by those who talk to be understood, but by those who
> write to be admired. (*Lives*, 1: 40)

In *Idler* 77, on 'Easy Poetry', Johnson had written that Cowley possessed 'the power of
writing easily beyond any other of our poets' (*Idler*, 242).[10]

For Johnson, then, Cowley's poetical lightness of touch was not an incidental or
external grace of language but profoundly connected to the human meaning of his
poems. In his paragraphs on 'The Chronicle', and on the *Anacreontiques*, Johnson
writes with approval of a 'levity' in Cowley that was for him one of the great and
characteristic delights of poetry. And in registering what he seems to have enjoyed
most, Johnson does not insist on the moral gravity and monumental severity of his own
poems. His enthusiastic taste for 'The Chronicle', and for the *Anacreontiques*, shows
rather the openness of his mind to poetry where pleasure, though it remains rational,
does at least equal instruction. And, of course, Johnson's enthusiasm for poems and
collections of verses where pleasure is not the servant but the partner of morality, exists
as a critical guide to open-minded readers of Cowley in *any* age, indicating where, in
first making contact with his poems, they might most pleasurably begin.

The Diagnostics of Failure: Cowley's *Mistress*

In turning to the poems in Cowley's *Mistress* (1647), a very much larger collection
of short pieces than the *Anacreontiques* or the *Miscellanies* from *Poems* (1656),
Johnson allows some praise, but was also deeply irritated, and at the heart of his

commentary is an uncompromizingly negative criticism. Johnson's impatience with the vacuous and trivial in Cowley's poetry is conveyed here by the pulsing beat of his prose, and his mocking briskness: 'His praises are too far-sought and too hyperbolical, either to express love or to excite it: every stanza is crouded with darts and flames, with wounds and death, with mingled souls, and with broken hearts' (*Lives*, 1: 40). To say 'every stanza' is, of course, an exaggeration, but the comment is in general terms true. When writing of 'mingled souls', Johnson obviously has a poem such as Cowley's 'Platonick Love' in mind, a piece that begins with a metaphysical cliché:

> Indeed I must confess,
> When *Souls* mix 'tis an *Happiness*;
> But not compleat till *Bodies* too combine,
> And closely as our minds together joyn;
> But half of Heaven the *Souls* in glory tast,
> 'Till by Love in Heaven at last,
> Their *Bodies* too are plac't.
> (*The Mistress*, 12)

When Johnson writes of 'wounds' and 'broken hearts' a number of lines from 'My Heart Discovered' will best underpin the observation:

> But, oh, what other *Heart* is there,
> Which sighs and crowds to her so near?
> 'Tis all on flame, and does like *fire*,
> To that, as to its *Heaven*, aspire,
> The wounds are many in't and deep;
> Still does it bleed, and still does weep.
> (*The Mistress*, 15)

Throughout the course of his criticism, Johnson is typically unembarrassed to borrow from past criticism he considers useful and sound, and in examining Cowley's *Mistress*, he quotes Addison on 'mixed wit': 'wit which consists of thoughts true in one sense of the expression, and false in the other' (*Lives*, 1: 41). Addison had written of Cowley in *The Spectator*, No. 62 (a paper which begins with an eloquent tribute to the French critic of wit, Dominique Bouhours) that: 'observing the cold regard of his mistress's eyes, and at the same time their power of producing love in him, he considers them as burning glasses made of ice'. The reference is to the opening lines of 'The vain Love':

> What new-found *Witchcraft* was in thee;
> With thine own *Cold* to *kindle Me*?
> Strange art! like him that should devise
> To make a *Burning-Glass of Ice*.
> (*The Mistress*, 17)

Addison's next example is of Cowley who 'Finding himself able to live in the greatest extremities of love ... concludes the torrid zone to be habitable' (*Lives*, 1: 41), and is a reference to the fourth stanza of the first poem in the collection, 'The Request':

> Come arm'd with flames, for I would prove
> All the extremities of mighty Love.
>   Th'excess of heat is but a fable;
> We know the *torrid* Zone is now found *habitable*.
> (*The Mistress*, 4)

The third example that Johnson cites from Addison ('Upon the dying of a tree, on which he had cut his loves, he observes that his flames had burnt up and withered the tree' [*Lives*, 1: 41]) refers to the opening stanza of 'The Tree':

> I Chose the flouri'shingst *Tree* in all the Park,
>   With freshest Boughs, and fairest head;
> I cut my Love into his gentle Bark,
>   And in three days, behold 'tis *dead*;
> My very *written flames* so violent be
>   They 'have burnt and wither'd up the Tree.
> (*The Mistress*, 70)

From these examples we can see what Johnson means when he writes that Cowley, like other poets, expresses love metaphorically by flame and fire, but is at the same time idiosyncratic: 'that which is true of real fire is said of love, or figurative fire, the same word in the same sentence retaining both significations' (*Lives*, 1: 41). Love is only metaphorically 'flames' in the above stanza; but the tree is burnt, as surely as it is chosen and engraved. In the final stanza it is referred to as 'blasted'.

Johnson thought that Addison's 'representation' of 'mixed wit' was 'sufficiently indulgent'; and as he read through the *Mistress*, the mixing that Addison had defined seemed increasingly tiresome to him: 'that confusion of images may entertain for a moment, but being unnatural it soon grows wearisome' (*Lives*, 1: 41). Cowley's 'mixed wit', that is, was precisely not 'general nature', but one of 'the pleasures of sudden wonder' that are soon exhausted. Ultimately, Johnson condemns the *Mistress* because he finds Cowley's professions of love feigned or false, manufactured for purely artificial effect. There is an element of profound personal distaste evident in the temper of Johnson's prose at this point. Echoing Pope, who echoes Boileau, who is imitating Horace, the classic grounds for Johnson's objection to emotional emptiness in poetry are tellingly unrolled:

> Cowley's *Mistress* has no power of seduction; 'she plays round the head, but comes not at [to] the heart'. Her beauty and absence, her kindness and cruelty, her disdain and inconstancy, produce no correspondence of emotion. His poetical account of the virtues of plants and colours of flowers is not perused with more sluggish frigidity. The compositions are such as might have been written for penance by a hermit, or for hire by a philosophical rhymer who had only heard of another sex; for they turn the mind only on the writer, whom, without thinking on a woman but as the subject for his talk, we sometimes esteem as learned and

sometimes despise as trifling, always admire as ingenious, and always condemn as unnatural. (*Lives*, 1: 42)[11]

The frisson of this passage implies a countervailing Johnsonian standard of how a woman might be properly thought of by a man, and in this it draws on the affections of Johnson's personal friendships with many real women in life.[12] But when Johnson says of the poems in the *Mistress* that 'they turn the mind only on the writer', we are prepared for the thought not only by earlier eighteenth-century criticisms of Cowley,[13] but also by the comparison from a completely different context between Shakespeare's *Othello* and Addison's *Cato*: 'the composition refers us only to the writer', wrote Johnson in his *Preface to Shakespeare*, 'we pronounce the name of *Cato*, but we think on Addison' (*Shakespeare*, 7: 84). In his claim that Cowley's *Mistress* might have been written for penance by a hermit or for hire by a philosophical rhymer who had only heard of another sex, the suggestion, almost, is that the poems gave Johnson the appearance of having been forced out of the poet, as a paid exercise or duty, in which he had no emotional stake. Here, like other metaphysicals, Cowley becomes one of Johnson's Epicurean deities, writing 'without interest and without emotion', his courtship 'void of fondness' (*Lives*, 1: 20). How accidental to the conception of the *Mistress* are the women themselves, comes out clearly in this stanza from 'The Wish'. The woman within the poem is one of the items on the list of desirable domestic commodities in Cowley's dream of Horatian retirement:

> Ah, yet, E're I descend to th'Grave
> May I a *small House*, and *large Garden* have!
> And a *few Friends*, and *many Books*, both true,
>   Both wise, and both delightful too!
>   And since *Love* ne're will from me flee,
> A *Mistress* moderately fair,
> And good as *Guardian-Angels* are,
>   Only belov'd, and loving me!
> (*The Mistress*, 22-23)

Cowley's coldness in love, the chilling ingenuity of his verses of love, was for Johnson unnatural and therefore radically *un*true. His eye and mind are not on the women. What is said to them, and of them, is therefore strained and contrived. Johnson's boldness in criticizing Cowley's *Mistress* is one of the moments in the 'Life of Cowley' that make it a critical manifesto for the entire *Lives*.

This is not, in the event, however, all there is to Johnson's judgment of the *Mistress*. One poem, at least, Johnson enjoyed deeply: Cowley's 'Against Hope', or as Johnson called it, 'On Hope', which he had quoted in the preceding section of the 'Life' (*Lives*, 1: 33-34). Aside from the congeniality of the theme, it is easy to discern the reason for Johnson's unusual delight in this piece. Cowley's style was here fitted to his subject:

> It must be ... confessed of these writers that if they are upon common subjects often unnecessarily and unpoetically subtle, yet where scholastick speculation can

be properly admitted, their copiousness and acuteness may justly be admired. What Cowley has written upon Hope shews an unequalled fertility of invention. (*Lives*, 1: 33)

Cowley's 'Against Hope' is part of a pair.[14] Its arguments are matched and answered by 'For Hope', its sequel and antithesis within the collection. The poet is personally committed to both views, or neither view. But if we think of Johnson's praise of the metaphysicals' 'unequalled fertility of invention' at this point, we see that unlike the poems written to, or about, a mistress, Cowley does not pretend to be speaking under the compulsion of some personal feeling in this poem. Johnson is accordingly able to admire the originality with which Cowley realized his theme. It may be a cliché to call hope, as Cowley does in the first stanza, a 'Vain *shadow*!' But he then asks us to think of the disappearance of shadows at midday when the sun is high, or overhead, and after it has set:

> *Hope*, whose weak *Being* ruin'd is
> Alike if it *succeed*, and if it *miss*;
> Whom *Good* or *Ill* does equally confound,
> And both the *Horns* of *Fates Dilemma* wound.
> Vain *shadow*! which dost vanish quite,
> Both at full *Noon*, and perfect *Night!*
> (*The Mistress*, 41)

In the second stanza, the state of disappointed hope is represented as that poverty which ensues when legacies eat up an inheritance, a thought which Cowley offers with a certain exasperated outspokenness: 'Thou bring'st us an *Estate*, yet leav'st us *Poor*, / By clogging it with *Legacies* before!' Cowley's mind then dances to the idea of '*Joys*' as marriageable virgins, '*deflowr'd*' by the time we possess them. From there, he leaps to the thought of good fortunes as profitless, high-tariff imports. And from there, to the notion that anticipated pleasures evaporate in advance of the thing enjoyed. So '*Joy*', 'like *Wine*, kept close does better tast; / If it take air before, its spirits wast' (42). The unhesitating directness of these thoughts (so different from Donne's 'scholastick speculations'), the rapid shifts of association, the pace with which such varied images succeed and flow one into another, here substantiate Johnson's claim for Cowley's 'unequalled fertility of invention'. Johnson appreciated a Cowley at ease with himself in this poem. Not that Cowley has forsaken his guiding theme. It is wittily recalled in the final stanza in the rueful lines against false hope of a successful catch in a male lover's chase after women:

> *Brother* of *Fear*, more gaily clad!
> The *merr'ier Fool* o'th' two, yet quite as *Mad*:
> Site of *Repentance*, Child of fond *Desire*!
> That blow'st the *Chymicks*, and the *Lovers* fire!
> Leading them still insensibly on
> By the strange *witchcraft* of *Anon*!
> By *Thee* the one does changing *Nature* through

> Her endless *Labyrinths* pursue,
> And th'other chases *Women*, whilst She goes
> More ways and turns than *hunted Nature* knows.
> (*The Mistress*, 42)

Qualities of the Whole: The Case of Cowley's Diction

Cowley's diction, says Johnson, is 'negligent': 'He seems not to have known, or not to have considered, that words being arbitrary must owe their power to association, and have the influence, and that only, which custom has given them' (*Lives*, 1: 58). But if at this point we recall Johnson's thoughts on the admissibility of diction from *Rambler* 168, we can also see that Johnson is prefacing his commentary by rising to a resonant statement of general principle, a principle that is reinforced in his *Essay on Criticism* by Pope:

> Expression is the *Dress* of *Thought*, and still
> Appears more *decent* as more *suitable*
> (*Essay*, lines 318-19).

The principle of diction that Johnson had hitherto refrained from applying to Shakespeare is now applied, where elegance is required, to Cowley:

> Language is the dress of thought; and as the noblest mien or most graceful action would be degraded and obscured by a garb appropriated to the gross employments of rusticks or mechanicks, so the most heroick sentiments will lose their efficacy, and the most splendid ideas drop their magnificence, if they are conveyed by words used commonly upon low and trivial occasions, debased by vulgar mouths, and contaminated by inelegant applications. (*Lives*, 1: 58-59)

Johnson's belief (on both occasions) is that while words are only words, negligent diction, in that it tends to licence obscurity, may defeat the reader's attention, just as gold may fail to repay the cost of extraction from the ore. Words matter because although they have only that influence which custom has given them, they are at the same time the vehicle of thought, and therefore of truth, which does not change: 'Truth indeed is always truth, and reason is always reason; they have an intrinsick and unalterable value, and constitute that intellectual gold which defies destruction' (*Lives*, 1: 59). Writing from the point of view of the creator of poetry, Dryden in his 'Preface to *Fables*' (1700) had said that the words 'are the colouring of a work, and in the order of nature are the last to be considered'.[15] Johnson, writing as a reader of poetry, sides with the diametrically opposite view: 'The diction, being the vehicle of the thoughts, first presents itself to the intellectual eye; and if the first appearance offends, a further knowledge is not often sought' (*Lives*, 1: 59).

To know a poem in depth, Johnson suggests, is to collaborate with the verbal surface of language through which this depth is revealed. Without the instantaneous lexical pleasures, the moral resources of poetry cannot be unlocked.

As before, an idea of the interdependence of delight and instruction informs Johnson's sense of the relationship between expression and thought at this point:

> Whatever professes to benefit by pleasing must please at once. The pleasures of the mind imply something sudden and unexpected; that which elevates must always surprise. What is perceived by slow degrees may gratify us with the consciousness of improvement, but will never strike with the sense of pleasure. (*Lives*, 1: 59)

Where the diction of poetry is careless, no such pleasure can be felt. Thus Cowley:

> makes no selection of words, nor seeks any neatness of phrase; he has no elegances either lucky or elaborate: as his endeavours were rather to impress sentences upon the understanding than images on the fancy he has few epithets, and those scattered without peculiar propriety or nice adaptation. It seems to follow from the necessity of the subject, rather than the care of the writer, that the diction of his heroick poem is less familiar than that of his slightest writings. He has given not the same numbers, but the same diction, to the gentle Anacreon and the tempestuous Pindar. (*Lives*, 1: 59)

The historical 'justice' of these remarks, once again, will depend on the evidence of the poems. Pat Rogers has suggested that Johnson is condemning Cowley for failure to adopt a conventionally skin-deep linguistic decorum:

> Johnson deepens and refines the prevailing idea of propriety when he comes to examine stylistic issues, but he certainly does not abandon the principle of correctness. Cowley and his peers fall down because their linguistic means are not in keeping with the poetic effects they propose: it is a breach of decorum.

And for Rogers, who admits that Johnson is 'more eloquent, more intelligent and more detailed than the run of commentaries', Johnson's 'entire discussion of the metaphysical poets draws on the familiar notions of his age'.[16] But when Johnson says that Cowley 'makes no selection of words, nor seeks any neatness of phrase', the criticism must *first* be interpreted in the light of the poetry he is bringing to mind. We may think of the very many awkward expressions in Cowley's poem, such as those that Johnson has earlier condemned (in a substantial section of the final part of the 'Life') from the *Pindarique Odes* (*Lives*, 1: 42-48). And we may call to mind the many items of domestic or familiar vocabulary in Cowley. '*Grape*', 'gowty', 'chips', 'lung'd', 'justle', '*Stock*', 'dig', 'purge', 'mint', '*Bet*', '*Ink*', '*Sack*', '*Clinches*', '*Slime*', '*Chinks*' and '*Key-holes*' all appear in the *Miscellanies*.

Favourite sources of diction are the realms of house-keeping, and of legal contracts, particularly as applied to the buying and selling of estates. Contractual language is a regular feature of the *Mistress*, where it is applied to the making and breaking of contracts of love. Thus, in 'The Given Love', we have the term '*Under-Rates*' in the line: 'But not at *Under-Rates to sell*' (*The Mistress*, 7), and in the same poem 'joyntyre', which Johnson defined in his *Dictionary* as an 'Estate settled on a wife to be enjoyed after her husband's decease'. There is also '*Simony*' ('The Bargain'), '*Competency*', in the lines from 'Resolved to be Beloved': 'But I must sweat in *Love*, and labour yet, / Till I a *Competency* get' (*The Mistress*, 30); '*Servient*', in the phrase '*Form Servient*' from 'The Soul'; '*entail'd*', in the phrase '*entail'd Estate*', from 'For Hope', and in the same poem '*Earnest-Money*' and '*Moveables*': 'Thy *Portion* yet in *Moveables* is great' (*The Mistress*, 43).

In admitting *both* the familiar and the technical into his poetry, Cowley does indeed - we see - make no 'selection of words'. Johnson's implicit standard in this comment is Dryden. He was later to write in the 'Life' that there was before the time of Dryden:

> no poetical diction: no system of words at once refined from the grossness of domestick use and free from the harshness of terms appropriated to particular arts. Words too familiar or too remote defeat the purpose of a poet. (*Lives*, 1: 420)

Thus Cowley, writing without the example of Dryden to guide him, can conceive of his mistress's maidenhead in the specialist terminology of the seventeenth-century construction industry:

> Slight, outward *Curtain* to the *Nuptial Bed!*
> Thou *Case* to buildings not yet finished!
> ('Maidenhead', *The Mistress*, 59)

But whatever feelings about propriety of diction might be aroused (not discounting the modern reader's response to the 'propriety' of this image), technical vocabulary is clearly too abundant in Cowley's poetry to ignore. What can be said in support of Johnson's opinion of the 'selection' of words is also true of the accompanying charge: that Cowley seeks no 'neatness of phrase'. But the 'neatness' Johnson here has in mind is not part of a narrowly Augustan cultural paradigm impervious to the standards of other times. There are, for example, lines such this, from 'Silence':

> I'll bind that *Sore* up, I did ill reveal.
> (*The Mistress*, 61)

Or the lines from 'Loves Ingratitude' where the weeds of love:

> Strait will ... choak up and devour
> Each wholsom *herb* and beauteous *flower!*
> (*The Mistress*, 44)

Many lines in Cowley's poetry creak and groan under the strain of such verbal clumsiness. In 'The Monopoly' we learn that:

> ... *Cupids Forge* is set up here.
> (*The Mistress*, 51)

Johnson's point that Cowley seeks no 'neatness of phrase' is, then, closely connected to his complaint that Cowley makes no selection of words. Cowley's expressions rest too often on words which have no more than a functional convenience in the lines, and frequently the poet commences with a graceful and confident forward march, only to fall flat on his face, as in the opening of 'Resolved to Love':

> I wonder what the *Grave* and *Wise*
>   Think of all us that *Love*.
> (*The Mistress*, 55)

Which superficially resembles, but does not carry through, the successful turn of Donne's 'The good-morrow':

> I wonder by my troth, what thou, and I
> Did, till we lov'd?

Here, as in many other places in his poetry, the crippling of the lines seems to come from the weight Cowley is in the habit of placing on his pronouns. He often puts them in prominent positions, such as at the beginning of two contrasting stanzas of 'My Fate', from *The Mistress*:

> Me, mine example let the *Stoicks* use ...
> You who mens *Fortunes* in their faces read ....
> (*The Mistress*, 56)

In the opening stanza of 'Silence' the thought turns on the juxtaposition of Cowley's personal pronouns:

> Curse on this *Tongue*, that has my *Heart* betray'd,
>   And his great *Secret* open laid!
>   For of all persons chiefly *She*,
>   Should not the ills I suffer know;
>   Since 'tis a thing might dang'rous grow,
>   Only in *Her* to *Pity* Me:
> Since 'tis for *Me* to *lose* my 'Life' more *fit*,
> Than 'tis for *Her* to *save* and ransome it.
> (*The Mistress*, 61)

In the succeeding poem from *The Mistress*, Cowley, typically, uses the personal pronoun 'I' as a rhyme word, coming at the end of a line:

> But now, by *Love*, the mighty *Phalaris*, I
>   My *burning Bull* the first do try.
> ('The Dissembler', *The Mistress*, 62)

It is of interest here that in his *Dictionary*, where Cowley is rarely quoted, Johnson defines by a sudden surge of quotations from Cowley nine different uses of the pronoun 'that'. This is shortly followed by a succession of quotations illustrating uses of the definite article.

Thus is Johnson's complaint that the diction seems frequently humdrum or mundane verified by the detail of Cowley's poems. The reservation appears to go with Johnson's persistent suggestions about the coldness of Cowley. Sometimes, Cowley's exceptionally flat vocabulary seems part of a failure both to imagine and to feel. When Cowley is content with what first comes to hand the strain and pretension of fabricated emotional states is often exposed for what it really is: an artful posture, as here in the repeated 'what' of the poet's lament in 'Weeping':

> Ah, mighty Love, that it were *inward Heat*
>> Which made this precious *Limbeck* sweat!
> But what, alas, ah what does it avail
>> That she weeps Tears so wondrous *cold*,
>> As scarce the *Asses hoof* can hold,
> So *cold* that I admire they fall not *Hail*.
> (*The Mistress*, 66)

But that Cowley's epithets are few, and that they are 'scattered without peculiar propriety or nice adaptation' (*Lives*, 1: 59), can also be ascertained from the poetry. The 'propriety' Johnson has in mind here seems nothing more than the quite simple demand that the words should be there for a purpose, and that they should be those words and not others. What, for example, is gained from calling the '*Quire*' of '*Years to come*' in 'The Resurrection' (from Cowley's *Pindarique Odes*) 'well-fitted'? What is added to the idea of '*pride*' (in 'The Muse', the next in the collection) by the epithet '*goodly*'? And does the poet have any particular reason for his choice of epithets in the line:

> ... innocent *Loves*, and *pleasant Truths*, and *useful Lies* [?]
> (*Pindarique Odes*, 23)

Often, it seems, Cowley's epithets are used loosely, as a kind of metrical filler. His mind does not always appear to be *on* the object he is talking about.

But is Johnson here relying on a set of historically located standards, culturally remote from our own expectations as readers of poetry, to point this out? The problem is not confined to the fact that Cowley's epithets are weak or vague, or that there is frequently no special reason, no *peculiar* propriety, for the ones he chooses. The choice seems sometimes to countermand his intentions, and in ways which do not require the so-called 'familiar notions' of Johnson's age to detect them. Thus in the fourth stanza of his poem 'To Mr Hobs', Cowley's point is that the great seas of the world are as nothing to the ocean sailed by the 'nobler *Vessel*' of Hobbes's wit. So why, at the end of a list of the seas, does he call the Mediterranean 'slender-limb'd'? In thinking of the many narrow channels and passages on the Mediterranean coast, Cowley has forgotten that the comparison depends on evoking the *greatness* of the seas. In the poem 'To Dr Scarborough', similarly, there is little force in Scarborough's 'successful *care*':

> By wondrous *Art*, and by successful *care*
> The *Ruines* of a *Civil War* thou dost *alone repair*.
> (*Pindarique Odes*, 35)

It is probable that Cowley was content with any merely adequate epithet of three syllables.

According to Johnson, Cowley's neglect of diction is persistent and pervasive, a part of his temperament as a poet. Thus the relative absence of 'familiar' vocabulary in the *Davideis* Johnson is inclined to see as a consequence of the epic and biblical material and not as significant evidence of Cowley's care. That there *are* fewer items of familiar diction in the *Davideis* than in Cowley's 'slightest writings' seems on inspection true. Johnson's diagnosis is an impression based on what 'seems to follow'. It is informed partly by Johnson's sense of Cowley's habits elsewhere, and partly by his knowledge of the influence of 'the necessity of the subject' (*Lives*, 1: 59). In the first note to Book 1 of the *Davideis*, Cowley writes of the obligation he felt to open his poem with an Invocation or Proposition, according to the traditions of epic verse:

> though I could have found out a better way, I should not (I think) have ventured upon it. But there can be, I believe, none better; and that part, of the *Invocation*, if it became a *Heathen*, is no less Necessary for a *Christian Poet*. ('Davideis, A Sacred Poem', 24)

That it was indeed 'necessity' which inhibited the use of familiar diction here, Johnson argues by pointing to the uniformity of the *Pindarique Odes* and the *Anacreontiques*. Anacreon is 'gentle', Pindar 'tempestuous'. Cowley's versions of both, says Johnson, exhibit the 'same diction' (*Lives*, 1: 59). In a literal sense this is true. The concluding lines of the first of the *Anacreontiques* ('Love') rhymes '*Things*' with 'strings'. The rhyme is repeated in the opening stanza of Cowley's 'Second Olympique Ode of Pindar':

> *Queen* of all Harmonious things,
> *Dancing Words* and *Speaking Strings*,
> What *God*, what *Hero* wilt thou sing?
> (*Pindarique Odes*, 1)

In 'Drinking' (from the *Anacreontiques*), the earth 'gapes for drink again', while in the 'First Nemeæan Ode' the word reappears to describe two serpents with 'gaping *Mouths*'. The '*starry Diadems*' of '*God-descended Kings*' in 'The Praise of Pindar' recalls the same striking word in 'The Epicure', No. VIII of the *Anacreontics*:

> Crown'd with Roses we contemn
> *Gyges* wealthy *Diadem*.
> (*Miscellanies*, 36)

But while such repetitions can be found, Johnson may be mainly suggesting that the vocabulary of both collections is drawn from the same stock or fund of diction, and that it encompasses an identical range.

Cowley and the Structure of the Johnsonian Critical Judgment

With Shakespeare in his *Preface* of 1765, Johnson had attempted to respond to the critical challenge posed by the greatest poet in English. With the subject matter of the 'major' *Lives*, 'Milton', 'Dryden' and 'Pope', Johnson was writing revaluative criticism on poets of established reputation, whose fame had expanded after their deaths, and was continuing to grow. With Cowley, Johnson's subject was a minor poet of initial celebrity who at his death had exerted an enormous influence on his poetical successors and was a seminal presence in the history of seventeenth- and eighteenth-century English poetry.[17] The effort Johnson expends in trying to restore this (in his opinion) *unfairly* neglected and forgotten author to public attention in the later years of the eighteenth century is an underestimated mark of his distinction as a critic.[18]

But its quality cannot be historicized without a fuller charting of the criticism's relation to the poems it is responding to. Compared with Milton, Johnson saw Cowley as a poet whose significance was ultimately circumscribed; but while he shared the doubts of his age about his conceited style, his essay on Cowley is nevertheless a substantial judgment, as considered in its way as his treatment of poets far greater than Cowley, and less in need of critical assistance. As in the *Preface*, Johnson finds in features of Cowley's style signs of the essential quality of a human mind in all its pathos of thwarted desire and deviant obsession. And by surveying the whole, he exposes for his first readers, as he does for us, distinctions of *relative* value. The 'Life of Cowley' is built out of a sense of the relativities between the bad, the not so bad, the good and the exceptional parts of Cowley. These may be single lines, groups of lines, whole poems, or whole collections of verse. The *Davideis* bored him; he had grave misgivings about the *Pindarique Odes*; the *Mistress* left him cold. But the *Anacreontiques* and the *Miscellanies* (as both the source of supreme individual works and as whole collections of poems), call forth examples of praise higher than Johnson ever lavishes on poems or collections by any other poet.

Within his sense of the whole, Johnson has responded to poetry of entirely different levels of ambition and quality, and to the spectrum of a dazzling variety. To do justice to this variety the 'Life' contains some of Johnson's most generous praise but also damning remarks, and the full range of his capacity for poetical pain and poetical pleasure.[19] Johnson was able to move without strain between expressions of passionate delight and frank contempt. We have his wry humour at some feature of Cowley's poetical style, or mental eccentricities, or a grave and serious statement on the potential profanity of Sacred History in verse - as in his extended comments on the *Davideis*. Passing to this poem at the end of his account of Cowley, we see that Johnson, with restrained gravity, had suggested here the heroic poem's fundamental mistake - the poet's very choice of Sacred History.

Cowley's success in imitating classical material in the *Pindarique Odes* may have been mixed, but his poetical version of a scriptural narrative was doomed from its initial conception. Resting his praise of Cowley on 'invention' - a strength of all good verse according to Johnson - Cowley's version of the story of David failed because the narrative left no room to invent. Johnson here looks forward to his famous passage at the conclusion of the 'Life of Waller', where he writes that: 'The ideas of Christian Theology are too simple for eloquence, too sacred for fiction, and too majestick for ornament' (*Lives*, 1: 292). In the 'Cowley' too, there is no opportunity for imaginative flights:

> Sacred History has been always read with submissive reverence, and an imagination over-awed and controlled. We have been accustomed to acquiesce in the nakedness and simplicity of the authentick narrative, and to repose on its veracity with such humble confidence as suppresses curiosity. We go with the historian as he goes, and stop with him when he stops. All amplification is frivolous and vain: all addition to that which is already sufficient for the purposes of religion seems not only useless, but in some degree profane. (*Lives*, 1: 49-50)

For Johnson, the poet can only repeat in the simplest terms what he finds in the scriptural texts. Where Boileau had distinguished the true sublime by reference to scriptural simplicity, Johnson, with the pages of Cowley's *Davideis* open before him (and doubtless with Boileau's thoughts on religion and poetry in his head), wrote along similar lines: 'Such events as were produced by the visible interposition of Divine Power are above the power of human genius to dignify. The miracle of Creation, however it may teem with images, is best described with little diffusion of language: "He spake the word, and they were made"' (*Lives*, 1: 50).[20] Cowley's variety, then, the fact that his poetry was sometimes so fine and sometimes so flawed, seems in this the first of the *Lives* to have helped bring out for the first time since the *Preface* the full resonance of Johnson's repertoire of critical response. Johnson's critical range emerges in so far as Cowley was *not* a Dryden, or a Milton, or a Pope.

For the modern as for the eighteenth-century reader, Johnson's 'Life of Cowley' indicates where to look first, and what to look for, in Cowley's poems. Johnson founds his judgment on that which makes Cowley unique; on those qualities which distinguish him from all other poets both major and minor. Johnson identifies Cowley's poetic distinction as existing on at least four separate levels: on that of the *genre*:

> No author ever kept his verse and his prose at a greater distance from each other. (*Lives*, 1: 64)

On that of the *verse collection*:

> Such an assemblage of diversified excellence [as that of Cowley's *Miscellanies*] no other poet has hitherto afforded ... surely those verses [the *Pindarique Odes*]

are not without a just claim to praise; of which it may be said with truth, that no one but Cowley could have written them. (*Lives*, 1: 35; 48)

On that of the *individual poem*:

> The ode on Wit is almost without a rival .... *The Chronicle* is a composition unrivalled and alone ... [Cowley's verses on Crashaw] apparently excel all that have gone before them, and in which there are beauties which common authors may justly think not only above their attainment, but above their ambition. (*Lives*, 1: 36; 37; 39)

And, finally, on the level of the *individual line* (in the *Davideis*):

> he has given one example of representative versification, which perhaps no other English line can equal ...
> > *Which runs, and as it runs, for ever shall run on.*
> (*Lives*, 1: 62-63)

To this sense of the *levels* on which Cowley stands supreme, Johnson, while building up a 'character' (in Dryden's sense) of Cowley's poetry, adds a conception of his characteristic quality: the essential genius present to a greater or lesser degree everywhere in that poetry. He tells us where, in addition, amongst Cowley's many poems and collections, this genius is manifest:

> The *Anacreontiques* ... of Cowley give now all the pleasure which they ever gave. If he was formed by nature for one kind of writing more than another, his power seems to have been greatest in the familiar and the festive. (*Lives*, 1: 40)

By reference to his 'power', Johnson conveys to us how Cowley *as a whole* is unusual, or remarkable, either negatively, as in his account of 'The fault of Cowley' or with detached neutrality: 'the power of Cowley is not so much to move the affections, as to exercise the understanding.... Cowley gives inferences instead of images ... his endeavours were rather to impress sentences upon the understanding than images on the fancy' (*Lives*, 1: 37; 51; 59). It is typical of Johnson's engagement with the subject matter of his criticism (the literature) that he can suggest not only the nature of Cowley's power, but how it can be misused, or fail to be properly realized as a power, in actual poems. In ways which link the criticism of Cowley to the biographical morality of other 'Lives', Johnson returns regularly in the 'Life' to the theme of Cowley's wasted potential. Too often, for Johnson, Cowley's finest effects are uselessly squandered, or counteracted by another part of his nature:

> that confusion of images may entertain for a moment, but being unnatural it soon grows wearisome ... all the power of description is destroyed by a scrupulous enumeration.... what might in general expressions be great and forcible he weakens and makes ridiculous by branching it into small parts.... In the perusal of his *Davideis*, as of all Cowley's works, we find wit and learning unprofitably squandered.... His rhymes ... disappoint the ear, and destroy the energy of the

line…. a passage, in which every reader will lament to see just and noble thoughts defrauded of their praise by inelegance of language …. (*Lives*, 1: 41; 45; 53; 55; 60)

The rise and fall of these statements follows the pattern of the vanity of human wishes - where failure disappoints, destroys, disintegrates or defrauds the hope or expectation of human life from within, and the 'balance' of the judgment, as a weighing rather than a rating or scoring, reflects this collapse, and constitutes Cowley as a tragic phenomenon. Johnson's account of the vulnerability of Cowley's human temperament, and human imperfections includes at the same time an affectionate and sociable sympathy with Cowley's likeable quirks and obsessions that seems more reminiscent of *Rasselas*, or of the forms of self-awareness encapsulated in Johnson's own letters, diaries and prayers, and looks ahead to Wordsworth's recollection of Cowley as 'that able writer and amiable man'.[21] This positive taste emerges in an only partly concealed amusement at the prospect of Cowley seen as the victim of temptations he proved unable to resist: 'Cowley delighted in it [the confusion of images], as much as if he had invented it' (*Lives*, 1: 41). Johnson's rich vein of critical humour at the expense of Cowley is as often indulgent or forgiving or participative as it is scornful, and it is of course because Johnson saw poetry as a human matter, man-made for human consumption, that he can express in the 'Life of Cowley' what its known limits are: 'Such events as were produced by the visible interposition of Divine Power are above the power of human genius to dignify' (*Lives*, 1: 50).

Characteristic of Johnson's perspective in the 'Life of Cowley' is the fact that Johnson sets his remarks on any particular poet, and on any particular poem, in a framework created by a sense of the merits and functions of all poets and of all poems. What Cowley, considered as a whole, does, is placed in the context of what poetry, viewed as a whole, *can* do. The Johnsonian principle adopted wholeheartedly by Wordsworth in the following century, as by Roland Barthes in a different sense in the twentieth,[22] is the principle of *pleasure*. Against this principle, in the 'Life of Cowley', Cowley's poetry is constantly tested and judged. Thus 'The great pleasure of verse arises from the known measure of the lines and the uniform structure of the stanzas…. One of the great sources of poetical delight is description…. Whatever professes to benefit by pleasing must please at once' (*Lives*, 1: 47; 51; 59). Such a stress on the pleasures or potential pleasures of Cowley's poetry[23] suggests the liveliest incentive to look at the poems afresh.[24]

In the spirit of this acknowledgment, finally, we see that Johnson is often harder on Cowley than the majority of those modern critics who have touched on his work.[25] Johnson, who is writing for readers of poetry who are, like him, 'outside the academic fold', highlights different poems and is bolder in both praise and blame; and by comparison with the modern academic critic Johnson appears often to be plucking quotations and examples from the page he happens to have open before him. But Johnson's Cowley is a reader's Cowley for precisely these reasons. In writing a 'Preface' to Cowley, and not merely (as its intrinsic literary quality almost instantly made it) a 'Life', Johnson returns us to the experience of the poems in a spirit fitted to discriminate and enjoy them. Bringing Johnson's 'Life' into proximity with the poetry is an attempt to participate in his pleasures and to understand his pains. And when the poetry of the past is opened up thus, Johnson's criticism seems to do most to overwhelm the historicity of critical history; to yield an experience of criticism as a reflected grace of the experience of poetry.

Notes

[1] Johnson reports this opinion twice - in his 'Life of Milton' (*Lives*, 1: 154), and in the 'Life of Cowley' itself (*Lives*, 1: 56). He appears to have derived Milton's estimate of Cowley from a note in Thomas Newton's *Paradise Lost ... A New Edition* (1749). Cf. also the 'mighty Cowley' of Katherine Philips, a tribute she accorded to him in the year of his death. See *Poems: By the most deservedly Admired Mrs Katherine Philips: The Matchless Orinda* (London, 1667).

[2] Beside the attention that has been given to Wordsworth, Keats, Milton or Pope, or in recent years even to Dryden, critical analyses of Cowley in academic monographs are remarkably rare. T.S. Eliot has made a few appreciative and a few depreciative remarks on Cowley in his essay on Dryden of 1921 (*Selected Essays*, 308); but the most influential critics and critical theorists have had little to say on Cowley's behalf; there is a marked absence of theoretical 're-readings' of Cowley to accompany those available on Milton, Shakespeare or other 'Renaissance' or 'Cavalier' poets. Even granting that choices have to be made, it is symptomatic that the literary historian Michael Alexander could devote only a single phrase to the poetry of Cowley in over four-hundred pages of text. See *A History of English Literature* (London: Macmillan, 2000).

A full, scholarly, edition of Cowley's writings with Commentary (six volumes projected) has been commenced. See Thomas O. Calhoun, Lawrence Heyworth, Robert B. Hinman, William B. Hunter and Allen Pritchard, eds., *The Collected Works of Abraham Cowley* (Newark: University of Delaware Press, 1989-). At the time of writing, vol. 1 (1989): *Poetical Blossomes, The Puritans Lecture, The Puritan and the Papist, The Civil War*, and vol. 2, Part 1 (1993) *Poems: The Mistress*, had appeared in print. Of the several modern selections from Cowley, the one giving most weight to Johnson's insights and tastes is the edition by David Hopkins and Tom Mason, *Abraham Cowley: Selected Poems* (Manchester: Carcanet Press, 1994).

[3] See, for example, W.R. Keast, 'Johnson's Criticism of the Metaphysical Poets', *ELH* 17 (1950): 59-70. Keast complains of Johnson's failure to engage with issues that interest modern critics; but he does not apparently conceive how Johnson's interests may *usefully* differ from theirs. It is again the *general* discussion of the metaphysical poets in relation to the 'concepts of tradition' - as distinct from the criticism of Cowley in the particular case - that dominates the commentary of W.J. Bate. See *The Achievement of Samuel Johnson*, 212-16.

[4] 'To Mr. Nichol', *The Letters of Samuel Johnson*, ed. Bruce Redford, 5 vols. (Oxford: Clarendon Press, 1992-94), 3: 122. The 'Lives' of Cowley and Waller appeared together, as *Prefaces*, in vol. 1 of the first edition of the *English Poets*, 1779.

[5] Birkbeck Hill refers the reader of the 'Life of Cowley' to vols. 7-9 of *The Works of the English Poets*, 3nd ed. (London: J. Heath, 1802). It seems likely that Johnson was actually working from the 1656 folio of *Poems* (containing the *Miscellanies, The*

Mistress, Pindarique Odes and the *Davideis*), and/or from any or all of the 12 'editions' of *The Works* printed between 1668 and 1712, and the 3 editions of Richard Hurd's *Select Works* of Cowley (London, 1772, 1777). (For a full description of the successive editions of Cowley, see M.R. Perkin, *Abraham Cowley: A Bibliography* (Folkstone: Dawson, 1977). It is notable that although Johnson appears to treat the *Anacreontiques* as a separate collection, the poems of this type are printed under the running header of *Miscellanies* in 1680-81 and in other folios. I quote in this chapter from the separately paginated collections included in the 1680-81 *Works*.

[6] For example: 'Cowley's first piece, which ought to be inscribed *To my Muse*, for want of which the second couplet is without reference. When the title is added, there will still remain a defect; for every piece ought to contain in itself whatever is necessary to make it intelligible', and the comment that: 'In his verses to lord Falkland ... there are ... some striking thoughts; but they are not well wrought' (*Lives*, 1: 35-36).

[7] See, for example, the following lines:

> Methinks *Heroick Poesie* till now
> Like some fantastick *Fairy Land* did show,
> *Gods, Devils, Nymphs, Witches* and *Gyants* race,
> And all but *Man* in *Mans chief work* had place.
> Thou like some worthy *Knight* with sacred Arms
> Dost drive the *Monsters* thence, and end the *Charms*.
> In stead of those dost *Men* and *Manners* plant,
> The things which that rich *Soil* did chiefly want.
> Yet ev'en thy *Mortals* do their *Gods* excell
> Taught by thy *Muse* to *Fight* and *Love* so well.
> (*Miscellanies*, 24)

[8] For a full and authoritative account of Cowley's translations of Anacreon see Tom Mason, 'Cowley and the Wisdom of Anacreon', *CQ* 19 (1990): 103-37.

[9] Johnson significantly does not require that poetry be serious in order to be lasting.

[10] David Hume had made an exception for Cowley's *Anacreontiques* on the same terms as Johnson when he wrote that a few of them 'surprise us by their ease and gaiety'. *The History of England, from the Invasion of Julius Caesar to the Revolution in 1688*, 8 vols. (London, 1770), 7: 339.

[11] The Delaware editors suggest that Johnson is here 'catching the tone of Cowley's own remarks on *The Mistress* in the preface to F1 [*Poems* 1656]', and 'is in part inspired to these remarks by the "accusation of lasciviousness" advanced by censurers like Elys'. (See Edmund Elys's *An Exclamation to All those that love the Lord Jesus in sincerity, against an apology written by an ingenious person for Mr. Cowley's lascivious and profane verses* [London, 1670]). The editors continue: 'Johnson's judgment had, and continues to have, considerable impact on those who study literature at one remove from the texts' (*Works* 2: Part 1, 220). The possibility that Johnson's adverse criticism of Cowley at this point validates his positive judgments on other occasions - and might conceivably come from having the text in front of his eyes - is curiously not entertained.

[12] For discussion of Johnson's relationships with Eva Garrick, Elizabeth Carter, Charlotte Lennox, Hester Thrale, Elizabeth Montagu, Hannah More and Fanny Burney, see Norma Clarke, *Dr Johnson's Women* (London and New York: Hambledon and London, 2000). See also Isobel Grundy, 'Samuel Johnson as Patron of Women', *AJ* 1 (1987): 59-77, and Jaclyn Geller, 'The Unnarrated Life: Samuel Johnson, Female Friendship, and the Rise of the Novel', in *Johnson*

Revisioned, 80-98.

[13] The unusual and distinctive *weight* of Johnson's observations can be gathered from a comparison with the same general *ideas* in John Oldmixon, *The Arts of Logick and Rhetorick* (London, 1728) (on Cowley's *Mistress*): 'almost all the Thoughts in those Love-Verses are false, because they are unnatural, Full of Affectation and Point, and aiming rather to shew the Author's Wit, and even Learning, than his Tenderness and Passion, by which only he could reach and move his Mistress's Heart' (38).

[14] The Delaware editors point out that 'Against Hope' 'first appears in Richard Crashaw's *Steps to the Temple*, where its stanzas alternate with those of Crashaw's poem on hope' (*Works* 2: Part 1, 272).

[15] *Essays*, 2: 275.

[16] *Cambridge History*, 4: 377.

[17] For an earlier but still highly illuminating account of Johnson's role in the history of Cowley's reception, see Arthur H. Nethercott, 'The Reputation of Abraham Cowley (1660-1800)', *PMLA* 38 (1923), 588-641. Nethercott writes that 'Early in his famous Life of Cowley ... Johnson indicated the only sane attitude to take to Cowley' (621), and points out that the tendency from the publication of the *Lives* 'has been to overlook Cowley's good points and to fasten only upon his bad ones' (623).

[18] Contrary to W.J. Bate's suggestion that the issues of the 'Life of Cowley' are 'relatively minor compared with those in the *Preface to Shakespeare*' (*The Achievement of Samuel Johnson*, 215), my contention is that the critical *occasion* differs, but that the critical 'issues' (the humanity and emotional content of the poetry that Johnson is responding to) are similar in both magnitude and kind.

[19] Cf. the many substantiating references to the 'Life' in William Edinger's *Samuel Johnson and Poetic Style* (Chicago and London: University of Chicago Press, 1977). Edinger's emphasis falls on the 'Life' as a locus classicus of Johnsonian theories of language, or 'familiar notions' (as Rogers has claimed). But the 'Life of Cowley' is also a part of history in the sense that brings the past into the present; as a performance of the judging intelligence informed by emotional needs.

[20] See Boileau's Preface to his *Traité du Sublime* (1674) (English translation in *The Works of Monsieur Boileau*, 3 vols. [London, 1711-13]), and the lines on Christian epic poetry (586-671) from his *Art Poétique* (also 1674), first translated into English by Dryden and Soame in 1683. (*Poems of John Dryden*, 1: 348-50).

[21] William Wordsworth, 'An Essay, Supplementary to the Preface, 1815'. See *Prose Works of William Wordsworth*, ed. W.J.B. Owen and J.W. Smyser, 3 vols. (Oxford: Clarendon Press, 1974), 3: 71. Wordsworth claims to have had a copy of the 1681 ('seventh edition') of Cowley's *Works* on his shelves and reveals that 'twenty-five years ago', i.e. in 1790, 'the booksellers' stalls in London swarmed with the folios of Cowley'.

[22] See Roland Barthes, *Le Plaisir du texte* (Paris: Éditions du Seuil, 1973).

[23] Susan Manning seems right to sense the urgency of retrieving this criterion from the age of Hume and of Johnson. See 'Whatever Happened to Pleasure?', *CQ* 30, no. 3 (2001): 215-32.

[24] Johnson is reported by Boswell in 1773 to have said that 'There is more sense in a line of Cowley than in a page of Pope'. See *Boswell's Life of Johnson*, 5: 345.

[25] David Trotter, for example, has sought to interpret Cowley's poetical oeuvre less judgmentally than Johnson through the history of seventeenth-century ideas; see *The Poetry of Abraham Cowley* (London: Macmillan, 1979). A similar emphasis appears in Robert B. Hinman's *Abraham Cowley's World of Order* (Cambridge, MA: Harvard

University Press, 1960), where Cowley's poetry is explained in terms of 'the extensive knowledge of seventeenth-century thought accumulated by modern research' (vii).

Chapter 5

Voice and Image: Critical Comedy, the Johnsonian Monster, and the Construction of Judgment

Critical Comedy in Johnson's *Lives*

In the last chapter, and in the one before, we saw how a simultaneous and parallel attention to the particularities of drama or poetry was able to place the text of Johnson's criticism in a different kind of historical light, the emphasis being on judgment rather than theory, on the present experience of relativities of pain or pleasure as an alternative to the traditional emphasis on criticism in its context of thought. In this next chapter, however, I will pick up the earlier thread that leads from Johnson's treatment of Minim, and turn first to the subversive comic and satirical temper of Johnson as it plays over a wider range of 'Lives' that we know so well but hear so faintly. For I would suggest that comic writing is of the essence of Johnson's critical presence as, for Johnson, 'comedy' was the prevailing spirit of Johnson's portraits of critics in the periodical papers, the essence of his appreciation of Cowley, was part of Shakespearean 'general nature' and of 'mingled drama'.[1] '[Shakespeare's] disposition', wrote Johnson, 'led him to comedy' (*Shakespeare*, 7: 69). And so, very often, did Johnson's. 'Offsetting the somber contemplator of death', writes Harold Bloom in *The Western Canon*, 'is Johnson the critical humorist, who teaches the critic not to be solemn, smug, or superior'.[2] In addition to the comic vision of human experience that he shared with Boileau, with Dryden and with Pope (but not at all with the Beatties, the Blairs, the Kameses, the Wartons, the Gerards, the Morgans, or any other of the famously contextualizing critics of his own day), Johnson does this, I shall suggest here, in a way that both roots him within and lifts him outside his culture - by his mastery of what today we call 'tone'.

'Tone' is a core ingredient of literary interpretation and critical realization. Historians of criticism must catch the tone if they are to know what is meant in a critical text. Tone expresses the extraordinary intimacy and intelligibility of a critical language as it engages with its critical object. This goes beyond the structures of grammar, conceptual and philological context, the role of the text in critical and literary history and so forth; it brings articulation, elocution, and intonation into the equation of critical meaning by which the literary critic is judged. Tone registers the difference (in John Searle's terms) between 'author meaning' and 'sentence meaning';[3] it gives us an *audible* intuition of the voice, tempo, facial expression and pulse of the speaker long before recordings on wax, vinyl, magnetic tape or compact disk could technically be made. In the case of Johnson, tone diverts us from the one-dimensional experience of reading a written text of criticism to the sense of the speaker talking to us aloud and suggests the speaker's spoken attitude *towards* the things he is saying. It adds substantially to the record we have from Boswell's *Life* or the *Memoirs* of Johnson by Mrs. Thrale.[4]

We cannot therefore begin to construct a history of criticism which features prominently the work of Samuel Johnson, or try to locate its place within history, unless we can read his tone. As ironists from Erasmus to Jane Austen knew well, tone marks the difference between appearance and reality in the literary as in the critical text, and we cannot have a history of criticism that makes meaningful mention of Samuel Johnson if we are dead to his tone - this apprehended ahistorically by direct appeal to our sense of humour in the present day. (The same would go for attempts to historicize the critical writings of Boileau, Pope and of Dryden, of Wordsworth, Coleridge, T.S. Eliot or Jacques Derrida; and it would go for many other writers who critical historians are interested in). As the idea of criticism has in the twentieth century given way to the sober concepts of literary 'scholarship' and 'research', the habits of mind these concepts express are in turn used to reclaim the critical past. But tone - this manifested in the comic apprehension of authors, their works, their language and the ideas that their critical texts contain - is a fact of the raw material, the primary data, of the history of criticism.

We have seen that comedy pervades Johnson's critical writings (and his idea of the critic) from his earliest years. From the various portraits of critical absurdity in the periodical papers written in the early 1750s, culminating in the masterpiece of Minim the critic in the *Idler* of 1759, Johnson's comic sense of the role of the critic guides his critical response to the major and minor authors who ultimately came within his sights. The tone that Johnson adopts is a part of his critical perspective, and part of his meaning. Sometimes terse and sardonic, at others self-mocking, infinitely light or buoyant, bathetic, po-faced or inscrutably deadpan, moving in Boileau's words as adapted by Pope from 'grave to gay, from lively to severe', Johnson's satirical humour is a delicate instrument of critical understanding, expression and control. 'Double, double, toil and trouble', he writes in summing up the pompous sublime of the odes of Gray in the *Lives* (3: 440). The agility of the allusion illuminates by contrast the turgid magnificence and strained mystique of these poems.

Comic hyperbole - the caustic tirade of Juvenalian railing, consciously pitched to convey an assault on the reader - only rarely emerges through the sustained gravity, economy, acerbity and restraint of Johnson's poetic imitations of the Roman poet in 1738 and 1749. But in the comments Johnson makes about Blackmore's medical writings in the *Lives of the Poets* thirty years later, we find this account of the inexhaustible obsessions of Blackmore's medical mind:

> I know not whether I can enumerate all the treatises by which he has endeavoured to diffuse the art of healing; for there is scarcely any distemper of dreadful name

which he has not taught his reader how to oppose. He has written on the small-pox, with a vehement invective against inoculation; on consumptions, the spleen, the gout, the rheumatism, the king's-evil, the dropsy, the jaundice, the stone, the diabetes, and the plague. (*Lives* 2: 250)

But in terms which bring the *Lives* into closer proximity to Johnson's Juvenal imitations, the rising trajectory is also here accompanied by a corresponding collapse; a tendency of Johnsonian critical prose in the direction of praise to conclude in bathetic descent. Of the overweening ambition and poetic poverty of Pope's *Essay on Man*, for example, Johnson wrote that 'Never were penury of knowledge and vulgarity of sentiment so happily disguised. The reader feels his mind full, though he learns nothing; and when he meets it in its new array no longer knows the talk of his mother and his nurse' (*Lives*, 3: 243). There is in the 'Life of Dryden' the subtle registration of anti-climax, or of high expectations refused, when Johnson reflects on Dryden's version of *The Tempest* vis-à-vis Shakespeare's play: 'The effect produced by the conjunction of these two powerful minds was that to Shakespeare's monster Caliban is added a sister-monster Sicorax; and a woman, who, in the original play, had never seen a man, is in this brought acquainted with a man that had never seen a woman' (*Lives*, 1: 341). 'So what?' is the question Johnson seems here to throw out.

In the 'Life of Waller', Johnson criticizes the use of mythology by reference to a ludicrous detail: 'A fiction, not only detected but despised', he writes, 'can never afford a solid basis to any position, though sometimes it may furnish a transient allusion, or slight illustration. No modern monarch can be much exalted by hearing that, as Hercules had had his *club*, he has his *navy*' (*Lives*, 1:295). Johnson's derision at the expense of mythology is closely connected with his amused contempt for pastoral imagery, as for example in the 'Life of Gay' (on Gay's *Dione*). The judgment of literature here develops into a kind of satire which bites, and the humour approximates to an unmitigated disdain for pastoral, with little warmth or sympathy for its infantilization of poetry:

A Pastoral of an hundred lines may be endured; but who will hear of sheep and goats, and myrtle bowers and purling rivulets, through five acts? Such scenes please barbarians in the dawn of literature, and children in the dawn of life; but will be for the most part thrown away as men grow wise, and nations grow learned. (*Lives*, 2: 284-85)

We hear this deflationary note again in the 'Life of Dorset'. Dorset had been praised in grovelling terms by Dryden as the equal in satire to Shakespeare in tragedy: 'Would it be imagined', asks Johnson in reply, 'that, of this rival to antiquity, all the satires were little personal invectives, and that his longest composition was a song of eleven stanzas?' (*Lives*, 1: 307). The pastoral dreams of poets about their own lives are comically represented in the 'Life of Savage'. In an account written as if from within the mind of Savage, Johnson imagines what Savage envisions his forthcoming exile in Wales will be like:

> As he was ready to entertain himself with future pleasures, he had planned out a
> scheme of life for the country, of which he had no knowledge but from pastorals
> and songs. He imagined that he should be transported to scenes of flowery felicity,
> like those which one poet has reflected to another; and had projected a perpetual
> round of innocent pleasures, of which he suspected no interruption from pride, or
> ignorance, or brutality.
>
> With these expectations he was so enchanted, that when he was once gently
> reproached by a friend for submitting to live upon a subscription, and advised
> rather by a resolute exertion of his abilities to support himself, he could not bear to
> debar himself from the happiness which was to be found in the calm of a cottage,
> or lose the opportunity of listening without intermission to the melody of the
> nightingale, which he believed was to be heard from every bramble, and which he
> did not fail to mention as a very important part of the happiness of a country life.
> (*Lives*, 2: 410)

John Philips's use of blank verse in preference to rhyme in his poem *Cider*
inspires a related rise and descent. By this Johnson evinces the stylistic and
metrical propriety required to anchor poetry in ordinary things. Johnson is thinking
of poetry not hierarchically but holistically here, of Philips's little masterpiece and
Milton's great epic as the best comment on each other: 'Contending angels may
shake the regions of heaven in blank verse', writes Johnson, 'but the flow of equal
measures and the embellishment of rhyme must recommend to our attention the art
of engrafting' (*Lives*, 1: 319-20). The notion of the totality and termination of a
poet's life is sometimes evoked when Johnson links the art of critical biography
with a sharp sense of the tragic absurdity we know from elsewhere in his writings.
There is the over-confidence and self-destructiveness of Edmund Smith, one of the
'murmurers at Fortune' (*Lives*, 2: 20), who, however Fortune's blows might strike:

> eat and drank till he found himself plethorick; and then, resolving to ease himself
> by evacuation, he wrote to an apothecary in the neighbourhood a prescription of a
> purge so forcible, that the apothecary thought it his duty to delay it till he had
> given notice of its danger. Smith, not pleased with the contradiction of a shopman,
> and boastful of his own knowledge, treated the notice with rude contempt, and
> swallowed his own medicine, which, in July 1710, brought him to the grave. He
> was buried at Hartham. (*Lives*, 2: 17-18)

It is that mock-pedantic placing of the exact date, 'July 1710', and the terse, utterly
matter-of-fact, sentence which follows, 'He was buried at Hartham', which
conveys at once the absurdity and the finality of Smith's sudden, altogether stupid
and gratuitous, self-inflicted, demise. Such deaths of the poets in the *Lives of the
Poets* call forth some of Johnson's most mordant humour, as in the following
anecdote from the 'Life of Addison':

> Lord Warwick was a young man of very irregular life, and perhaps of loose
> opinions. Addison, for whom he did not want respect, had very diligently
> endeavoured to reclaim him; but his arguments and expostulations had no effect.
> One experiment, however, remained to be tried: when he found his life near its
> end he directed the young lord to be called, and when he desired with great
> tenderness to hear his last injunctions, told him, 'I have sent for you that you may

see how a Christian can die'. What effect this awful scene had on the earl I know not; he likewise died himself in a short time. (*Lives*, 2: 117)

Elsewhere Johnson brings a *reductio ad absurdum* to his more directly literary observations, as when, again in the 'Life of Addison' he is analysing the internal logic of lines from Joseph Addison's celebrated *Letter from Italy*:

> Fir'd with that name—
> I bridle in my struggling Muse with pain,
> That longs to launch into a nobler [bolder] strain.

On which he comments:

> To *bridle* a *goddess* is no very delicate idea: but why must she be *bridled?* because she *longs to launch*; an act which was never hindered by a *bridle*: and whither will she *launch*? into a *nobler strain*. She is in the first line a *horse*, in the second a *boat*; and the care of the poet is to keep his *horse* or his *boat* from *singing*. (*Lives*, 2: 128)

Among the smaller 'Lives', Johnson reflects in similar vein on the *Elegies* of the poet James Hammond, who in a typically dreary poem, says Johnson, 'Like other lovers ... threatens his lady with dying' (*Lives*, 2: 315). As Johnson recounts it here the contested story of Hammond's romantic experience affords a similar opportunity. As 'the son of a Turkey merchant' Hammond 'had some office at the prince of Wales's court, till love of a lady, whose name was Dashwood, for a time disordered his understanding'. Johnson goes on to explain that Hammond apparently became as a result of this encounter 'unextinguishably amorous' while his mistress became 'inexorably cruel' (*Lives*, 2: 312). In these and many other examples the critical point to be made, the essential judgment registered of man and works, is experienced as a presence by today's reader of Johnson through the play of the mock-heroic. This is greatly superior in point and control, I would suggest, to the desperate coterie puns of any transliterated post-Saussurean critical text, and Johnson's criticism by comparison rises above its context of origin at such points to enter the world where human beings have always laughed the same way. Combined with a participative sympathy in the petty tragedies of any writer, the less-than-serious note is part of the sum total of Johnson's critical attitude; more pervasive as it is not explicit; heard in the voice not seen on the page. The comedy of Johnsonian criticism is as indispensable to the comprehension of Johnson's whole mode of relation to critical history as it is to the enjoyment of a Jane Austen novel. 'The tears of lovers', Johnson had remarked of poems by Cowley and Donne, 'are always of great poetical account' (*Lives*, 1: 26).

From Hagstrum to Hinnant, from Krutch to Keast, from Wellek to Wain, the voice of comedy has not always rung in the ears of modern commentary on the criticism of Johnson. The ironic or sceptical commitments of postmodern critics to an endless play have not replaced the range and pertinence of Johnsonian humour, and perhaps no text by a major critic till the time of George Eliot has been able to match the Johnsonian harnessing of play to a purpose, of the joke to the judgment.

The tones he locates in his most quietly comedic moments in the *Preface* and the *Lives* are wedded to Johnson's appreciation of the sublime indispensability of fools, the deep delight in human pretension articulated in Dick Minim. But if Johnson's refusal to be paralysed by awe at the poetry of the English tradition is the characteristic of a critical *voice* that transcends its time - beyond any difference in *theory* - it is matched by his age's equal and opposite refusal to be paralysed by him. And so we turn to Johnsonian criticism as the *object* of satire.

James Gillray and the Satirical Image of Johnson as Critic

To picture Samuel Johnson in one's mind's eye is to instantiate the whole of what he did, what he is and what he was, out of the stream of time - in a present moment of apprehension. To *see* him pictured, in words, in paint or in ink, is however to place or to frame him historically. Thomas Babington Macaulay's vividly conjured visualization of Johnson in his notorious 1831 review of Croker's edition of Boswell's *Life* fixes Johnson, bundled with his critical mentality, judgments and ideas, to a particular instant in the history of criticism. In the Johnson whose eyes and mouth move with 'convulsive twitches', whose 'gigantic body ... huge massy face, seamed with the scars of desease', we have fully formed the caricature whose gruff, neurotic and combative habits, low and gross appetites, deafness and blindness to life's finer things, generated 'cartoon' ways of conceiving his criticism for years to come.[5] Johnson the psycho-physical 'case' (the word 'case' is George Watson's)[6] is a critical being to whom we can all feel superior. Macaulay's image historicizes Johnson as a gothic Gargantua able both to horrify and delight those who recall his figure to mind.

The complex history of attacks on Johnson's criticism that precede the Macaulayan moment of 1831, and are its condition of possibility, is perhaps not yet completely charted. Commentators have noticed the disparities between the mood of the times at the appearance of Johnson's *Lives* and his rough or derisive treatment of Milton's personality and shorter poems, Gray's *Odes*, eighteenth-century pastoral poetry, some parts of Prior and Hammond and even (or more especially) areas of Dryden and Pope. As a comparison between Johnson's opinions and those of his near-contemporary Joseph Warton would suggest, Johnson may indeed be aesthetically out of step.[7] And yet pre- and post-Victorian readers of Johnson's criticism have often overlooked the reasons why this division arose, preferring to think historically that Johnson was simply a symptom of reactionary consciousness, stubbornly 'conservative', or sentimentally 'Tory'; or that he had failed to escape from an overwhelming enthusiasm for Dryden and Pope. We have seen that views of this kind have crystallized in such twentieth-century verdicts on Johnson that his criticism is 'Not for enlightenment about the authors with whom it deals ... and not for direct instruction in critical thinking'.[8]

But such a stark division between the critical present and the critical past may also have obscured the fact that Johnson was attacked by Whig and Tory alike, and that Johnson's harshest criticism was reserved for exhausted linguistic and generic traditions which new genius had failed to refresh. Gray, according to Johnson, has 'a kind a strutting dignity and is tall by walking on tiptoe'; his 'art and his struggle are too visible, and there is too little appearance of ease and nature'; Gray 'thought his language more poetical as it was more remote from common use' (*Lives*, 3: 440; 435). Other eighteenth-century poets are condemned with equal vigour for their 'mythology' or their 'imitation' whatever its exact source may be, while Shakespeare, Johnson's 'poet of nature', as I have suggested, forms the criterion against which the poetry of Cowley, Milton, Dryden and Pope can be positively *and* negatively judged. Be that as it may, the critical history that depicts Johnson as the representative 'classical' critic retains its power, and has never been extinguished by the contemporary observation that Johnson was also a critic *of* the classical.[9] But Johnson's hostility to examples of gratuitous classicizing by English poets precisely suggests why it is that some of his most eloquent contemporaries and successors were confounded and shocked. Thus Cowper could write to William Unwin in 1779 that:

> As a poet, he [Johnson] has treated him [Milton] with severity enough, and has plucked one or two of the most beautiful feathers out of his Muse's wing, and trampled them under his great foot. He has passed sentence of condemnation upon 'Lycidas', and has taken occasion, from that charming poem, to expose to ridicule (what is indeed ridiculous enough) the childish prattlement of pastoral compositions, as if 'Lycidas' was the prototype and pattern of them all. The liveliness of the description, the sweetness of the numbers, the classical spirit of antiquity that prevails in it, go for nothing.[10]

For Cowper there was no essential conflict between the 'classical' and that characteristic element of 'pre-romantic' taste, the 'antique'.

What needs to be further examined in this connection is however the part played in advancing Johnson's critical notoriety by the most talented caricaturists of the eighteenth century.[11] The images that I shall now go on to discuss combine with comments by Cowper, Warton and others to register a critical reception that seems with regard to Johnson in a partial state of denial. Such images vitalize critical issues in compellingly pictorial form, and they engage an aesthetic politics not co-extensive with party.

The political and satirical cartoon was coming into its own at about the time of the *Lives*, and cartoon images of a politically compromised Johnson had begun to appear from the time of his £300 per year pension from Lord Bute. In later years, cartoons featuring Johnson abandoned their political thrust to focus on such topics as Johnson's eating habits, the personal relationship between Johnson and Mrs. Thrale,[12] or more significantly between Johnson and Boswell.[13] A famous series of illustrations to Boswell's Hebridean *Tour* engraved by Thomas Rowlandson from drawings by Samuel Collings remains relatively amiable in its treatment of Johnson, though Johnson is more cruelly and scandalously represented in others. Satirically effective in a different way are cartoons devoted to Johnson's dining manners, and here we find the evocation of the Rabelaisian figure of 'Gargantua's mouth' discussed by David Amigoni in his essay on Boswellian and later Victorian responses to Johnson's body.[14] All the images conspire to construct a Johnson who could have no more feeling for the graces of poetry than for gracious living.

It is, however, two particularly compelling images of Johnson by James Gillray that relate most specifically to his contemporary repute as a critic, and together these wreak a highly pointed revenge on the harshness of Johnson's opinion of his country's poetical favourites. In so doing they take us deeper than any of the caricatures devoted to Johnson's politics or pension, his personal relations or his purely physical habits, into the values at the heart of his critical achievement and its relation to literary judgment.[15] They illuminate the role of Johnson in the eighteenth-century history of criticism in ways the verbal text of this narrative cannot materialize. My interpretation and contextualization of these memorable and magnificent pieces is the subject of what remains of this chapter. Considered in the setting of other satirical prints of the period, and with reference to written reactions to Johnson's criticism, they are part of the essential background to the construction of Macaulay's Johnsonian monster.

Old Wisdom

Old Wisdom Blinking at the Stars was published in what Gillray's biographer Draper Hill calls his 'busy year' of 1782.[16] Gillray here depicts the head of Johnson on the body of an owl - the symbol of Judgment (1). This monstrous hybrid may to a certain extent recall Pope's famous line in his satirical portrait of Sporus from the *Epistle to Dr Arbuthnot*: 'A Cherub's face, a Reptile all the rest'.[17] But while the face in this image is far from cherubic, the engraving anticipates a favourite Gillrayan device which is also the stock-in-trade of the period's graphic satire, just as it articulates in visual language the satirist's conception of 'Parts that none will trust'.[18] The literary and aesthetic origins of this device may be partially suggested by the 'incongruous mixture' of imagery discussed by Diana Donald in relation to Gillray's *Shakespeare Sacrificed* of 1789. The visual juxtapositions would remind the eighteenth-century spectator of the opening lines of Horace's *Ars Poetica*:

> If some mad painter, by his fancy led,
> Should join a horse's neck and human head,
> And upon limbs from various beasts should bring
> Plumage from birds of every coloured wing,
> So that a handsome female face should grow
> Down to a fish of hideous form below,
> Could you, this picture if allowed to see,
> Gaze on the sight from boisterous laughter free?[19]

'Horace's words', according to Donald, 'offered Gillray a positive programme for a new kind of satire, which through burlesque could express something of the mania and extremism of post-Revolutionary politics',[20] and the lines serve to assert the relevance of Horace's Augustan standard as a necessary reference point for the 'revolutionary' play of comic and bizarre. Thus are human heads and faces in other prints variously joined with the bodies of asses, dogs, pigs, cattle, sheep, vultures, a rattle-snake and a squirrel, a dragon, a lion, a bear, horses, a crab, wasps and bees, geese, cormorants and other beasts whose mingled beauty and horror mostly evoke

Figure 5.1   *Old Wisdom Blinking at the Stars.* **James Gillray (1782)**

the hypocrisy of political figures, or the stupid conduct of the military and ministers of state.[21] Here Johnson, eyes narrowed and looking ahead, wings folded, sulks lugubriously under the busts of a severe-featured Milton and a disdainful Pope, both the subjects of two major, and extremely controversial, 'Lives'.[22] In depicting Johnson as the contemporary judge of both Puritan and Catholic poets, *Old Wisdom* dramatizes the independently poetic politics of Johnson's critical and aesthetic role.

Two other poets are obscured by Johnson's colossal head. The crown of bays just visible in outline may suggest the figure of Dryden. However the poet on the extreme left of the picture we can only guess. Material to the primitivistic power of this engraving is a perspective adopted by Gillray in many of his later plates - the contrast between the relative detail of the face and the sketchiness of the rest of the picture.[23] The eyes ('blinking' according to the caption) draw attention to Johnson's personal weakness of vision but also - in common with other contemporary prints - to the cruelty and absurdity of literary legislation itself. Johnson's closing of the eyes, it could be argued, indicates ambiguously not dullness or glumness only, but shrewd appraisal. The casual outlines of the remaining parts of the image show folio volumes arranged on shelves behind. Gillray establishes a hierarchical scale of poetry and criticism in this print. Johnson stands high on the bibliographical pedestal of his *Lives of the Poets* and his *Dictionary* but *below* the poets he blinks at. The implied attitude to these poets does not therefore *entirely* eliminate Gillray's critical respect.

But the detailed attention to Johnson's face serves not just to intensify the critical focus on the subject, the real Samuel Johnson. The particulars allude to a prior artistic model, a 1769 portrait of Johnson by Reynolds (2), that both assists and resists the mythologization of Johnson. This complicates and situates the apparent crudity of the young engraver's bold technique, and the visual bluntness of the satire. Compared with this original, Gillray catches precisely the fall of the hair, combed forward over the forehead from the crown. The half-closed eyes of the Reynolds portrait are also recalled. But Gillray systematically coarsens, externalizes, subverts and de-idealizes the classical heroism of Johnson's features in their inner agony of thought or expression. Modifications include Johnson's complexion. In the coloured version of the print this is pink and puffy; the lower lip is extended outwards, the eyebrows are owlishly arched and the nose is given an additional length and droop. Gillray would on a number of later occasions make it his business to burlesque Reynolds.[24] He is said to have respected the artist, and in 1778 had been admitted to the Royal Academy schools, from when, according to Draper Hill, 'a rapid improvement in the standard of Gillray's draftsmanship' occurred. 'Without doubt', writes his biographer, 'the most commanding figure [for Gillray] was Sir Joshua Reynolds himself'.[25] But Gillray's satire of Johnson seems also to strike at the glorifying style of his victim's most famous iconographer, and the uncritical memorialization registered by it. The symbolism of the owl may also intimate that Gillray's mind was playing over the history of Pope iconography, as Morris Brownell has suggested, and was combining within this image ideas from that and written sources.[26]

Figure 5.2   *Samuel Johnson.* **Joshua Reynolds (1769)**

But Gillray's satire also subtly and tactically conveys a paradoxical admiration for, and acknowledgment of, Johnson, on his own terms so to speak. To deflate the pomposity of old Johnsonian wisdom (blended in the figure of owlish stupidity) is only to extrapolate the critical irony that Johnson directed at himself - in such contexts we have seen as the 1759 *Idler* papers on Minim (in the matter of criticism), in the famous tenth chapter of *Rasselas* (on the nature of poetry, also 1759), or in the *Preface to Shakespeare* (1765) where Johnson heroically and mockingly, seriously and unseriously, fixes on himself as a critic and editor of Shakespeare's plays:

> Perhaps, what I have here not dogmatically but deliberatively written, may recal the principles of the drama to a new examination. I am almost frighted at my own temerity; and when I estimate the fame and the strength of those that maintain the contrary opinion, am ready to sink down in reverential silence; as Aeneas withdrew from the defence of Troy, when he saw Neptune shaking the wall, and Juno heading the besiegers. (*Shakespeare*, 7: 80-81)

Draper Hill writes that Gillray's personal conduct was 'enigmatic' and that in the eyes of one contemporary he 'seemed to affect a total indifference to the men and events upon which he commented'.[27] But his satire evokes his subject's centrality, complexity and charismatic appeal (and not *just* his physical grossness) as a necessary and countervailing condition of the work of creative destruction. The reference to Reynolds internalizes Johnson's celebrity and importance within the frame of the travesty, and as Sporus to Pope, or in the inventive distortions of Pope's own body to his detractors, Johnson to Gillray is so much more than a satirical *victim*.

Johnson is reported by Mrs. Thrale to have disliked a later (1775) portrait by Reynolds (engraved by John Hall in 1787 and reproduced as the Frontispiece to this volume) depicting the tortured features of a short-sighted Johnson his face pressed close against the pages of a book he is attempting to read. Commentators seem sure that in the anecdote she recorded Mrs. Thale has misremembered Johnson as 'looking into the slit of his pen', and the expression of intense concentration or pain clearly refers to the same image that seems to have caused irritation, and prompted a protest.[28] Writes Mrs. Thrale:

> When Sir Joshua Reynolds had painted his portrait looking into the slit of his pen, and holding it almost close to his eye, as was his general custom, he felt displeased, and told me 'he would not be known by posterity for his *defects* only, let Sir Joshua do his worst'. I said in reply, that Reynolds had no such difficulties about himself, and that he might observe the picture which hung up in the room where we were talking, represented Sir Joshua holding his ear in his hand to catch the sound. 'He may paint himself as deaf if he chuses (replied Johnson); but I will not be *blinking Sam*'.[29]

Of the quotations that Johnson had given in his *Dictionary* to define the verb 'to blink', meaning 'To see obscurely', one had been taken from Act ii, scene ix of Shakespeare's *Merchant of Venice* where the modern, now rather old-fashioned expletive seems first to be hinted: 'What's here?' exclaims Arragon to Portia as the silver casket is unlocked, 'the portrait of a blinking idiot'. *Old Wisdom Blinking at the Stars* mocks the earlier painting by Reynolds of that other 'blinking Sam' who is the 'bloody Sam', the 'portrait of ... [that] blinking idiot' who wrote the *Lives of the Poets*; or in the words of William Blake's lampoon of that other critical creature of darkness from *An Island in the Moon* (?1784):

> Lo the Bat with Leathern wing
> Winking & blinking
> Winking & blinking
> Winking & blinking
> Like Doctor Johnson.[30]

The cultural service Gillray performs here for contextualist critical history is to adapt the newly evolving satirical idiom to pictorialize the interplay between Johnson's notoriously poor eyes and his putative defects of critical vision in the *Lives*. But the throw of his satirical net also catches the poets that Johnson is dazzled by and is blinking at. The 'Stars' in the title prefigure an attitude to poetical celebrity in its modern 'Hollywood' sense. The shabby, tinsel nature of Milton's marbled eminence and Pope's is disparagingly caught in the resplendently crude, pale yellow star spikes that decorate the heads of this established élite.[31] Milton's expression is surly disapproval; Pope displays the pride and superiority to the rest of the world that is not contradicted by Johnson's biographical and critical 'Life'. In this poetical community half of the history of poetry is hidden symbolically behind Johnson's head. The visible portion is saluted by cheap statuary and plaster busts. The image recalls Pope's own story of having the portraits of the great poets of the past around him to keep him humble.[32] But the scene is also reminiscent of the classical garbage heap that is Timon's villa.[33]

A final allusion signalled within the bounds of the image is more directly literary. Open on the floor of the room in which Johnson is perched is a copy of *The Beauties of Johnson*. *The Beauties of Samuel Johnson LLD consisting of Maxims and Observations Moral, Critical, and Miscellaneous* was first published one year before the appearance of Gillray's print. Taken in the first instance from the edition of Shakespeare, the periodical papers of the *Rambler* and the *Idler* and in later editions including entries drawn from Boswell and Mrs. Thrale, these 'beauties' are mocked by the palpably unbeautiful image of Gillray's engraving. In the same way Reynolds's idealized portrait is undercut by a Johnson 'known by posterity for his *defects* only', and in this the image by Gillray suggests not the book of beauties layed out on the floor, but the *Deformities of Samuel Johnson* published by James Thomson Callendar in 1782. Both prepare the way for Macaulay's slide between Johnson's physical enormity and the alleged deformities of his criticism - the criticism other than unqualified praise that is - in the *Lives of the Poets*.

Dr Pomposo

A comparable sense of Gillray's role in criticizing the critic, also directed at the

Figure 5.3 *Apollo and the Muses, Inflicting Penance on Dr Pomposo, Round Parnassus.* James Gillray (1783)

Lives, is my second and perhaps better known example of 1783: *Apollo Muses Inflicting Penance on Dr. Pomposo, Round Parnassus* (3).[34] Here the Johnsonian figure, like a convict being marched to the gallows for his crimes, stripped to the waist and wearing a dunce's cap, is that of a huge cart-horse or bear. Johnson had been dubbed Dr. Pomposo by Charles Churchill in his satirical poem *The Ghost*,[35] and had appeared with the actual fur-covered body of a bear in other prints, mostly satirical illustrations of moments from Boswell's *Tour*. Johnson's 'bearish' qualities in conversation and manner were well known, and friends and enemies alike refer to him as 'Ursa Major' - the coinage may have been Boswell's father's.[36] In the figure of a bear Johnson is sometimes depicted on two legs, as in the anonymous *Scottish Worship of an English Idol; his High Priest attending* of 1786.[37] In other prints he can appear on all fours, as in the scurrilous image of *Bossy Bounce preparing for the Scottish Professors to Kiss* also of this year.[38] Both this and its companion print, *A Tom Tit twittering on an Eagle's Back-side*,[39] were pasted by Horace Walpole into his personal copy of Boswell's book. The treatment of Johnson in the series of sketches by Samuel Collings etched by Rowlandson and designed to respond to the *Tour* are as I have suggested relatively restrained. Boswell is the fool and stooge scoffed at in Macaulay's Croker review: Johnson, his foil, is depicted as the massive hero of modern letters in comic or farcical situations drawn from everyday life as a tourist in Scotland; but his image also retains vestiges of the detachment, grandeur, knowing geniality and serenity of the genuine sage.[40]

Like *Old Wisdom*, however, *Apollo and the Muses* stands out as a satire on Johnson's specifically *critical* qualities.[41] But the engraving forges once again the link so essential to Macaulay's account, between Johnsonian physical and aesthetic grossness, between moral qualities and artistic ones, between beliefs and character, as these were developed within the definition of the ideal from Pope's *Essay on Criticism* of 1711. Here the humility, flexibility, clear-sightedness and evaluative stability of the ideal critic join in a being 'Unbiass'd, or by *Favour* or by *Spite*; / Not *dully prepossest*, nor *blindly right*'. 'Tho' Learn'd, well-bred; and tho' well-bred, sincere', writes Pope, such a critic is also 'Modestly bold, and Humanly severe' (*Essay*, lines 633-36). Gillray's intimacy with the movements in critical taste aligns his portrait with such protests against blind Johnsonian judgment as the second volume, in 1782, of Joseph Warton's *Essay on the Genius and Writings of Pope* or, in the same year, Fitz-Thomas's *Remarks on Dr. Johnson's Life and Critical Observations on the Works of Mr Gray*,[42] and, as mentioned above, the 1782 *Deformities of Samuel Johnson*. It is also a critical counterpart to some of the sentiments of the *Monthly Review*. The tone of exasperation in the *Monthly*'s treatment of those 'Lives' published in 1781 builds to a head as the reviewer regrets 'Instances ... in which the Critic's judgment seems altogether under the dominion of predilection or prejudice'.[43] The seemingly wilful cruelty of 'the old Colossus' in his condemnation of the 'beauties of Milton, Prior, Gray &c &c' was later lamented in comparably ethical terms by Anna Seward,[44] who wrote from Lichfield in a letter to Thomas Park in 1797:

> After Johnson rose himself into fame, it is well known that he read no other man's writings, living or dead, with that attention without which public criticism can have no honour, or, indeed, common honesty. If genius flashed upon his maturer eyes, they ached at its splendour, and he cast the book indignantly from him. All his familiarity with poetic compositions, was the result of juvenile avidity of perusal; and their various beauties were stampt upon his mind, by a miraculous strength and retention of memory. The wealth of poetic quotation in his admirable Dictionary, was supplied from the hoards of his early years. They were very little augmented afterwards.
>
> In subsequent periods, he read verse, not to appreciate, but to depreciate its excellence. His first ambition, early in life, was poetic fame; his first avowed publication was in verse. Disappointed in that darling wish, indignant of less than first-rate eminence, he hated the authors, preceding or contemporary, whose fame, as poets, eclipsed his own.[45]

Gillray in *Old Wisdom* had recalled the graphic and poetically verbalized figure of Pope's dunciadic owl, and in *Apollo and the Muses* he lists on Johnson's pyramidical dunce's cap the 'Lives' where he is charged with offending the Muses: Milton, Otway, Waller, Gray, Shenstone, Lyttelton are legible on the forward face though a similar number inscribed on the side are not. Johnson carries over his right shoulder a placard which reads: 'For defaming that Genius I could never emulate, by criticism without Judgment; - and endeavouring to cast the beauties of British Poetry into the hideous shade of oblivion'. This phrase 'the Beauties of British Poetry' may recall the comparative deformities of British Criticism, shown to be falsely called 'beauties' by the satirical exposure of *Old Wisdom Blinking at the Stars* and is one of several points of cross-fertilization between these two prints. Here also the image of books engraved within the frame of the picture carries the moral of the whole composition and reinforces it, as in the inscriptions on the winged volumes flying about before Johnson's feet - *An Essay on the Milk of Human kindness dedicated to Dr Johnson as a Man* and *An Essay on Envy dedicated to Dr Johnson as an Author*. Johnson's putative jealousy of the men and the authors treated in the *Lives* again indicates Gillray's effort to fuel the flames of the ethical attack on Johnson's critical performance in terms derived from Pope, and in the usage of classical standards to fault him. As the failed dramatist too ready to find fault with Shakespeare, he cannot admit the greatness of Milton or Gray. Such sentiments offer a more acidic version of the ready moralizing about Johnson that was beginning to emerge - more strongly after his death - in the writings of Warton, in (as we have seen) Cowper's letters, Robert Anderson's *Life of Johnson* of 1795, the *Letters* of Anna Seward, and in Macaulay's later observation that Johnson 'took it for granted that the kind of poetry which flourished in his own time, which he had been accustomed to hear praised from his childhood, and which he had himself written with success, was the best kind of poetry'.[46] Anderson had praised Johnson's criticism of Shakespeare, Dryden and Pope, but attacked his criticisms of minor eighteenth-century poets, writing of his 'degrading estimate of the exquisite compositions of Prior, Hammond, Collins, Gray, Shenstone and Akenside'.[47] In his edition of Pope of 1797, Warton's tone (while more sympathetic in certain ways) had combined a sense of regret with the slightly hysterical or shrill:

> Johnson's taste was formed for the Didactic, the Moral, and the Satyric; and he had no true relish for the higher and more genuine species of poetry. Strong couplets, modern manners, present life, moral sententious writings alone pleased him. Hence his tasteless and groundless objections to the Lycidas of Milton, and to the Bard of Gray. Hence his own Irene is so frigid and uninteresting a tragedy; while his imitations of Juvenal are so forcible and pointed. His Lives of the Poets are unhappily tinctured with this narrow prejudice, and confined notion of poetry which has occasioned many false and spurious remarks and many ill-grounded opinions, in a work that might have been, and was intended to be, a manual of good taste and judgment.[48]

The Johnsonian Monster and the History of Criticism

The narrative of *Apollo and the Muses* is, finally, significant of developing conditions within the history of criticism in the later eighteenth century and gives visual drama to a parting of ways. Opportunistic though the work of Gillray may be, it is both symptom and agent of crucial changes in, or broadenings of, poetical taste. Its satirical moral is doubtless developed within what we would call a contemporary politics of gender. In the critical idiom of the present day, the coarseness of modern (masculine) manners, as symbolized by Johnson's massive form, will always in the fullness of time be tamed by the superior, finer, feminine and above all classical values whose defence in Cowper, Warton and others merges so imperceptibly with 'pre-romantic' resistance to Johnson; poetry will always ultimately have its revenge upon literary criticism. The critic, once the 'Muse's Handmaid' at the time of Pope, becomes her oppressor in the work of Johnson but then is finally subdued as her slave. The suggestion in Gillray's cartoon image, as it is in Warton's note to Pope - along with other occasions where Warton saw himself as defending the 'classical', initially in concert with, but ultimately *against* an offensively English Johnson - is that Johnson is revealed unfit by his very nature as a critic of poetry. Johnson and Warton could at one time write in praise of Pope's *Essay on Criticism* (for example) on very similar grounds;[49] but in the course of their careers their opinions divided over the poetry of Gray, over pastoral poetry, Thomson and even over Pope, not because Johnson had excessively esteemed the poetry in Warton's opinion but because he had not valued Pope highly enough.[50] And just as the major achievement of Warton's lifetime was his work on Pope, so his warm encomium on Boileau and the 'classical purity' of Erasmus goes beyond anything to be found in the writings of Johnson.[51] But the explicit divergences between the two critics become apparent with Warton's response to the *Lives of the Poets* in his second volume of his *Essay on Pope* in 1782, and relations between the leading personalities responsible for shaping critical history in the later years of the eighteenth century become at this point increasingly complex.[52] Shifting contemporary values are re-distributed through areas of the literary and national past that defy the categorizations of critical history. Thus Warton could write enthusiastically of modern poets' return to a specifically British mythology in preference to classical imagery, but could also *complain* with reference to Johnson's 'Lives' of Shenstone and Gay for example that the critic preferred 'the dungeons of the Strand to the valleys of Arcadia'.[53]

Macaulay's Johnson is pre-figured in Warton's growing frustration with Johnson's tastes (as they play against the patterns of their personal relationship over many years and Warton's residual respect for Johnson to the end), but Warton's irritation remains largely unexposed. Gillray's treatment more clearly taps into reactionary class attitudes that keep Johnson's judgments firmly in their place. Gillray's shockingly adept visual portrayal thus prepares the wider culture beyond literature and criticism for the Johnsonian monster of Macaulay's prose. Johnson, according to Macaulay, is one of the 'heads which will live for ever on the canvass of Reynolds',[54] and his account of Johnson's physical eccentricities may have been suggested by Reynolds's observation of the 'strange antic gestures' whose representation adds drama to his portrait of 1769.[55] But Johnson perhaps had a stronger sense of the immortalizing harshness of the satirical image, and he recognized the place of Gillray's Johnsonian hero-villain in ensuring his own durability. Johnson once walked in upon a discussion of *Apollo and the Muses* taking place at Sir Joshua Reynolds's house, and is reported to have said to Dr. Farr, who was present:

> Sir, I am very glad to hear this. I hope the day will never arrive when I shall neither be the object of calumny or ridicule, for then I shall be neglected and forgotten.[56]

Johnson may have protested to Mrs. Thrale that he would not be 'known to posterity for his *defects* only'. But he rightly anticipated the memorializing power these 'defects' can have.

In the novel *England, England* by Julian Barnes, the character of Dr Samuel Johnson is played by an overweight and out-of-work actor dressed up in Johnsonian garb in a diorama representation of the Cheshire Cheese, this part of an English Heritage theme-park attraction on the Isle of Wight.[57] This is only the latest in a long line of Johnsonian comic mythologizations which help to perpetuate fictions of his critical-historical role. The final consequence of Gillray's concerted satirical attack on the *Lives of the Poets* in the two cartoons discussed in this chapter is dual. On the one hand they conspire to create the image of a *necessarily* clod-like Johnson, blind and deaf to the Stars and the Muses, and distanced from us by history. On the other hand they deflect, indeed, transfuse and translate into the immediacy of the visual medium something of Johnson's own critical shockingness just as they play to the shocked reactions against it of the age's most ardent lovers and judgers of poetry. Ultimately they remind us of the enduring nature of Johnson's ability to challenge convention today, when the mass of Johnsonian scholarship runs the risk of sinking the criticism in an image that is not the same as Macaulay's but reproduces a Johnson too tolerantly human, too staidly familiar and predictably wrong in his judgments to be worth taking issue with. Gillray, this satirical parasite 'who lived like a caterpillar on the green leaf of reputation',[58] was ready to eat away at the respect accorded to Johnson by the time of the *Lives*. His images live in the mind, as they do in the eye, as permanent reminders of Johnson's critical recalcitrance. As a channel for discharging emotion, they play a powerful and necessary defamiliarizing role. The satirical engravings of Gillray bring into focus the paradox (made famous by John Stuart Mill) of judgments which strike home on the one hand, and our seeming need on the other to mock, disrespect and despise them. They begin to explain the deep-seated psycho-pathography[59] of modern historical accounts of Johnson as critic.

Notes

[1] Johnson's appreciation of the comic in Shakespeare and Cowley may indeed be profound; but his criticism *of* such poets has been traditionally regarded as a vehicle for moral teachings: 'Johnson's best criticism', writes Leopold Damrosch Jr., 'combines literary with moral judgment' (*The Uses of Johnson's Criticism*, 104). Much recent scholarship on Johnson's writings within this tradition has been devoted to Johnson's socio-political views, on gender, race, slavery, politics, the law and colonial expansionism, and scholars have thus incorporated Johnson into debates about the massive seriousness of massive human and social issues that concern us now. Johnson has begun to enjoy in these terms a new life as a twenty-first-century moralist. Commentators most sensitive to Johnsonian comedy have nevertheless continued to focus on the wise and witty conversational remarks remembered by Johnson's friends and acquaintances, the Johnsonian inner life that is communicated through the social observations of Boswell, Reynolds or Mrs. Thrale. As Isobel Grundy has shown, Johnson's comic spirit is represented by passages from the periodical narratives, and from moments in *Rasselas* (See 'On Reading Johnson for Laughs', *The New Rambler* [1978]: 21-25). To these examples one could add the Johnsonian verse parodies and lighter poems, and the implicit sociability of such exquisite pieces as 'To Mrs. Thrale, On Completing her Thirty-Fifth Year' (*Poems*, 292-93). Even the *Dictionary* is not free from comic definitions. Latterly, fictionalizations of Johnson by novelists such as Julian Barnes in *England, England* and Beryl Bainbridge in *According to Queeney* have relied on an appeal to the tragic in combination with the ludicrous sense. It is generally recognized that to miss the comedy is to miss the complexity and contradictoriness of Johnson.

[2] Harold Bloom, *The Western Canon: The Books and School of the Ages* (New York: Harcourt Brace, 1994), 192.

[3] See 'Literary Theory and Its Discontents', *Beyond Poststructuralism*, ed. Wendell V. Harris (University Park, PA: Penn State University Press, 1996), 101-35.

[4] Despite the impressive thoroughness of W.K. Wimsatt's treatment in *The Prose Style of Samuel Johnson* (New Haven: Yale University Press, 1941) - on style as meaning, antithesis, parallelism, diction, etc. in Johnson's writing - he has little to say about Johnson's *tone*.

[5] Thomas Babington Macaulay, *Critical and Historical Essays contributed to the Edinburgh Review*, 2nd ed., 3 vols. (London, 1843), 1: 407. Macaulay's 'Boswell's Life of Johnson' was printed in the *Edinburgh Review* 54, no. 107 (September 1831): 1-38.

[6] George Watson, *The Literary Critics* (1962; rpt. London: Penguin Books, 1968), 82.

[7] For Warton, Johnson had offended not only against contemporary enthusiasm for Milton and Gray - in their *continuity* with the gothic, 'sublime' and descriptive passages of Dryden and Pope - but against the whole body of values that the Augustan revolution had prized

from the time of Queen Anne. See, for example, his *Essay on the Genius and Writings of Pope*, 2 vols. (London, 1756 and 1782), 1: 139.

[8]   F.R. Leavis, 'Johnson as Critic', 187.

[9]   See, most recently, the references to Johnson in the essay by John Osborne on 'Drama, after 1740' in the *Cambridge History*, 4: 206, and alluded to here.

[10] See Cowper's letter to 'The Rev. William Unwin (The 'Thresh his Old Jacket' Letter)', 31 October 1779, *The Correspondence of William Cowper*, arranged by Thomas Wright (London: Hodder and Stoughton, 1904), 1: 164-65. See also 'To the Rev. William Unwin', 5 and 17 January 1782, *Correspondence*, 1: 421-24 and 428-32 for Cowper's attack on Johnson's opinion of Prior.

[11] The most complete survey to date of satirical images of Johnson is Morris Brownell's chapter, 'Johnson Caricatured and Illustrated', in *Samuel Johnson and the Arts* (Oxford: Oxford University Press, 1989), 91-104. The survey is not, however, exhaustive, and Brownell's discussion of individual prints is often tantalizingly brief. I aim here more fully to integrate two of the leading caricatures into the issues arising from Johnson's critical reputation and writing.

[12] Among the cartoons featuring Mrs. Thrale are *Signor Piozzi Ravishing Mrs Thrale* (?1784) (LWL 784.0.14), which portrays Piozzi serenading Mrs. Thrale with his cello.

[13] See, for example, *Boswell and the Ghost of Dr Johnson* (?1791). This image is discussed in detail by Morris Brownell in '"Dr Johnson's Ghost": Genesis of a Satirical Engraving', *HLQ* 50, 4 (1987): 338-57.

[14] David Amigoni, '"Borrowing Gargantua's Mouth": biography, Bakhtin and grotesque discourse - James Boswell, Thomas Carlyle and Leslie Stephen on Samuel Johnson', in *Victorian Culture and the Idea of the Grotesque*, ed. Colin Trodd, Paul Barlow and David Amigoni (Aldershot: Ashgate, 1999), 21-36.

[15] For fuller details of the range of caricatures featuring Johnson see my essay, 'The Johnsonian Monster and the *Lives of the Poets*: James Gillray, Critical History and the Eighteenth-Century Satirical Cartoon', *BJECS* 25, no. 2 (2002): 217-45.

[16] Draper Hill, *Mr. Gillray the Caricaturist: A Biography* (Greenwich, Conn.: Greenwood Press, 1965), 23. The image (LWL 782.3.10.1) was published on 10 March 1782 by W. Rennie and is found in both coloured and uncoloured impressions. Draper Hill makes no mention of this print, but it has been reproduced in Mary Dorothy George, *Hogarth to Cruickshank: Social Change in Graphic Satire* (London: Allen Lane, 1967), 127, Fig. 119. William Kurtz Wimsatt, *The Portraits of Alexander Pope* (New Haven and London: Yale University Press, 1965), notes its appearance in C.B. Tinker, ed., *Dr. Johnson and Fanny Burney: Being the Johnsonian Passages from the Works of Mme. D'Arblay* (New York: Andrew Melrose, 1911), facing page 150.

[17] *Imitations*, 120, line 331.

[18] *Imitations*, 120, line 332.

[19] From *The Art of Poetry* with translations in prose and verse by Daniel Bagot (Edinburgh and London, 1863), 3, lines 1-8.

[20] Diana Donald, *The Age of Caricature: Satirical Prints in the Age of George III* (London: New Haven and London: Yale University Press, 1996), 73.

[21] E.g. *The Vulture of the Constitution* (1789). For numerous other examples see *The Works of James Gillray from the Original Prints with the addition of many subjects not before collected* (London, 1849).

[22] Johnson's 'Life of Milton' had appeared in the 1779 group of 'Lives'; the 'Life of Pope' in 1781.

[23] Compare, for example, *The Morning after Marriage - or - A Scene on the Continent* (1788).

[24] Draper Hill, 3. These parodies date from somewhat later in Gillray's career. Diana Donald

notes pertinently in connection with Reynolds that 'ersatz grandiosity and lapses into vulgar naturalism ... often characterized [his] botched attempts at the sublime, and ... could therefore, simply as a style, symbolize the gap between professed ideology and realpolitik which Gillray increasingly sought to embody' (*The Age of Caricature*, 73).

[25] Draper Hill, 19; 20.

[26] Cases in point would include the owls in Book 1 of Pope's *Dunciad Variorum* of 1729.

[27] Draper Hill, 5.

[28] *Boswell's Life of Johnson*, 4: 450: 'There is no known portrait of Johnson by Reynolds in which he is represented as looking into the slit of a pen, &c., but it is probable that Mrs. Piozzi is inaccurately describing this painting' (Appendix H).

[29] *Anecdotes of the Late Samuel Johnson, LL.D.*, *Johnsonian Miscellanies*, 1: 313.

[30] See *William Blake's Writings*, ed. G.E. Bentley, Jr., 2 vols. (Oxford: Clarendon Press, 1978), 2: *Writings in Conventional Typography and Manuscript*, 888.

[31] Wimsatt notes suggestively of the Gillray representation of Pope's bust that it is 'a token image of approximately the Roubiliac type' (266). The fact that Johnson is supposedly 'blinking' at a highly classicized and rococo Pope complicates once again his conventional critical role within the 'classic to romantic' story of critical life.

[32] 'Pope to Caryll', 25 June 1711, *The Correspondence of Alexander Pope*, ed. George Sherburn, 5 vols. (Oxford: Clarendon Press, 1956), 1: 120: 'I know too well the vast difference betwixt those who truly deserve the name of poets and men of wit, and one who is nothing but what he owes to them; and I keep the pictures of Dryden, Milton, Shakespear, &c., in my chamber, round about me, that the constant remembrance of 'em may keep me always humble'.

[33] See 'Epistle 4 To Richard Boyle Earl of Burlington', *Epistles*, 142-48.

[34] LWL 783.7.29.1. Published 29 July 1783. The image has been reproduced by J.C.D. Clark, *Samuel Johnson: Literature, religion and English cultural politics from the Restoration to Romanticism* (Cambridge: Cambridge University Press, 1994), 242, and its relationship to Reynolds's portraits of Johnson is briefly discussed by Nicolas Penny, *Reynolds* (London: Weidenfeld and Nicholson, 1986).

[35] *The Ghost* (1762), *The Poetical Works of Charles Churchill*, ed. Douglas Grant (Oxford: Clarendon Press, 1956), book 2, 80-81, 86-89; book 4, 165-69. The publication of *The Ghost* coincides with Johnson's receipt of his pension from Lord Bute, and Gillray's recall of 'Dr Pomposo' implicitly revisits this earlier and more established satirical theme.

[36] See *Boswell's Life of Johnson*, 5: 384. The editors suggest the name was first applied to Johnson by Gray in conversation with Bonstetten. Anna Seward writes of the depiction of Johnson in Boswell's *Tour*: 'How strongly our imagination is impressed when the massive Being is presented to it stalking, like a Greenland bear, over the barren Hebrides....' Letter of 27 August 1785, *The Letters of Anna Seward written between the years 1784 and 1807*, 6 vols. (Edinburgh, 1811), 1: 81.

[37] LWL 786.0.15.

[38] LWL 786.4.19.2. 'Published 19 April 1786 by S.W. Fores, at the Caricature Warehouse No. 3, Piccadilly. My friend delin[eavi]t. I fecit'.

[39] LWL 786.4.19.1. 'Published 19 April 1786 by S.W. Fores, at the Caricature Warehouse No. 3, Piccadilly. My friend delin[eavi]t. I fecit'. Johnson and Boswell are portrayed climbing a steep slope in the Scottish Highlands, both on all fours. Johnson, ahead, is saying 'Come Bossy' while Boswell, in tow behind, has his tongue extended to lick his hero's back-side, and is saying (or we are rather to suppose thinking to himself) 'I shall record this'.

[40] See the set of twenty plates by Rowlandson after Samuel Collings (1786).

[41] A third, anonymous, satire directed at the *Lives* is *The Ghost of Sir Richard Blackmore Appearing to Johnson While Writing the Life of Blackmore*. This image is discussed by

Morris Brownell, 96, and reproduced (Plate 16).

[42] Anna Seward, Letter of 20 March 1794, *Letters*, 3: 352, suggests that the *Remarks* were actually little known in their time and that Fitz-Thomas had supplied her with a copy.

[43] See John Ker Spittal, ed., *Contemporary Criticisms of Dr. Samuel Johnson, his Works, and his Biographers* (London: John Murray, 1923), 291.

[44] Seward calls Johnson 'the old Colossus' in her Letter of 7 November 1784, *Letters*, 1: 10, and berates him (as on many other occasions) for his attacks on Milton, Prior and Gray in a Letter of 27 October 1786, *Letters*, 1: 207.

[45] Letter of 21 December 1797, *Letters*, 5: 31.

[46] *Critical and Historical Essays*, 1: 397-98.

[47] Robert Anderson, *The Life of Samuel Johnson LLD. with Critical Observations on his Works* (London, 1795), 204.

[48] See *The Works of Alexander Pope, Esq.: In nine Volumes Complete with Notes and Illustrations* (London, 1797), 1: 173n.

[49] Warton writes of Pope's *Essay on Criticism* in his *Essay on Pope*, 1: 98. For Johnson's exceptionally high praise of the *Essay on Criticism* see *Lives*, 3: 94.

[50] Warton's *Pope*, 3: 162n. Warton writes especially strongly of Johnson's apparent contempt for Pope's *Essay on Man*.

[51] *Essay on Pope*, 1: 189-90; 178-79.

[52] For a recent discussion of Warton's and others' critical reactions to Johnson's *Lives of the Poets* see Tom Mason and Adam Rounce, '"Looking Before and After"?: Reflections on the Early Reception of Johnson's Critical Judgments', *Johnson Re-Visioned*, 134-66.

[53] Warton's *Pope*, 1: 66n.

[54] *Critical and Historical Essays*, 1: 407.

[55] See *Johnsonian Miscellanies*, 2: 222. Penny suggests that 'The gestures [made by Johnson's hands in the 1769 portrait] are surely intended as a dignified version of these "gesticulations"' (240).

[56] *Johnsonian Miscellanies*, 2: 419-20. The anecdote, by Mrs. Rose, explains that the admirers of Gray were laughing at Dr. Farr's account of *Apollo and the Muses* when Johnson arrived, but that 'Johnson was not at all surly on the occasion' (420).

[57] *England, England* (London: Picador/Jonathan Cape, 1998).

[58] From *The Athenaeum* (October 1831), 632-33. Quoted by Draper Hill, 5.

[59] I use the term to refer to the biography or narrative history of illness. 'Psycho-pathography' implies a disability of mind within the stricken individual (in this case the eighteenth-century literary critic).

Chapter 6

From Image to History: Johnson's Criticism and the Genealogy of Romanticism

Johnson, Europe and the Romantic Revolt: Stendhal

The need to respond to the critical past through caricature is also, of course, a mode of resistance to its historical influence, to its role as a condition of possibility for the present of criticism; but the most intractable obstacle to an unimpeded relationship between Johnson and the modern reader, after initial reaction to his criticism had settled down, is the intervening presence of 'the romantic'; or rather the idea of 'the romantic' as this is codified by the historical mode. One piece of evidence that has failed to engage critical historians strongly enough is that Johnson was not especially short of early nineteenth-century 'radical' admirers of his criticism, on both sides of the Channel, nor - if we think of the various American women readers encouraged and inspired by Johnson's humanitarian anti-racist, anti-slaving views[1] - on both sides of the Atlantic Ocean. In Britain Johnson was celebrated for his views on life and on literature by Mary Wollstonecraft and by Sir Walter Scott (whose *Life of Dryden* has many detailed recollections of the Johnsonian 'Life'). Shelley's *Defence of Poetry* owes much to Johnsonian ideas on poetry opened to ironic inspection by the tenth chapter of *Rasselas*, the criticism of Shakespeare, and the *Lives*. In France, meanwhile, Johnson's *Preface to Shakespeare* was received into the wider culture of Europe with the French translations of Shakespeare's plays. Jean-Baptiste Antoine Suard included a French translation of parts of Johnson's *Preface* in *Variétés littéraires* (1769), while a German translation of part of the *Preface to Shakespeare* appeared in 1816 and an Italian version in 1819.[2]

More locally suggestive of Johnson's participation in the Europeanization and globalization of Shakespeare that took place in the later eighteenth century (and is a logical validation of Johnson's principle of 'general nature') is the fact that in his 1818 'Qu'est-ce que le Romanticisme?' Johnson's passage from the *Preface to Shakespeare* on the 'classical' unities of time and place was translated unacknowledged by Stendhal to bolster his contemporary manifesto of romanticism and to launch an attack on classical form.[3] The extended parallels between Johnson and Stendhal are recorded in a printing of the French and English texts in an Appendix to Doris Gunnell's study *Stendhal et l'Angleterre* of 1909;[4] but the same passage of Johnson was, in addition, more freely adapted as part of the exchange between the personae of 'L'Académicien' and 'Le Romantique' in Stendhal's *Racine et Shakspeare* of 1823-25. Neither of these continuities appears to have had much influence on the shape of the official narrative of literary criticism from Johnson's time to the 'romantic age';[5] but the complicating historical value of these parallels is more than the observation of a curious Franco-Johnsonese: Stendhal had here begun to imagine out the patterns and transitions linking Johnson's thought to a superior *logic* of the romantic. The dialogue accordingly comes to a Johnsonian head in the reflection by Stendhal's 'Le Romantique' on the theatrical meaning of 'illusion':

> Quand on dit que l'imagination du spectateur se figure qu'il se passe le temps nécessaire pour les événements que l'on représente sur la scène, on n'entend pas que l'illusion du spectateur aille au point de croire tout ce temps réellement écoulé. Le fait est que le spectateur, entraîné par l'action, n'est choqué de rien....[6]

Or as Johnson had affirmed: 'The truth is, that the spectators are always in their senses....' (*Shakespeare*, 7: 77).

Stendhal on other occasions in his writings accuses Johnson of the myopic pedantry of the traditional neo-classical critic; but here the turn of Stendhal's prose, more subtly than the bald plagiarism of 'Qu'est-ce que le Romanticisme?', exploits the rhetorical and logical shift which takes place in the *Preface* as Johnson moves from reasoning *with* the 'criticks' he will ultimately oppose. Johnson's *reductio ad absurdum* had been to sketch the logic of a putative 'delusion': the spectator, once transported from reality, is 'in a state of elevation above the reach of reason, or of truth, and from the heights of empyrean poetry, may despise the circumscriptions of terrestrial nature'. The mock-heroic flight of these expressions anticipates the dryly laconic Johnson we have explored in the *Lives*, and it captures the comic melodrama of critical contestation, and sense of the endless futility and ultimate folly of the literary critic, within the *Preface*. Johnson's observation that 'There is no reason why a mind thus wandering in extasy should count the clock, or why an hour should not be a century in that calenture of the brains that can make the stage a field' (*Shakespeare*, 7: 77), is counterpointed by the simple statement of personal conviction (quoted above) that begins the paragraph. But whatever the conscious intent of Stendhal as an agent of historical change, (and his mixture of derogatory and appreciative comments on Johnson elsewhere), the English critic enters *in practice* into the European history of criticism both on the side of Shakespeare, and on the side of the romantic. As Gunnell herself has remarked when commenting upon the Stendhal who sought from Johnson the arguments he needed to revolutionize the drama in France: 'Cela ne manque pas de piquant'.[7]

A Precursor of English Literary Radicalism: Johnson and Wordsworth on Dryden, Poetry and Pope

Within the English tradition, Johnson's criticism and the terms of the Wordsworthian aesthetic are connected in ways that are less overt, but fundamental to the purposes of both writers; and their juncture provides the most appropriate (and, one hopes, rectifying) historical retrospective on what we have observed thus far.[8] Thus Stendhal's aside (when describing a statue of Johnson in London) that Johnson was 'le père du *romanticisme*',[9] the critical progenitor of a romantic aesthetic, is resisted by almost all that Wordsworth *explicitly* said about Johnson. Wordsworth made a concerted attempt to historicize Johnson as a figure of the last age; to 'write over' him, in the psycho-critical terms made current in the twentieth century by Bloom. And just as Wordsworth sees Johnson as antithetic to his personal directions as a new-generation poet (and as the part of history he has left behind), it is Wordsworth's construction of 'events' in the historical world of criticism, and not the plagiary by Stendhal, that critical historians and scholars of Wordsworth have tended to esteem. In this penultimate chapter I shall suggest that such an evaluation of Johnson by a romantic critic poses as a foundational historical 'fact', but that its 'factuality' conceals the parricidal psychology of Wordsworth. It has authorized fictionalizations of critical history that are unwarranted in their departure from the text and have proved impossible to erase. [10]

The relationship between Johnson and Wordsworth thereby introduces us to one of the ironies of the critical past that disrupt the heroic flow of criticism's progress from the past into the present; it enables us to trace the specifically romantic phase in the construction of the pervasive assumption that Johnson's criticism is not, after all, 'for direct instruction in critical thinking' and to explain why postmodern commitments to romantic thought (mapped in detail by such scholars as Jonathan Arac and Andrew Bowie[11]) have signally failed to deflect the ingratitude of this view; indeed, since the view supports powerful scholarly vested interests in literary periodization, postmodernism has shown little interest in questioning established modes of relation between the eighteenth-century past and the nineteenth century.

Wordsworth's sense of the fissure between present and past is decisive and absolute: he used the example of Johnson's own poetry to call into question the taste of the last age in his Appendix to the *Lyrical Ballads*, and quoting Johnson's 'The Ant', vigorously condemned the poetical diction which marred the work of the most recent poets:

> In process of time metre became a symbol or promise of this unusual language, and whoever took upon him to write in metre, according as he possessed more or less of true poetic genius, introduced less or more of this adulterated phraseology into his compositions, and the true and the false were inseparably interwoven until, the taste of men becoming gradually perverted, this language was received as a natural language: and at length, by the influence of books upon men, did to a certain degree really become so. Abuses of this kind were imported from one nation to another, and with the progress of refinement this diction became daily

more and more corrupt, thrusting out of sight the plain humanities of nature by a motley masquerade of tricks, quaintnesses, hieroglyphics, and enigmas.[12]

In contrast to Johnson's verse, Wordsworth's own poems would seek to 'imitate, and, as far as possible to adopt, the very language of men', and in the third of his three 'Essays upon Epitaphs' Wordsworth complained that in the epitaphs of the eighteenth century, 'there is scarcely one which is not thoroughly tainted by the artifices which have overrun our writings in metre from the days of Dryden and Pope'. He believed that the artifices introduced by Dryden had been extended to further degrading effect by Pope and that Lord Lyttelton, for example, had been misled in his epitaphs by false taste. For this Wordsworth attacked Pope 'whose sparkling and tuneful manner had bewitched the men of letters his Contemporaries, and corrupted the judgment of the Nation through all the ranks of society'.[13] In his unpromisingly titled 'Essay, Supplementary to the Preface' (1815) Wordsworth had given a similar but fuller account of Pope's damaging influence on poetical manners:

> He bewitched the nation by his melody, and dazzled it by his polished style, and was himself blinded by his own success. Having wandered from humanity in his Eclogues with boyish inexperience, the praise, which these compositions obtained, tempted him into a belief that Nature was not to be trusted, at least in pastoral Poetry.[14]

Wordsworth goes on to deploy a logic of cause and effect to link the style of Johnson's poetry to the taste for such polished verse, and he casts Johnson in the role of his critical adversary, the leader of the nation of readers dazzled and bewitched by Pope. Wordsworth could object to 'undue exertion of those arts ... [as] the cause why Pope has for some time held a rank in literature, to which, if he had not been seduced by an over-love of immediate popularity, and had confided more in his native genius, he never could have descended'.[15] But Johnson did not - as a matter of fact - think that Pope's 'exertion' was *always* 'undue'. In his 'Life of Dryden' Johnson explained how the English ear had been 'accustomed to the mellifluence of Pope's numbers' (*Lives*, 1: 453), and how elegance was missing from English verse before Dryden, when there was 'no poetical diction: no system of words at once refined from the grossness of domestick use and free from the harshness of terms appropriated to particular arts' (*Lives*, 1: 420). Johnson here seems not only chronologically but also instinctively closer to the cultural-historical moment of Dryden's and Pope's poetry than Wordsworth. In his 'Life of Pope' Johnson defended Pope's *need* for an elegant diction when translating Homer as a reasoned response to the taste of Pope's contemporary readers: '"necessitas quod cogit defendit", that may be lawfully done which cannot be forborne': 'Time and place will always enforce regard. In estimating this translation consideration must be had of the nature of our language, the form of our metre, and above all, of the change which two thousand years have made in the modes of life and the habits of thought'. Even Virgil, Johnson went on to say, had had to take intelligent stock of the mood of the day and had had to adorn Homer's nature: 'he found ... the state of the world so much altered, and the demand for elegance so much increased, that mere nature would be endured no longer; and perhaps, in the multitude of borrowed passages, very few can be shewn which he has not embellished' (*Lives*, 3: 238-39).

But Johnson's defence of Pope comes with important reservations and these open the way for Johnson's 'Wordsworthian turn'. We see that Johnson is himself a potential source of anxieties that Wordsworth may have experienced when he thought of his poetical and critical roots in the eighteenth century. Once viewed through the filter of a Wordsworthian 'radical' psychology, these attitudes are eventually to rebound upon Johnson, so that Wordsworth's reaction to Johnson becomes in time foundational to the convention of historical thinking about criticism. In the paragraph from the 'Life of Pope' that follows his defence of Pope's Homeric translations Johnson almost if not quite admitted that Pope's pursuit of elegance had encouraged an unhealthy and undesirable development in English taste. The ambition and decline of historical individuals, great military heroes, and other examples of aspiring humanity that mark the *Vanity of Human Wishes* are here reproduced in the trajectory of rise, evaporation and (inescapable) fall detectable in the cycles of literary taste:

> There is a time when nations emerging from barbarity, and falling into regular subordination, gain leisure to grow wise, and feel the shame of ignorance and the craving pain of unsatisfied curiosity. To this hunger of the mind plain sense is grateful; that which fills the void removes uneasiness, and to be free from pain for a while is pleasure; but repletion generates fastidiousness, a saturated intellect soon becomes luxurious, and knowledge finds no willing reception till it is recommended by artificial diction. Thus it will be found in the progress of learning that in all nations the first writers are simple, and that every age improves in elegance. One refinement always makes way for another, and what was expedient to Virgil was necessary to Pope. (*Lives*, 3: 239)

The idea of historical development that emerges from this passage stands in undisrupted linearity with Wordsworth. Johnson is saying that refinement was 'necessary' to Pope, and that the advance of refinement was part of a natural and desirable process in a nation's emergence from barbarity. But in this Johnson also anticipates Wordsworth's negative claim that Pope had 'corrupted the judgment of the Nation'. On the one hand, Johnson sympathized with Pope's need for embellishment. On the other, he used morally charged vocabulary such as 'fastidiousness', 'saturated', and 'luxurious' to suggest how such elegance was not *always* the goal of good poets. Johnson did not feel Wordsworth's outraged aversion to refined poetry and he held back from the kind of moral condemnation that Wordsworth heaped on the later ages of poetry for its deliberate and perverse desertion of nature. For Johnson, the power to excel in elegance and refinement may not have been the greatest of poetical virtues but was nevertheless *of* value, a legitimate and sometimes necessary constituent of good poetry. For Wordsworth, more simply, this power was usually an abuse:

The earliest poets of all nations generally wrote from passion excited by real events; they wrote naturally, and as men: feeling powerfully as they did, their language was daring, and figurative. In succeeding times, Poets, and Men ambitious of the fame of Poets, perceiving the influence of such language, and desirous of producing the same effect without being animated by the same passion, set themselves to a mechanical adoption of these figures of speech, and made use of them, sometimes with propriety, but much more frequently applied them to feelings and thoughts with which they had no natural connection whatsoever. A language was thus insensibly produced, differing materially from the real language of men in *any situation* .... Poets, it is probable, who had before contented themselves for the most part with misapplying only expressions which at first had been dictated by real passion, carried the abuse still further, and introduced phrases composed apparently in the spirit of the original figurative language of passion, yet altogether of their own invention, and characterised by various degrees of wanton deviation from good sense and nature.[16]

Here, in his 1802 Appendix to *Lyrical Ballads*, Wordsworth thought that poets had sought the refined while nature remained to be explored. Johnson registers sympathy for the poets of later ages and extends fellow-feeling to them, even if he did not say they were better poets. Moreover, Johnson is writing as a poet who had himself followed in the footsteps of Pope but had substantially abandoned public modes of poetry for prose.[17] But if Johnson was more sympathetic to Pope's polished style than was possible for Wordsworth, he viewed the successors of Pope more harshly than did Wordsworth. Johnson did not think that Dryden's and Pope's poetry was itself seriously corrupted. Dryden had taught us '"sapere et fari", to think naturally and express forcibly' (*Lives*, 1: 469); but Gray (mistakenly in Johnson's opinion) 'thought his language more poetical as it was more remote from common use: finding in Dryden "honey redolent of Spring", an expression that reaches the utmost limits of our language, Gray drove it a little more beyond common apprehension, by making "gales" to be "redolent of joy and youth"' (*Lives*, 3: 435). We have seen that for many of his immediate contemporaries Johnson's negative criticism of Gray was among the most controversial and puzzling judgments in the whole *Lives of the Poets*. The surprising thing, perhaps, for a Wordsworth whose opinion of Gray was not exactly remote from Johnson's, is that he does nothing whatsoever to rescue Johnson from the derision that descended on his head. He cannot *feel* the historical affinity that connects them.

Because Johnson believed that the utmost limits of our language had been reached in the poetry of Dryden and Pope, he could write with undisguised warmth of the 'treasure of poetical elegances' that he found in Pope's translation of Homer (*Lives*, 3: 238). Thus there was clearly a place for the conscious expression of 'art' in Johnson's framework of taste, and despite its shortcomings as drama, Johnson could write approvingly of Milton's *Comus* in his 'Life of Milton': 'A work more truly poetical is rarely found; allusions, images, and descriptive epithets embellish almost every period with lavish decoration' (*Lives*, 1: 167-68). The inspiration for this praise contrasts with the marked absence of poetical embellishment that Johnson celebrated when he made the claim that Shakespeare was 'one of the original masters of our language' (*Shakespeare*, 7: 70). Such a standard recalls the criteria of expressive simplicity developed from the writings of Boileau, Bouhours, Rapin, Dryden and Pope, and Johnson evoked similar values in the 'Life of Cowley' to suggest how the metaphysical poets had missed the 'sublime' (*Lives*, 1: 20-21). But these criteria are ultimately the basis for a further cultural transformation into the critical present of the Wordsworthian consciousness. The Johnsonian past crowds in upon 'romanticism' at this point:

> If there be, what I believe there is, in every nation, a stile which never becomes obsolete, a certain mode of phraseology so consonant and congenial to the analogy and principles of its respective language as to remain settled and unaltered; this stile is probably to be sought in the common intercourse of life, among those who speak only to be understood, without ambition of elegance. The polite are always catching modish innovations, and the learned depart from established forms of speech, in hope of finding or making better; those who wish for distinction forsake the vulgar, when the vulgar is right; but there is a conversation above grossness and below refinement, where propriety resides, and where this poet seems to have gathered his comick dialogue. (*Shakespeare*, 7: 70)[18]

The oedipal elimination of the 'father of romanticism' may have been as necessary to Wordsworth at *his* historical moment as the elegancies of the Homer translation were at an earlier moment to Pope. But if this suggests the depth of the need which drives Wordsworth and Johnson to opposite cultural extremes, a salutary comparison can be drawn with their treatments of Dryden at this point.

Wordsworth complained to Walter Scott in 1805 - the time Scott was working on his edition of Dryden - that Dryden was not 'as a *Poet*, any great favourite of mine', and claimed that Dryden was lacking in the '*essentially* poetical'. Wordsworth based this view on the language of Dryden's poetry, but also on Dryden's decision to concentrate on what seemed the less congenial sides of human nature:

> I admire his talents and Genius greatly, but he is not a poetical Genius: the only qualities I can find in Dryden that are *essentially* poetical are a certain ardour and impetuosity of mind with an excellent ear: it may seem strange that I do not add to this, great command of language: *that* he certainly has and of such language also as it is most desirable that a Poet should possess, or rather should not be without; but it is not language that is in the high sense of the word poetical, being neither of the imagination or the passions; I mean of the amiable the ennobling or intense passions; I do not mean to say that there is nothing of this in Dryden, but as little, I think, as is possible, considering how much he has written .... Dryden had neither a tender heart nor a lofty sense of moral dignity: where his language is poetically impassioned it is mostly upon unpleasing subjects; such as the follies, vice, and crimes of classes of men or of individuals. That his cannot be the language of imagination must have necessarily followed from this, that there is not a single image from Nature in the whole body of his works; and in his translation from Vergil whenever Vergil can be fairly said to have had his *eye* upon his subject, Dryden always spoils the passage.[19]

When Dryden and Pope are compared in the 'Life of Pope', Johnson admits to a 'partial fondness' for the memory of Dryden (*Lives*, 3: 223); but as Johnson rose to the finale of his account of Dryden's achievement in the 'Life of Dryden', his tone becomes one of relative disinterest and detachment, and in this he transcends the first-person singular of Wordsworth's letter to Scott. Johnson's is not a radical dislodgement of the Augustan poet, and he found nothing culpable *per se* in Dryden's habitual concern with 'the follies, vice, and crimes' of men, or with evil passions. The passage is characteristic of the judgments of Johnson at their ahistorical extreme; and when it is compared with Wordsworth's assessment of Dryden, the estimate that Johnson gives seems almost totally to remove the valuer from the process of valuing. The result is a kind of prose poem in the mode of 'literary criticism'. The radically distanced tone, elegiacally tinged, seems closer to some of Wordsworth's own poetry than to the polemic of the latter's critical prefaces:

> The power that predominated in his intellectual operations was rather strong reason than quick sensibility. Upon all occasions that were presented he studied rather than felt, and produced sentiments not such as Nature enforces, but meditation supplies. With the simple and elemental passions, as they spring separate in the mind,[20] he seems not much acquainted, and seldom describes them but as they are complicated by the various relations of society and confused in the tumults and agitations of life....
>
> Dryden's was not one of the 'gentle bosoms': Love, as it subsists in itself, with no tendency but to the person loved and wishing only for correspondent kindness, such love as shuts out all other interest, the Love of the Golden Age, was too soft and subtle to put his faculties in motion. He hardly conceived it but in its turbulent effervescence with some other desires: when it was inflamed by rivalry or obstructed by difficulties; when it invigorated ambition or exasperated revenge. (*Lives*, 1: 457-58)

When Johnson described the passions of Dryden's poetry as 'complicated by the various relations of society and confused in the tumults and agitations of life', and said he had difficulty in exhibiting 'the genuine operations of the heart', he creates the conditions of possibility for Wordsworth's more directed remark that Dryden wanted 'a tender heart'. Once again, the equivocality of Johnson's description provides the authority of precedent for Wordsworth's more explicitly hostile view.

Such a principle can be appreciated through Johnson's and Wordsworth's attitudes to rural nature, a value that Wordsworth took as a measure of the cultural distance between himself and the leading Augustans. Wordsworth thought that the simplicity of passion so notably missing from Dryden could best be found amongst people in rural surroundings, and amongst the poor. He defended his choice of 'Humble and rustic life' in the Preface to his *Lyrical Ballads* on the grounds that: 'in that condition, the essential passions of the heart find a better soil in which they can attain maturity, are less under restraint, and speak a plainer and more emphatic language; because in that condition of life our elementary feelings co-exist in a state of greater simplicity, and, consequently, may be more accurately contemplated, and more forcibly communicated'.[21] The failure to attend to 'realities' of rural nature was one of Wordsworth's principal indictments of all the Augustan poets, and Pope and Dryden, he believed, had failed to perceive clearly or imagine vividly the scenes of nature before their eyes. In a tone that falls scarcely short of contempt, Wordsworth berated two admired passages from Dryden and Pope in his 'Essay, Supplementary to the Preface' - the description of night from Dryden's *The Indian Emperour* (1667),[22] analysed with warm appreciation by Rymer in his Preface to Rapin, and Pope's famous 'moonlight' scene from his translation of the *Iliad*.[23] For Wordsworth, as his comments on these passages suggest, only those passions which harmonized and combined with the background of rural nature could be considered natural. For Johnson, wherever there was Man, there was Nature - the business of the poet was 'the essential passions of the heart' wherever these were found.

This is not to say that the description of rural nature was not *part* of Johnson's conception of the poetry of nature, as is made abundantly clear in the *Lives of the Poets* by Johnson's praise of the *Seasons* of Thomson (*Lives*, 1: 298-99). The appearance of the *Seasons* marks poetry's return to nature for Wordsworth, and common poetical terrain is revealed again when Johnson praises Shakespeare's inanimate nature: he notes in the *Preface* Shakespeare's skills as 'an exact surveyor of the inanimate world' and begins his account of Shakespeare's claims to originality as a poet who 'gives the image which he receives, not weakened or distorted by the intervention of any other mind' (*Shakespeare*, 7: 89-90). Through all these passages, the verbal correspondences bring into question both the authority and reliability of Wordsworth's account of critical history and that of later historians of criticism whose map of history Wordsworth had drawn.[24]

One further example - from Johnson's and Wordsworth's criticism of the epitaph - will suffice to suggest how a reconceptualization of this history along less culturally specific and external lines may be textually grounded. Wordsworth thought he was refuting Johnson's account of the epitaph (which appears in a series of notes printed at the conclusion of his 'Life of Pope' but composed some years earlier[25]). Johnson (a writer of epitaphs himself) had objected to Pope's epitaph on Robert and Mary Digby on the grounds that it 'contains of the brother only a general indiscriminate character, and of the sister tells nothing but that she died' (*Lives*, 3: 263), a comment that seems to arise from Johnson's concern that poetry could be *too* general, vague and indistinct. Wordsworth took issue with Pope (*and* with Johnson) in his three 'Essays upon Epitaphs', written in 1810, where he complained that the characters depicted in the epitaphs fail to achieve their full emotional weight - not because they are *too* general, but because they are *not general enough*. Wordsworth objected in terms drawn from the tradition of Boileau, Rapin and Bouhours that Johnson placed too much store by particularity: 'the writer of an epitaph is not an atomist, who dissects the internal frame of the mind; he is not even a painter, who executes a portrait at leisure and in entire tranquillity':

> It suffices ... that the trunk and the main branches of the worth of the deceased be boldly and unaffectedly represented. Any further detail, minutely and scrupulously pursued, especially if this be done with laborious and antithetic discriminations,

> must inevitably frustrate its own purpose ... for, the understanding having been so busy in its petty occupation, how could the heart of the mourner be other than cold?[26]

And he summed up his thoughts about the epitaph thus:

> Let an Epitaph, then, contain at least these acknowledgements to our common nature; nor let the sense of their importance be sacrificed to a balance of opposite qualities or minute distinctions in individual character; which if they do not, (as will for the most part be the case,) when examined, resolve themselves into a trick of words, will, even when they are true and just, for the most part be grievously out of place; for, as it is probable that few only have explored these intricacies of human nature, so can the tracing of them be interesting only to a few.[27]

Wordsworth is here refuting Johnson according to standards that are themselves substantially derived from his works. 'Nothing can please many, and please long', Johnson had famously written in his *Preface to Shakespeare*, 'but just representations of general nature': 'Particular manners can be known to few, and therefore few only can judge how nearly they are copied' (*Shakespeare*, 7: 61). With an irony characteristic of the unheroic progress of critical history at any time, Johnson is transforming the criteria derived from Boileau, Rapin and Bouhours later used in his critique of Cowley and the metaphysical poets, and Wordsworth and Johnson achieve their clearest congruence at this point. Wordsworth's objection to detail 'minutely and scrupulously pursued' and to discriminations 'unfeelingly' laboured,[28] recalls, for example, Johnson's dislike of the 'laboured particularities' by which the metaphysical poets, as Johnson wrote in his 'Life of Cowley', 'broke every image into fragments':

> The fault of Cowley, and perhaps of all the writers of the metaphysical race, is that of pursuing his thoughts to their last ramifications, by which he loses the grandeur of generality, for of the greatest things the parts are little; what is little can be but pretty, and by claiming dignity becomes ridiculous. Thus all the power of description is destroyed by a scrupulous enumeration .... (*Lives*, 1: 45)

Johnson, the Romantic Shakespeare and A.W. Schlegel

In determining that the eighteenth-century development shows (in Johnson's conception) 'a progress of English poetry toward an ideal technical norm attained especially by Pope',[29] we have seen how the twentieth-century historian of criticism, René Wellek, necessarily turns his back on the inferences to be drawn from Johnson's 'fastidiousness', 'saturated' and the 'luxurious'. Wellek seems here to commit himself to a type of historical narrative that underplays the manifest continua between Johnson and the romantic critics;[30] but a certain amount of detailed comparison between what Johnson says *in his own words*, and the judgments that are assigned to him by the major romantic critics, is necessary to convey this point.

Schlegel, not unlike Wellek himself in the twentieth century, complained of Johnson that he had simply confused art and life. In his comprehensive course of lectures on the history and development of European drama, Schlegel made frequent mention of Johnson; yet he seems to have felt no substantial common cause with any of the eighteenth-century English critics of Shakespeare: he wrote that 'I must separate myself from them entirely'.[31] On the subject of such critics' alleged mistreatment of Shakespeare, he complained that 'I have hardly ever found either truth or profundity in their remarks; and these critics seem to me to be but stammering interpreters of the general and almost idolatrous admiration of his [Shakespeare's] countrymen'.[32] Among the occasions of Schlegel's *explicit* discontent with Johnson over Shakespeare in his *Lectures* is his rejection of Johnson's praise of Shakespearean 'mingled drama', and it is here that Johnson's confusion of art and life is said to occur. Johnson was culpable according to Schlegel not because he applied standards of eighteenth-century order and decorum to Shakespeare and found him wanting, but because he did not respect the aesthetic hierarchy. While

> in real life the vulgar is found close to the sublime ... the merry and the sad usually accompany one another ... it does not follow that because both are found together, therefore they must not be separable in the compositions of art'.[33]

The irony is that while Schlegel could jettison Johnson's account of 'mingled drama' in one 'Lecture', he embraced a 'romantic drama' plainly reminiscent of Johnson in another. Schlegel's appeal to the 'romantic drama'[34] recalls what Johnson had said, one half century earlier, of Shakespeare, whose 'plays are not in the rigorous and critical sense either tragedies or comedies, but compositions of a distinct kind; exhibiting the real state of sublunary nature, which partakes of good and evil, joy and sorrow, mingled with endless variety of proportion and innumerable modes of combination' (*Shakespeare*, 7: 66).[35] Johnson is writing of 'sublunary nature' while Schlegel is preoccupied with standards of 'art'; but the rhythms of his account collapse the categories of the classical and the romantic at this point:

> We may safely admit, that the most of the English and Spanish dramatic works are neither tragedies nor comedies in the sense of the ancients: they are romantic dramas. [While] [t]he ancient art and poetry rigorously separate things which are dissimilar... the romantic delights in indissoluble mixtures; all contrarieties: nature and art, poetry and prose, seriousness and mirth, recollection and anticipation, spirituality and sensuality, terrestrial and celestial, life and death, are by it blended together in the most intimate combination.... It does not (like the Old Tragedy) separate seriousness and action, in a rigid manner, from among the whole ingredients of life; it embraces at once the whole of the chequered drama of life with all its circumstances.[36]

Schlegel's view of Johnson may, like Wordsworth's, have been necessary historically, and a similar conclusion, based again on a common rhetorical turn, could be drawn with respect to Coleridge and Johnson. In his 'Lecture on Classical and Romantic Drama' of 1810, Coleridge had proclaimed that Shakespeare's plays 'are in the ancient sense neither tragedies nor comedies, nor both in one, but a different genus, diverse in kind, nor merely different in degree, - romantic dramas, or dramatic romances'. Coleridge was here reminiscent in part of Johnson's defence of Shakespeare's neglect of the dramatic unities of time and place: 'if only the poet have such power of exciting our internal emotions as to make us present to the scene in imagination chiefly, he acquires the right and privilege of using time and space as they exist in the imagination, obedient only to the laws which imagination acts by'. And again in 1812 Henry Crabb Robinson reported Coleridge as giving a definition of the Shakespearean drama in terms which come very close to those of Johnson in the *Preface*: 'The ancient drama, he observed, is distinguished from the Shakespearean in this, that it exhibits a sort of abstraction, not of character, but of idea.... Shakespeare imitates life, mingled as we find it with joy and sorrow'.[37]

On the issue of the characters of Shakespeare, Johnson's thinking proved especially troubling to his romantic successors (and threatens their self-proclaimed eminence as the antagonists of the critical past). Schlegel preferred Pope to Johnson. He interpreted the latter's remark that in the writings of other poets 'a character is too often an individual; in those of Shakespeare it is commonly a species' (*Shakespeare*, 7: 62) as an unambiguous dismissal of the particular. But Schlegel, like some later critics, here misrepresents the words that Johnson actually used: 'A character which should be merely a personification of a naked general idea', he complained, 'could neither exhibit any great depth nor any great variety. The names of genera and species are well known to be merely auxiliaries for the understanding, that we may embrace the infinite variety of nature in a certain order'.[38] What Schlegel understands Shakespearean character-making to be reveals however a close affinity to Johnsonian structures, and is a partial consequence of them. Johnson had written that Shakespeare's specificity of characterization freed his persons from the localizations of particular 'manners', and thus created the 'general nature' that is apt to please many and please long. Schlegel claimed that:

> It is the power of endowing the creatures of his imagination with such self-existent energy, that they afterwards act in each conjuncture according to general laws of nature.... The characters which Shakespeare has so thoroughly delineated have undoubtedly a number of individual pecularities, but at the same time they possess a significance which is not applicable to them alone.[39]

Schlegel was doubtless more enthusiastic about the supernatural aspects of Shakespeare's characters than Johnson, who wrote in the *Preface to Shakespeare* that 'Even where the agency is supernatural the dialogue is level with life' and that 'Shakespeare approximates the remote, and familiarizes the wonderful; the event which he represents will not happen, but if it were possible, its effects would probably be such as he has assigned' (*Shakespeare*, 7: 64-65). But Schlegel also believed that the power of the supernatural characters was precisely the fact that Shakespeare had brought them *within* nature. This similarity is focused in a turn having a common ancestry in Addison's remarks on Shakespeare:

> [T]his Prometheus not merely forms men, he opens the gates of the magical world of spirits, calls up the midnight ghost, exhibits before us the witches with their unhallowed rites, peoples the air with sportive fairies and sylphs; and these beings, though existing only in the imagination, nevertheless possess such truth and consistency, that even with such misshapen abortions as Caliban, he extorts the assenting conviction, that were there such beings they would so conduct themselves. In a word, as he carries a bold and pregnant fancy into the kingdom of nature, on the other hand, he carries nature into the regions of fancy, which lie beyond the confines of reality. [40]

The fact that this quality was what Johnson seems partly to have meant by the 'species' in Shakespeare was conveniently (or necessarily) ignored.

The Irony of Historicization: Johnson and Hazlitt

The contradictions of Wordsworth's and Schlegel's historically successful bids to 'overwrite' Johnsonian criticism in England and Germany were ramified in the domestic context by Hazlitt, whose treatment of Johnson on Shakespeare was endorsed by Leigh Hunt as a 'masterly exposition'.[41] Hazlitt is the source of one of the most outspoken attacks by a major romantic on Johnson's criticism of Shakespeare. Quoting Schlegel's praise of Shakespeare in his Preface to 'The Characters of Shakespeare's Plays', Hazlitt wrote of it as giving 'by far the best account of the plays of Shakespear that has hitherto appeared'. He claimed that 'our own countryman, Dr. Johnson, has not been so favourable to him', and reprimanded Johnson as 'neither a poet, nor a judge of poetry'. Johnson, according to Hazlitt, responded only to the prosaic in Shakespearean language, and (echoing Schlegel's assertion) had neglected the vividly particular one-of-a-kind that typifies Shakespeare: 'He in fact found the general species or *didactic* form in Shakespear's characters, which was all he sought or cared for; he did not find the individual traits, or the *dramatic* distinctions which Shakespear has engrafted on this general nature, because he felt no interest in them'.[42]

But 'Characters ... ample and general', as we have seen from the *Preface to Shakespeare*, 'were not easily discriminated and preserved, yet perhaps no poet ever kept his personages more distinct from each other' (*Shakespeare*, 7, 64). This interdependence of particularity and generality in Johnson's criticism is echoed by Hazlitt's affirmation of generality (as this is stated in *The Champion* for 13 November 1814): 'It is the business of poetry, and indeed of all works of imagination, to exhibit the species through the individual'. Such extension beyond an imprisoning individuality to the whole species was itself a function of the 'imagination', a term which had assumed a more specialized significance since the time of Johnson. Without imagination, 'the descriptions of the painter or the poet', according to Hazlitt, 'are lifeless, unsubstantial and vapid'.[43] These proclamations square well with Johnson's ideal from the tenth chapter of *Rasselas*: 'The business of a poet ... is to examine, not the individual, but the species; to remark general properties and large appearances' (*Rasselas*, 43).

Finally, Hazlitt objected to Johnson's apparent insensitivity to the 'poetical' aspects of Shakespeare's language; but he nevertheless paid frequent attention to the natural speech of the characters within the plays. And even where Hazlitt complained of Johnson that he 'might cut down imagination to matter-of-fact, regulate the passions according to reason, and translate the whole into logical diagrams and rhetorical declamation',[44] his criteria are not fundamentally distanced. 'The characters of Shakespear', wrote Hazlitt, 'do not declaim like pedantic school-boys, but speak and act like men, placed in real circumstances'.[45] For Johnson:

> It will not easily be imagined how much Shakespeare excells in accommodating his sentiments to real life, but by comparing him with other authors. It was observed of the ancient schools of declamation, that the more diligently they were frequented, the more was the student disqualified for the world, because he found nothing there which he should ever meet in any other place. The same remark may be applied to every stage but that of Shakespeare. (*Shakespeare*, 7: 63)

Implications for Critical History

The consequence of all such omissions, plagiaries, re-transcriptions and distortions, - by Stendhal, Wordsworth, Schlegel, Coleridge and Hazlitt - is the deficit view that historians of criticism have tended to take of Johnson's major critical tastes and the standards that flow from them. Originally designed to clear a space for the work of the romantics, this view - the product of a particular cultural moment and the creative needs of a romantic imagination - has transformed into an institution of critical history and a controlling narrative archetype. But it is a perspective resulting in historical claims that include highly contestable interpretations of the critical text: that Johnson did not appreciate Shakespeare as widely or well as his successors; that his account of the achievement of Dryden and Pope is not stringently critical; that versification and diction are an index of the most significant form of literary change in the age of Johnson and the standard by which change is judged. But in these last two respects the romantic critics of the nineteenth century, followed by the critical historians of the twentieth, have also tended to obscure how Johnson prepared the way, however unknowingly, for the more open and thoroughgoing attack on the work of Dryden, Pope (and Johnson himself) conducted by the romantics. Thus Wordsworth, for example - somewhat less equivocally than Johnson - was later to say that 'Poets, and Men ambitious of the fame of Poets' had in 'succeeding times' induced 'various degrees of wanton deviation from good sense and nature'.[46]

In order to expose the defects of the tradition of Pope, Wordsworth writes of 'the real language of men'. Hazlitt, in order to distinguish the Shakespearean from the artifice dominant in other kinds of drama, was to claim (in 1818) that the characters in Shakespeare's plays 'are real beings of flesh and blood; they speak like men, not like authors'.[47] But it was in 1779 that Johnson had criticized 'a voluntary deviation from nature in pursuit of something new and strange' in the metaphysical poets ('Life of Cowley', *Lives*, 1: 35),[48] and in 1765 that Johnson had written that 'Addison speaks the language of poets, and Shakespeare, of men' (*Shakespeare*, 7: 84). Wordsworth's challenge to the later ages of poetry echoes likewise the sequence of transitions from nature to art that can be found in the following passage from the *Preface to Shakespeare*:

> It may be observed, that the oldest poets of many nations preserve their reputation, and that the following generations of wit, after a short celebrity, sink into oblivion. The first, whoever they be, must take their sentiments and descriptions immediately from knowledge; the resemblance is therefore just, their descriptions are verified by every eye, and their sentiments acknowledged by every breast. Those whom their fame invites to the same studies, copy partly them, and partly nature, till the books of one age gain such authority, as to stand in the place of nature to another, and imitation, always deviating a little, becomes at last capricious and casual. Shakespeare, whether life or nature be his subject, shews plainly, that he has seen with his own eyes; he gives the image which he receives, not weakened or distorted by the intervention of any other mind. (*Shakespeare*, 7: 89-90)

Both Johnson and Wordsworth place the emphasis on the genuineness of 'true passion' whose discriminations, in Johnson's phrase, are 'the colours of nature'. Both write of 'general nature' and of the 'permanent' and the 'durable' in their consonance with what Johnson called 'the uniform simplicity of primitive qualities' (*Shakespeare*, 7: 70). Wordsworth was to declare that 'our elementary feelings co-exist [with each other and with nature] in a state of greater simplicity, and, consequently, may be more accurately contemplated, and more forcibly communicated'.[49] Both criticize the effect upon the traditions of poetry of such eighteenth-century departures from 'nature' evident in the poetry of Gray, who (for Johnson) 'thought his language more poetical as it was more remote from common use' (*Lives*, 3: 435), and who (for Wordsworth) 'was more than any other man curiously elaborate in the structure of his own poetic diction'.[50] From correspondences of this kind it is apparent that there is an irony of consequence in the history of critical approaches to 'artificial diction' that Wellek, for example, *qua* historian, symptomatically neglects to bring out.[51] The extent of the overlap, resting as it does on key terms central to the priorities of both Wordsworth and Johnson, dissolves the categories from which history is made and transforms the historical narrative of 'classic to romantic' to a different kind of story. Similarly, the *Cambridge* historian's belief, nearly half a century later, that Johnson's criticism 'tended to adhere to neoclassical principles of generic purity, decorum and poetic justice' lacks reference to (or apparent knowledge of) 'facts' of history that could scarcely be missed in a reading of the Johnsonian text not hopelessly fettered by an overdetermining context of contemporary theories. Johnson's contempt for the 'petty cavils of petty minds', his famous praise of 'mingled drama', and his pointed attack on decorum of character all come to mind:

His adherence to general nature has exposed him to the censure of criticks, who form their judgments upon narrower principles. Dennis and Rhymer think his Romans not sufficiently Roman; and Voltaire censures his kings as not completely royal .... But Shakespeare always makes nature predominate over accident; and if he preserves the essential character, is not very careful of distinctions superinduced and adventitious. His story requires Romans or kings, but he thinks only on men (*Shakespeare*, 7: 65).[52]

We have seen that the phrase 'poetic justice' (as opposed to the 'poetical justice' considered in an earlier chapter) is used by Johnson at *no* point in his printed writings; but to comprehend the relation between the historicization of Johnson and the standards of the present scene, we must turn at last to the relationship between this moral purpose, modern and Johnsonian ideas of history, and the contrastingly earnest social moralism, as applied to the critical past, of today's cultural radicals.

Notes

[1] For details see James G. Basker, 'Multicultural Perspectives: Johnson, Race, and Gender' in *Johnson Re-Visioned*, 64-79.

[2] See Jean-Baptiste Antoine Suard, 'Observations sur Shakespeare' (1769), in *Variétés littéraires*, 4 toms. (Paris: Lacombe, 1768-69), 4: 65-94; G.G. Bredows nachgelassene Schriften, ed. J. Kunisch (Breslau, 1816); *Tragedie di Shakespeare* tradotte da Michele Leoni (Verona, 1819). For evidence that Johnson's commentary on Shakespeare was also a continuing matter of controversy in France, see Paul Duport, *Essais Littéraires sur Shakspeare*, 2 toms. (Paris: Constant Le Tellier Fils, 1828), where there are many references to Johnson's notes, and where many take issue with Johnson.

[3] See 'Des Unités de Temps et de Lieu', in 'Qu'est-ce que le Romanticisme?' (1818), *Oeuvres Complètes*, 35 toms. ed. Pierre Martino, *Journal Littéraire*, nouvelle edition, 3 toms. (Champion: Paris, Genève, 1970), 3: 110-119. Jay Bochner has argued that Shakespeare provided Stendhal with a stepping stone on which to base his own critical theories, and a model through which the French could come to understand more about their own position. See 'Shakespeare in France: A Survey of Dominant Opinion, 1733-1830', *Revue de Littérature Comparée* 39 (1965), 44-65.

Stendhal was not alone among the French critics to observe Johnson's enmity toward classical authority. See, for example, François Pierre Guillaume Guizot, *Shakespeare et son temps* (Paris, 1852). Guizot wrote that Johnson 'défend vigoureusement les libertés romantiques de Shakespeare contre les prétensions de l'autorité classique' (137). Guizot's knowledge of Johnson was evidently thorough: each of his notices to Shakespeare's plays includes some attempt to concur with or to contest Johnson's specific judgments. The work had first appeared in 1821 as a 'Vie de Shakspeare' in a revised edition of Le Tourneur's 1776 prose translation of Shakespeare and was later reprinted in both French and English versions.

[4] Doris Gunnell, *Stendhal et l'Angleterre* (Paris: Charles Bosse, 1909), 'Appendice B', 248-59.

[5] There is discussion of Johnson's continental influence as a critic of Shakespeare in Wellek's *A History of Modern Criticism*, 2: 110; but this does not seem radically to disrupt the narrative emplotment that guides Wellek's overall account, or, more particularly, his conception of the historical role of Johnson's criticism.

[6] *Racine et Shakspeare* (1823/25), *Oeuvres Complètes*, 37: 14.

[7] Gunnell, *Stendhal et l'Angleterre*, 249. The irony has been long ago remarked by Percy H. Houston, *Doctor Johnson: A Study in Eighteenth Century Humanism* (Cambridge MA: Harvard University Press, 1923). Houston complained pertinently that Johnson 'has not yet regained his former position as the sanest and most reasonable of Shakespearean critics because of the opprobrium heaped upon him by men who stole his wares and paid him with insult and contempt' (157).

[8] They raise important questions for those who (like Jonathan Arac) have attempted to read poststructuralist tradition in terms of a specifically romantic source. See *Critical Genealogies: Historical Situations for Postmodern Studies* (New York: Columbia University Press, 1987). Documentary evidence of how far the relationship between Johnson's criticism and Wordsworth has been deflected or played down by history, is the fact that there are so few references to Johnson (where we would most expect them) in the notes to the standard Owen and Smyser edition of Wordsworth's critical prose.

[9] See *Journal Littéraire* (1819), 3: 152. Stendhal had commenced Chapter 10 of his *Traité de L'Art de Faire des Comédies* in the *Journal Littéraire* (1813) by quoting as an epigraph Johnson's 'Nothing can please many, and please long, but just representations of general nature' (3: 16) from the *Preface to Shakespeare*.

[10] Criticism may have become more gender-conscious in ways that Johnson could not have conceived (though certain of the moral and egalitarian questions embraced by feminist criticism would be familiar to him in other forms); but criticism is also said to have become more 'scientific'. In the concluding essay of vol. 4 of the *Cambridge History* Michel Baridon gives an historical dimension to recent attempts to conceive of criticism in scientific terms, arguing that 'The transdisciplinary bridges built by Hobbes, Locke, Hume and Kant supply some of the strongest links between science and literary criticism from the age of Boileau to that of Herder' (778). He goes on to explain that Dryden's world image was shared by optics and by geometry, and ends by quoting Wordsworth's remark that the 'poet binds together by passion and knowledge the vast empire of human society': 'To define the poet's mission in such terms would have appeared very strange, if not preposterous, to Boileau, Pope and even Gray' (797). The objection is simply this: what else could Pope have meant by 'Eternal Nature' in his *Essay on Criticism* of 1711 or Johnson by 'general nature' in his *Preface* of 1765? The contrast between the 'age of reason' and the 'age of perfectability' is once again overworked by the historian of criticism to sustain a conventional historical explanation and cultural split. The demands of narrative coherence, the melodramatic appeal of revolutionary change, and a commitment to progress which flatters the present, lead him too far from the verifiable data of history, too far from what major English critics of the period actually say.

[11] Jonathan Arac, *Critical Genealogies*; Andrew Bowie, *From Romanticism to Critical Theory* (London: Routledge, 1997).

[12] *Prose Works* 1: 161-162.

[13] *Prose Works*, 2: 84; 75.

[14] *Prose Works*, 3: 72.

[15] *Prose Works*, 3: 72.

[16] *Prose Works*, 1: 160-61.

[17] If not, as David F. Venturo has shown, poetry's more intimate and familiar varieties, or his Latin verse. See *Johnson the Poet: The Poetic Career of Samuel Johnson* (Newark: University of Delaware Press, 1999). Johnson's life-long composition of Latin verse, independently of his career as an English poet, has also been rightly stressed by David Money. See 'Samuel Johnson and the neo-Latin Tradition', *Samuel Johnson in Historical Context*, 199-221.

[18] Johnson's confidence in the mean to be observed between ornament and grossness

anticipates here what we have seen he is later to say apropos Cowley's *Anacreontiques* in the 'Life of Cowley' (*Lives*, 1: 40). Such criteria are also reminiscent of Johnson's conception of 'Easy Poetry' as articulated in *Idler* 77 (1759). In the 'Life of Milton' Johnson wrote that Milton's expression was 'removed from common use' (*Lives*, 1: 190), while Addison, at the other extreme, 'sometimes descends too much to the language of conversation' (*Lives*, 2: 149). An example from Shakespeare is found in *The Tempest*, where Johnson discovered 'the native effusion of untaught affection' (*Shakespeare*, 7: 135).

[19] Letter 285, 'Wordsworth to Scott', 7 November 1805, *Letters of William and Dorothy Wordsworth*, ed. E. de Selincourt, 2nd. ed. rev. C.L. Shaver, 3 vols. (Oxford: Clarendon Press, 1967-69), 1: 641.

[20] Cf. *The Excursion*, Book 1, lines 341-47:

> ... much did he see of men,
> Their manners, their enjoyments, and pursuits,
> Their passions and their feelings; chiefly those
> Essential and eternal in the heart,
> That, 'mid the simpler forms of rural life,
> Exist more simple in their elements,
> And speak a plainer language.

The Poetical Works of William Wordsworth, ed. E. de Selincourt and Helen Darbishire, 5 vols. (Oxford: Clarendon Press, 1949), 5: 20.

[21] *Prose Works*, 1: 125. I quote from the 1850 text at this point.

[22] The full title is *The Indian Emperour, or, The Conquest of Mexico by the Spaniards*. For Wordsworth's response see *Prose Works*, 3: 73-74.

[23] For a detailed and highly suggestive comparison between this passage by Pope and Wordsworth's 'Nightpiece' see H.A. Mason, *To Homer through Pope: An Introduction to Homer's Iliad and Pope's Translation* (London: Chatto and Windus, 1972), 63ff. Mason contends that when Wordsworth fixed a title to his own poem, composed in 1798 and published in *Poems* (1815), 1: 301-302, he was recalling one of Pope's notes to the *Iliad* translation, and that there is 'a marked resemblance to Pope's translation' (65). Despite the vigour of his criticisms of Pope in his 'Essay, Supplementary to the Preface' (1815), 'Wordsworth is only superficially to be divided from the Augustans' (70). Such a finding has important implications for the contrastive thesis of 'classic to romantic'. On this issue see also Robert Griffin, *Wordsworth's Pope* (Cambridge: Cambridge University Press, 1995).

[24] Thus, for Wordsworth, the rural was a pre-condition of the natural, and therefore enduring, in human nature; but was also a means to an end, and to the kind of manners which germinate from those 'elementary feelings' (of rural life) which 'are more easily comprehended, and are more durable'. Wordsworth wrote to Coleridge in 1799 that: 'I do not so ardently desire character in poems like Burger's, as manners, not transitory manners reflecting the wearisome unintelligible obliquities of city-life, but manners connected with the permanent objects of nature and partaking of the simplicity of those objects. Such pictures must interest when the original shall cease to exist'. Letter 110, 27 February 1799, *Letters*, 1: 255.

[25] For *The Universal Visitor* in 1756. Hill notes Boswell's observation that this essay and an earlier one in *The Gentleman's Magazine* for December 1740 (593) were added to *The Idler* when it was collected in volumes. (*Lives*, 3: 254).

[26] *Prose Works*, 2: 57-59. The first of Wordsworth's 'Essays upon Epitaphs' first appeared in Coleridge's *The Friend* for 22 February 1810.

[27] *Prose Works*, 2: 59.

[28] *Prose Works*, 2: 58, 59.

[29] Wellek, 1: 103.

[30] The most illuminating exception to this general rule is G.F. Parker's fine chapter on Johnson and romantic criticism of Shakespeare, 'The Mind against the World', in *Johnson's Shakespeare*, 63-155.

[31] A. W. Schlegel, Lecture 22, *Lectures*, 346.

[32] Lecture 22, *Lectures*, 346.

[33] Lecture 23, *Lectures*, 371.

[34] Lecture 22, *Lectures*, 340-42.

[35] Henry Crabb Robinson reported Coleridge as saying that 'Shakespeare imitates life, mingled as we find it with joy and sorrow'. See *Diary*, in *Coleridge's Shakespearean Criticism*, ed. T. M. Raysor, 2 vols. (London: Constable, 1930), 1: 212. According to Crabb Robinson, Coleridge seems to have had mixed success in taking issue with Johnson's *Preface*. The *Diary* entry for 9 January 1812 reads: 'Evening, Coleridge's lecture on Johnson's Preface. C. succeeded admirably in the exposure of Johnson, and tho' he was sometimes obscure, the many palpable and intelligible *hits* must have given general satisfaction'. In the entry for 'Monday 13', however, we learn that Coleridge continued his remarks on Johnson's *Preface* but that these were 'Very feeble and unmeaning compared with the last. He had no answer to the general faults ascribed but the complaint of the generality of the imputation'. *Coleridge's Shakespearean Criticism*, 2: 173.

[36] Lecture 22, *Lectures*, 340-42; 344.

[37] See *Coleridge's Shakespearean Criticism*, 1: 197-98; 211-212. For a detailed account of Coleridge's debt to Schlegel, see Norman Fruman, *The Damaged Archangel* (New York: George Braziller, 1971).

[38] Lecture 23, *Lectures*, 363.

[39] Lecture 23, *Lectures*, 362; 363-64.

[40] Lecture 23, *Lectures*, 363. Cf. Addison, *Spectator* 419 (1 July 1712): 'Among the *English*, *Shakespear* has incomparably excelled all others. That noble Extravagance of Fancy, which he had in so great Perfection, thoroughly qualified him to touch this weak superstitious Part of his Reader's Imagination; and made him capable of succeeding, where he had nothing to support him besides the Strength of his own Genius. There is something so wild and yet so solemn in the Speeches of his Ghosts, Fairies, Witches and the like Imaginary Persons, that we cannot forbear thinking them natural, tho' we have no Rule by which to judge of them, and must confess, *if there are such Beings in the World, it looks highly probable they should talk and act as he has represented them*'. *The Spectator*, ed. Donald F. Bonds, 5 vols. (Oxford: Clarendon Press, 1965), 3: 572-73. (my emphases).

[41] *Leigh Hunt's Dramatic Criticism 1808-1831*, ed. L. H. Houtchens and C. W. Houtchens (New York: Columbia University Press, 1949), 167.

[42] *Works*, 4: 171, 174, 176.

[43] *A View of the English Stage*, in *Works*, 5: 204.

[44] William Hazlitt, 'On Shakespeare and Milton' (1818), *Works*, 5: 50.

[45] William Hazlitt, *A View of the English Stage*, in *Works*, 5: 205.

[46] Appendix to *Lyrical Ballads*, *Prose Works*, 1: 160-61.

[47] See William Hazlitt, 'On Shakespeare and Milton' (1818), *Works*, 5: 50.

[48] In his 'Essays upon Epitaphs' Wordsworth objects to the portrayal of the deceased in details 'minutely and scrupulously pursued' (*Prose Works*, 2: 59). '[A]ll the power of description', Johnson had written generally of the metaphysical poets, 'is destroyed by a scrupulous enumeration' (*Lives*, 1: 45). Such a principle links Wordsworth closely, if ironically, with the Augustan critical revolution of Boileau, Rapin and Bouhours.

[49] Preface to *Lyrical Ballads*, *Prose Works*, 1: 125.

[50] Preface to *Lyrical Ballads*, *Prose Works*, 1: 133.

[51] Houston had remarked that: 'It seems like the irony of fate that the last great upholder of the older criticism, the staunch supporter of the principles of reason and common sense,

should have prepared the way for the romantic enthusiasms of A. W. Schlegel and Manzoni, of Hazlitt and Coleridge'. *Doctor Johnson: A Study in Eighteenth Century Humanism*, 157.
[52] For further discussion of this point see Philip Smallwood, review of *The Cambridge History of Literary Criticism 4: The Eighteenth Century*, in *AJ* 10 (1999): 392-99.

Chapter 7

Conclusion: Johnson's Transfusion of the Critical Past and the Making of the Literary Canon

'Motion without Progress': Johnson's Historical Conceptualization of Literary Criticism

To conclude: critical historians have been driven by rhetorical imperatives, considerations of form, a different point of view, and by the sheer heterogeneity and complexity of the critical past to simplify history. But while critical history may have had to make past critical minds seem simple, a narrative composed only of simple minds does not make history make sense. With their tendency to objectivize, classify or compartmentalize the past, to disintegrate the unity of the critical life, or to flatten its contours of development, twentieth-century histories are too familiar and have been written in the same way too many times. As far as their assumptions about past criticism imply Johnson's underdevelopment (or arrested development) as a critic, their historical certainties, classifications and simplicities seem premature. We have seen that historical assumptions can intervene at too early a stage to short-circuit the process of historicization when more circumspection with regard to what we do not know about past critical minds is required, and when considerable quantities of textual detail in major critical texts remain open to different interpretations, or are clearly misinterpreted.

Johnson's criticism resists the reductive contextualism of a developmental narrative in at least three ways. First, any context whatsoever can be seen in a different kind of relation to the critical text, and as creatively connected to it rather than simply reflective of theory, the examples I have examined being Johnson's earlier critical thinking, his creative work, and prominent samples from his prose and poetical predecessors. Second, more concerted attention can be given to the critical text of Johnson's criticism than to any of its explanatory contexts, and Johnson's words can be read free of the hampering effects of historical data, my instances in the central chapters of this study being Johnson's reaction to specific dramatic situations encountered in Shakespeare and in the detail of Cowley's poetry. Third, the varieties of non-literary context, serious or satiric, can be artistically problematic texts themselves, and the critical text can inspire forms of visual response as vital to the milieu of criticism as the mass of minor theorists and critics conventionally permitted to constitute Johnson's critical relations. The spirit of eighteenth-century satirical caricature, in the ambiguity of its contact with Johnson, is my example here.

The relation that might in preference obtain between the Johnsonian critical past and the critical present, I conclude, is not historical in the sense limited by the negative satirical force of such caricature, by romanticism, cultural classification, or by the major forms of critical history.[1] It is best seen as translational in the sense brought to a focus in Johnson, and whose trans-historical forms are 'criticism' and 'literature'. Without ceasing to be new, new work is made out of old, or is recreated in the light of it. Thus the ideas, sensitivities, feelings, terminology and responses shaped within the critical context of the past of the eighteenth century are not committed to a thesis of *progress* in literary criticism. And in addressing questions that remain questions for us, and opening out the idea of context to a wider interpretation, the notion of 'transfusion' needs to figure more largely in historical representations of Johnson than does a revolutionary change, or any presumption of change for the better. '[T]he historical mode of the *Lives*', writes Greg Clingham in his *Johnson, Writing, Memory*, 'is unique in literary history in performing the work of *translation*'.[2] What Clingham has here claimed of the internal relationships between the poets within the *Lives of the Poets*, I would apply to the external relations between Johnson and the critics who precede him, and would propose as a model for thinking about our potential relation to his criticism today, his 'presence' in both present and past. But before going on to discuss the most significant aspect of the relationship between cultural radicalism and Johnson's criticism on this count, I will begin this concluding chapter with an instance of the historical basis for this claim.

From Dryden to Johnson

What is transfused by the historical relationship between Johnson and Dryden is both metacritical and performative. Dryden had defined 'criticism' in his 'Author's Apology for Heroic Poetry' as 'a standard of judging well';[3] but to admit into the concept 'criticism' the sum total of Dryden's collection of essays, dialogues, prefaces and epistles dedicatory in prose, or to include the many occasions where Dryden is alluding to, translating, adapting, and implicitly judging, placing, appreciating or otherwise interpreting other poets, or copying and re-stating other critics, is to concede to a definition of criticism that is not evidently reductive.[4] As poet, classicist and translator, Dryden transfused his source texts through translation, and to think of the Dryden who wrote apropos of Chaucer at the very end of his life that 'nothing [is] lost out of nature, though every thing is altered'[5] is to understand critical history, as Collingwood understood history, as a process of 're-enactment'.[6] Johnson called Dryden 'the father of English criticism', 'the writer who first taught us to determine upon principles the merit of composition' (*Lives*, 1: 410), and he spelt out an idea of criticism that he and Dryden fundamentally shared.[7] But it is ultimately Johnson's critical performance rather than his system, his practice in undertaking the same kinds of tasks that Dryden had faced in other contemporary and personal contexts, and not his adherence to or departure from prior categorical generalizations, which shapes an alternative narrative of history.

Johnson, pre-eminently, viewed what Dryden had said of Shakespeare as the paternal seed of all later attempts at Shakespearean criticism including his own: 'The account of Shakespeare', he writes of the *Essay of Dramatic Poesy*:

> may stand as a perpetual model of encomiastick criticism; exact without minuteness, and lofty without exaggeration. The praise lavished by Longinus, on the attestation of the heroes of Marathon by Demosthenes, fades away before it. In a few lines is exhibited a character, so extensive in its comprehension and so curious in its limitations, that nothing can be added, diminished, or reformed; nor can the editors and admirers of Shakespeare, in all their emulation of reverence, boast of much more than of having diffused and paraphrased this epitome of excellence, of having changed Dryden's gold for baser metal, of lower value though of greater bulk. (*Lives*, 1: 412)

Johnson quoted the entire passage from Dryden - recently alluded to in a study of the language of Shakespeare by Frank Kermode - at the end of his *Preface*.[8] Elements of its rhetorical organization are reflected in the *Preface* itself, and in a remark that seems to convey a debt both to the poetry and to the criticism, Johnson, in summing up his achievement, confessed to 'some partial fondness for the memory of Dryden' (*Lives*, 3: 223). In a comment which serves to bring out the historical significance and contemporary currency of 'classical' criticism, Johnson pays tribute in the 'Life of Dryden' to 'the criticism of a poet; not a dull collection of theorems, nor a rude detection of faults ... but a gay and vigorous dissertation, where delight is mingled with instruction, and where the author proves his right of judgement by his power of performance' (*Lives*, 1: 412).

The suggestion here, vis-à-vis Johnson and Dryden, must again be that the history of criticism requires an expansion in the *modes of relation* conventionally permitted between the critical text and the contexts by which it is known. The paradox once more is that the 'events' of criticism, of which Dryden's encomium on Shakespeare is one, are best conceived as history when they are best appreciated aesthetically. While the arrangement of past events in narrative terms is a pre-condition of history writing, if the reasons for change in the critical past are to be appreciated in the present, the reader of history needs to experience more of its moments as depths. This seems most strikingly evident in the passage from the 'Preface to *Fables*' where Dryden is introducing the *Iliad* of Homer. The combination of tone, language and rhetorical organization, in addition to content, all contribute indistinguishably here to an 'event' received as criticism then, but expressive of standards which implicate or indict criticism now:

> And this I dare assure the world beforehand, that I have found, by trial, Homer a more pleasing task than Virgil.... For the Grecian is more according to my genius than the Latin poet. In the works of the two authors we may read their manners and natural inclinations, which are wholly different. Virgil was of a quiet, sedate temper: Homer was violent, impetuous, and full of fire. The chief talent of Virgil was propriety of thoughts, and ornament of words: Homer was rapid in his thoughts, and took all the liberties, both of numbers and of expressions, which his language ... allowed him. Homer's invention was more copious, Virgil's more

confined.... our two great poets, being so different in their tempers, one choleric
and sanguine, the other phlegmatic and melancholic; ... the action of Homer,
being more full of vigour than that of Virgil, according to the temper of the writer,
is of consequence more pleasing to the reader. One warms you by degrees; the
other sets you on fire all at once, and never intermits his heat.[9]

Behind Dryden's appreciation are Longinus (translated into French by Boileau in
1674), the various 'Comparaisons' between Greek and Roman authors composed
by René Rapin,[10] and the comparisons between Greek, Roman, Italian, Spanish and
modern French poetry by Dominique Bouhours.[11] But Dryden draws back in this
passage from the detail of Homer's and Virgil's work, from the lines, passages and
speeches, episodes or books that he had grappled with close up as a translator, and
invites us to consider cross-cultural categories that precede textuality - 'genius',
'inclinations', 'temper' and 'talent'. A conscious elevation of style combines
medieval medical language (the 'choleric' and 'sanguine', the 'phlegmatic' and
'melancholic') with subdued alliterative touches - the 'full of fire', the 'copious'
and 'confined', or the creative 'vigour' of Homer when compared with 'Virgil'.
This too is the 'criticism of a poet'. And it is part of the aesthetic effect of the
passage that like the praise of Dryden's paragraph on Shakespeare by Johnson, the
comparison of Homer and Virgil is 'lofty without exaggeration'.

The visualizable gestures and conversational deferrals here (the move from the
polite aloofness of 'we' and 'the reader' to the familiar 'you' of the closing
sentence) may be closer to Montaigne than the dense metaphoric quality of
Johnsonian prose, the 'thorns and brambles' of Rymer's (Johnson, *Lives*, 1: 413),
or the fussy magisterialism of Wordsworth's. But Dryden's critical text is not at the
same time uniquely explained according to a critical teleology at this point. The
background in Longinus, Rapin and Bouhours suggests rather a structure of action,
feeling and thought that is uniformly and creatively traditional in its *combination
and unification* of ideas and emotions, intellectual reflection and poetic response.
Dryden's transitions from the 'Preface to *Fables*' were re-iterated in the 'Preface to
the Iliad', where Pope had again compared the habits and tempers of Virgil and
Homer (*Homer*, 7: 3-25; esp. 4-5). These habits and tempers were later re-enacted,
using different but equally comparable authors, and by reference to equally
necessary, urgent but complex and intractable divisions of quality, in Johnson. As
Johnson wrote in his *Preface to Shakespeare* of 1765, Addison's *Cato* was
composed in diction 'easy, elevated and harmonious'; Shakespeare's *Othello* was
'the vigorous and vivacious offspring of observation impregnated by genius'.
Addison speaks 'the language of poets, and Shakespeare, of men' (*Shakespeare*, 7:
84). Johnson, in his 'Life of Pope', can be seen to have woven elements drawn
from Pope's and Dryden's 'essays' on Homer and Virgil into his own 'parallel' (as
he called it) of Dryden and Pope:

The style of Dryden is capricious and varied, that of Pope is cautious and
uniform.... Dryden is sometimes vehement and rapid; Pope is always smooth,
uniform, and gentle. Dryden's page is a natural field, rising into inequalities, and
diversified by the varied exuberance of abundant vegetation; Pope's is a velvet

lawn, shaven by the scythe, and levelled by the roller.... If the flights of Dryden ... are higher, Pope continues longer on the wing. If of Dryden's fire the blaze is brighter, of Pope's the heat is more regular and constant. (*Lives*, 3: 222-23)[12]

Thus can Dryden's judgments of classical and medieval writing instance one of the several *different* kinds of historical organization (derived from a multi-dimensional cultural past) that I am suggesting we need in approaching the criticism of Johnson. Such a history creatively translates classical criticism into the present by giving a more plausible and interesting account of the past. It suggests the good things in criticism of the past that do not continue forever. But it also points to the perspective on the present of criticism that only the past can provide. The most desirable history would thus do more to maintain the ground for similarity and difference between critical past and present. As R.S. Crane determined as long ago as 1953, critical history in the period from 1650 to 1800 can be made and recorded regardless of the genres and doctrines to which poets conform. Such a history:

> would ... be free to exhibit critics speaking for themselves with respect to problems they themselves had formulated in the process of solving them, rather than problems set for them, after the event, by the historian.... Dryden and Johnson would still be the heroes of the story, but not because they helped to emancipate criticism from the tyranny of neoclassical rules.... [The history] could ... be expected to throw light not simply on the dead opinions and pronouncements of dead critics but on the permanent and still living problems of analysis and reasoning which critics in all times and traditions have faced, and concerning which we ourselves might easily profit, in a good many ways, by knowing in detail how they were defined and solved by our predecessors in the seventeenth and eighteenth centuries.[13]

As for the other English 'neoclassical' critics, Johnson quotes and refers to the writings of Dennis many times in the *Lives*. He substitutes in the 'Life of Addison' Dennis's remarks on Addison's *Cato* for a personal analysis, and he seeks through this process 'to rescue his [Dennis's] criticism from oblivion'. (Johnson is aware of the irony that 'at last, it will have no other life than it derives from the work which it endeavours to oppress' [*Lives*, 2: 133]). This tendency to provide for one's successors the unconscious thoughts and criteria by which one is consigned to history oneself, comes out in Johnson's careful assessment of Addison's own contribution to critical history in this 'Life'. Johnson writes here as a critical historian anxious to restore the context of the historical situation in which the past of criticism takes shape. He does so, however, in a spirit which suggests the critical past may still have something of permanent value to teach the present. 'It is not uncommon,' he writes, 'for those who have grown wise by the labour of others to add a little of their own, and overlook their masters. Addison is now despised by some who perhaps would never have seen his defects, but by the lights which he afforded them' (*Lives*, 2: 145-46). In his comments on the past of critical history that runs through Addison, Johnson is alive to the compromise the critic must make with posterity in order to discharge his contemporary function:

> That he always wrote as he would think it necessary to write now cannot be affirmed; his instructions were such as the character of his readers made proper. That general knowledge which now circulates in common talk was in his time rarely to be found. Men not professing learning were not ashamed of ignorance; and in the female world any acquaintance with books was distinguished only to be censured. His purpose was to infuse literary curiosity by gentle and unsuspected conveyance into the gay, the idle, and the wealthy.... (*Lives*, 2: 146)

Johnson sees Addison as the next necessary stage in the broadening of critical wisdom after Dryden:

> Dryden had not many years before scattered criticism over his *Prefaces* with very little parcimony; but, though he sometimes condescended to be somewhat familiar, his manner was in general too scholastick for those who had yet their rudiments to learn....
>   An instructor like Addison was now wanting.... (*Lives*, 2: 146)

And he looks to that part of the critical past that Addison has made his own as a check and a balance to the tendency of the present age to express superiority to Addison's achievements:

> Before the profound observers of the present race repose too securely on the consciousness of their superiority to Addison, let them consider his *Remarks on Ovid*, in which may be found specimens of criticism sufficiently subtle and refined; let them peruse likewise his *Essays on Wit* and on *The Pleasures of Imagination*, in which he founds art on the base of nature, and draws the principles of invention from dispositions inherent in the mind of man with skill and elegance, such as his contemners will not easily attain. (*Lives*, 2: 148)

In admitting the possibility of change for the better while wisely counselling against a consciousness of superiority to the critical past, Johnson is once again an advocate of 'direct instruction in critical thinking' and an example of it.

The Preface to Shakespeare and the Past of Criticism

It is when we turn back to the *Preface to Shakespeare* from passages on critics and criticism in the *Lives*, that we move the emphasis once more from what critics and historians have said of Johnson, to Johnson's own 'literary' image of the critical past. Johnson suggests here how the criticism of the present is itself swept along by the stream of time and is subject to the laws of nature, flux and perpetual change (though not necessarily progress) that are focused in Dryden's poetical translations, as they are in Johnson's conception of the past, I have earlier suggested, in *Rasselas*.

One especially pertinent passage that lends itself to evaluation within this re-creative classicism, and in twentieth-century literary-historiographical terms, is a poignant act of self-historicization:

> It is no pleasure to me, in revising my volumes, to observe how much paper is wasted in confutation. Whoever considers the revolutions of learning, and the various questions of greater or less importance, upon which wit and reason have exercised their powers, must lament the unsuccessfulness of enquiry, and the slow advances of truth, when he reflects, that great part of the labour of every writer is only the destruction of those that went before him. The first care of the builder of a new system, is to demolish the fabricks which are standing. The chief desire of him that comments an authour, is to shew how much other commentators have corrupted and obscured him. The opinions prevalent in one age, as truths above the reach of controversy, are confuted and rejected in another, and rise again to reception in remoter times. Thus the human mind is kept in motion without progress. Thus sometimes truth and errour, and sometimes contrarieties of errour, take each others place by reciprocal invasion. The tide of seeming knowledge which is poured over one generation, retires and leaves another naked and barren; the sudden meteors of intelligence which for a while appear to shoot their beams into the regions of obscurity, on a sudden withdraw their lustre, and leave mortals again to grope their way. (*Shakespeare*, 7: 99)

Such a passage is a rhapsody of vibrant imagery drawn from physical rhythms and celestial nature. Who could read it and not appreciate Johnson's representation of the past of criticism (apt, one might think, in the light of modern theorists' accounts of the 'literary' force of historical writing) as a transcendent *aesthetic* achievement?[14] One might notice here the balance of the phrasing - the rise and fall of the prose, the pith of the short first sentence compared with the rolling surge and descent of the second; then the sequence of brief direct statements (with their double 'thus') leading to the desolate and frightening finale. Remarkable too, is the vocabulary - the great weight of personal effort that is compressed into Johnson's linkage of the work of the critical commentator not with joy or delight but with 'labour'; the embodied abstractions at perpetual war in the persons of 'truth' and 'errour'; the decorousness and grace of the 'retiring' tide of knowledge and the chill farewell whereby the meteors of intelligence without warning 'withdraw' their luster; the contrast between the paired Latinate terms, 'corrupted and obscured', 'confuted and rejected' and the Anglo-Saxon 'grope' of the final sentence.

Like many modern critics, Johnson elsewhere could see the ever-accumulating weight of the past as a burden. The dead are dead but the living must be perpetually on their guard against their encroachments: 'had all the dead been embalmed', reflects Imlac, 'their repositories must in time have been more spacious than the dwellings of the living' (*Rasselas*, 169). But here the resistance of a critic against his own past has none of the noble resonance of the Wordsworthian revolt, and despite the correlations of Johnson and Wordsworth referred to in the previous chapter, Johnson, unlike the romantics, does not suggest that the past is *justly* and rationally consigned to history. Nor is there any evidence of a pre-Darwinian biology of criticism spiralling upwards from its primitive forms. Johnson, by contrast, sees the *telos* revealed by History within Criticism as persistently delusive. The motion is 'without progress'. The change in critical atmosphere or 'opinions prevalent' seems casual, unsystematic or arbitrary. The primary causes of alteration are for Johnson temperamental and individual rather than grandly epistemic. Yet because the fluctuations are viewed from inside the self (this being an aspect of Johnson's personal sense of bleak futility combined with Christian hope), the process seems coherent. It is part of nature. It attains a psychological plausibility. Johnson appeals to the *necessary* misapprehension which accompanies change. In terms of the modern theory of poetical development, this may suggest a form of Bloomian 'misprision'. But we may also recall that Johnson preferred the mingled dramas of Shakespeare to the inexorable movement of Greek tragedy. The rhythms of the Johnsonian past are accordingly linked to the reverses of a world where 'the loss of one is the gain of another; in which ... the malignity of one is sometimes defeated by the frolick of another; and many mischiefs and many benefits are done and hindered without design' (*Shakespeare*, 7: 66). This is less the oedipal 'anxiety of influence'[15] than the kind of critical play that modern critics like to refer to as 'carnivalesque'. So far as it is 'neoclassical', it recalls Plato's *Timaeus*, the flux of Lucretius, Ovid or Montaigne.[16] Johnson's imaginative participation in the pathos of editorial commentary on Shakespeare collapses the gulf between the historian and the material of history to achieve Collingwood's 'self-knowledge of the mind'.[17]

Historical Consciousness and the Value of Johnson as Critic

Johnson had called Dryden the 'father of English criticism' (*Lives*, 1: 410). And what can be said of Johnson's great predecessor in the history of criticism can be said, finally, of Johnson himself. We have seen that histories making reference to Johnson belong within the story-telling tradition, and involve the construction, maintenance and exploitation of myths; they may present their 'objects' and 'events' according to a system of textual transformation, interpolation, illustration and inference. But they are also for this same reason necessary elements in the creative translation of this past. They respond to cultural needs in their own time and place. They instate a role for the past as a barrier to cultural egotism and self-universalization. But a more developed historical consciousness than has proved possible in formal histories seems to be needed to restore respect for the unvarnished (textual) evidence of what criticism was in the hands of a man who lived, wrote and died before us. Only then, it seems, can the past of criticism reveal the possibilities of criticism that the present has failed to realize. The historical representation might then do more to accommodate John Stuart Mill's exhortation - praised in 'humanist' terms by Berlin - to tolerate rather than respect contrary views. Mill, wrote Berlin:

> once declared that when we deeply care, we must dislike those who hold opposite views. He preferred this to cold temperaments and opinions. He asked us not necessarily to respect the views of others - very far from it - only to try to understand and tolerate them; only tolerate; disapprove, think ill of, if need be mock or despise, but tolerate....[18]

It seems evident from the treatment of Johnson's 'opposite views' in modern historical accounts (such as the historicized readings of Johnson's criticism of Shakespeare by twentieth-century historians) that the tendency of historians is to continue to place the Johnsonian past and the critical present in separate compartments, these defined by massive cultural classifications that are externally related. Clearly, such doctrines as the 'reception aesthetics' of Hans Robert Jauss, with its notion of a 'fusion of the horizon of expectations' as the model for a new kind of literary history, have failed to remould the history of literary criticism in any significant way. Yet Jauss's ideas, in common with Collingwood's or Gadamer's 're-constructive' (or dialectical) concept of the relation between the present and the past, would seem to suggest the theoretical objections that must be raised against a present and a past of criticism that are too *simply* opposed. Equally to the point, from a resonantly 'postmodern' perspective, would be Michel de Certeau's Freudian sense of the present's systematic repression of the past (as 'other') in the 'pretty order of a line of progress', and the possibilities of this repression being overcome:

> In their respective turns, each 'new' time provides the *place* for a discourse considering whatever preceded it to be 'dead', but welcoming a 'past' that had already been specified by former ruptures.... But whatever this new understanding of the past holds to be irrelevant - shards created by the selection of materials, remainders left aside by an explication - comes back, despite everything, on the edges of discourse or in its rifts and crannies: 'resistances', 'survivals', or delays discreetly perturb the pretty order of a line of 'progress' or a system of interpretation. These are lapses in the syntax constructed by the law of a place. Therein they symbolize a return of the repressed, that is, a return of what, at a given moment, has *become* unthinkable in order for a new identity to *become* thinkable. [19]

My suggestion would be that overcoming the resistance to Johnson's critical 'survival' evident in the twentieth-century historical perspective requires a more lively and accommodating consciousness of what we have learnt from Johnson's critical 'sensations', as Johnson learnt from Dryden's, and as a necessary precondition of *our* reading of him - a clearer awareness of the irony of 'what we will not have been able to think without him' that Jacques Derrida has appreciated in Hegel.[20] I will therefore turn finally to this latest stage in the historicization of Johnson, and to the attitudes Johnson allegedly inspired as he shaped, and simultaneously inhabited, the so-called 'canon' of English literature. Such questions bring the issue of the critical past and the preoccupations of the critical present together on intimate terms.

Historical Closure: Johnson's Criticism and the English Literary Canon

The word 'canon', writes John Guillory in his book *Cultural Capital: the Problem of Literary Canon Formation*:

displaces the expressly honorific term 'classic' precisely in order to isolate the 'classics' as the object of critique. The concept of the canon names the traditional curriculum of literary texts by analogy to that body of writing historically characterized by an inherent logic of *closure* - the scriptural canon. The scriptural analogy is continuously present, if usually tacit, whenever canonical revision is expressed as 'opening the canon'.

'We may begin to interrogate this first assumption', Guillory continues, 'by raising the question of whether the process by which a selection of texts functions to define a religious practice and doctrine is really similar *historically* to the process by which literary texts come to be preserved, reproduced, and taught in the schools'.[21] For students of eighteenth-century literature, I would suggest, this historical process will incline for much of the time to the definition imposed upon English Literature by Samuel Johnson. He is 'the Canonical Critic' in Harold Bloom's phrase.[22] His work is the nexus of the idea of criticism and the idea of history. The components we have examined in this study - the conceptualization and valuation of Johnson's literary criticism, the theory of history, and the inherited models of critical history that actualize our idea of the past of criticism through the lens of the present - overlap. But the topic cannot be left, at last, without some comment on the relationship between the image of Johnson and the current politics of criticism 'after theory', between what Stefan Collini has called, somewhat disparagingly, 'grievance studies',[23] and what I would call Johnson's part in modern fantasies of dominance subversion.

According to Charles Altieri, in his 1983 essay 'An Idea and Ideal of a Literary Canon', 'Samuel Johnson is the canonical figure most useful for thinking about canons'. 'If we are less in need of discovering new truths than of remembering old ones', he writes, 'there are obvious social roles canons can play as selective memories of traditions or ideals'.[24] Johnson's interest in the great sixteenth- and seventeenth-century writers, 'which was almost inevitable', observes Robert DeMaria, doubtless 'carries cultural assumptions, as modern students of the literary canon must agree'.[25] But as attacks by modern cultural radicals on the élitist canon of English literature, or great literature, have become more commonplace, the interdependence of the canon and Samuel Johnson moves critical history into its most recent historical phase. This closely reflects the 'logic of closure' (a shutting of the door on the critical past) of which Guillory speaks. It has revived the simultaneous need to 'isolate' the classics of literary criticism that the modern revolution in criticism may achieve its goals. My conclusion is that these attacks have done too much to augment and too little to dismantle the vivid caricature of Johnson that originated with the first protesters against his critical judgments in the eighteenth century, and that they develop out of the standard tactics of romantic dissent.

At the same time, and as the first part of the parricidal irony of history I have focused upon, Johnson seems nevertheless to have helped certain critics of a radical persuasion to define the stereotypical elements of canon formation in Johnsonian terms. Thus Barbara Herrnstein-Smith complains that 'However much canonical works may be seen to "question" secular vanities such as wealth, social position, and political power, "remind" their readers of more elevated values and virtues ... they would not be found to *please long* and well if they were seen *radically* to undercut establishment interests....'[26] In this she echoes Johnson: 'Nothing can please many, and *please long*, but just representations of general nature' (*Shakespeare*, 7: 61).[27] Johnson argues from consensus over time in the opening pages of his *Preface* that two or more persons can actually share the same pleasures and pains, and that works or authors can transcend their originating contexts. For Herrnstein-Smith, however, in evoking the bogusness of a work's lasting appeal, such an argument would insinuate a false totality. According to the historical and critical standards she ascribes to the canon, Johnson and critics of a similar cultural persuasion would not be critiqued merely for their valuing *per se*. They attribute durability to things that do not deserve to last. Moreover such critics underpin a political continuity that runs counter to the culture of human rights. Johnsonian 'general nature' is thereby enmeshed in a movement whose particulars appear to do more to express liminality than flux. They reinforce a stubborn hypothesis about the splendid completeness and dominance of the literary past. Modern writers and modern critics have no choice but to feel this as oppressive.

But the juncture between Johnson's past role as a critic and the agency responsible for eighteenth-century canon creation also deepens the historical irony I have tried to outline in this study. It suffuses the relation between modern politico-sceptical theory and eighteenth-century values. For of all literary critics in English, Johnson on this issue drew the strictest possible distinction. On the one hand were the texts, belonging to the past, on which his own beliefs about God and the universe were ultimately founded. On the other was the canon of English poets. Johnson defined the word 'canon' in the first edition of his English *Dictionary* in 1755 with the following quotation: 'Canon ... denotes those books of Scripture, which are received as inspired and canonical, to distinguish them from either profane, apocryphal, or disputed books'. And in the 'Life of Waller', famously, where he uses language many have found hard to digest, Johnson argues with reference to the world of difference between poetic and sacred texts that:

> The topicks of devotion are few, and being few are universally known; but, few as they are, they can be made no more; they can receive no grace from novelty of sentiment, and very little from novelty of expression.
>
> Poetry pleases by exhibiting an idea more grateful to the mind than things themselves afford. This effect proceeds from the display of those parts of nature which attract, and the concealment of those which repel, the imagination: but religion must be shewn as it is; suppression and addition equally corrupt it, and such as it is, it is known already.... Omnipotence cannot be exalted; Infinity cannot be amplified; Perfection cannot be improved.
>
> The employments of pious meditation are Faith, Thanksgiving, Repentance, and Supplication. (*Lives*, 1: 291-92)

At the same time, of course, there is the canon in the sense belonging to literary criticism - a selective list of secular texts whose excellence or towering genius is no longer disputed. This was also coming into being *in*, or had come into being *by*, the eighteenth century. It was part of the taxonomic 'ordering of the arts' or the putative rise of literary history.[28] Such a canon could doubtless be partially attributed to the intervention of Johnson. One need only survey the citations in Johnson's *Dictionary*, as Anne McDermott has done, to define Johnson's 'golden age' of literature, and to see that 'Johnson's struggle to fix the language ... is, for him, a canonical act'.[29] Then there are the nominal subjects of Johnson's criticism, the authors we read to this day that he favoured by writing about. Dryden makes important critical comments on Chaucer or Shakespeare. But these seem largely overwhelmed by his commentary on the classical poets - the poetry of Ovid, Horace, Virgil, Lucretius, Juvenal, Homer and so forth that he at some time translated. Johnson's criticism displays by comparison an unprecedentedly *English* emphasis. His 'canon' is found in his collected editorial and prefatory work on Shakespeare, Cowley, Waller, Denham, Milton, Addison, Pope and the poetry of Dryden himself, plus such 'noncanonical worthies' (to quote Bloom again) 'as Pomfret, Sprat, Yalden, Dorset, Roscommon, Stepney, and Felton [sic]' (192). Johnson was indebted to a number of French literary critics, and this may suggest a commitment to transcend purely national criteria, as Pope had commanded in the *Essay on Criticism* (lines 400-401). However, such a *'poetic* collective identity' (as James Chandler has called it)[30] has led some critics to suspect a tie-up between an anglocentric canon and the rise of an English nationalism hostile to France. The line runs through Thomas Warton's *History of English Poetry* and collections such as Chalmers' Poets. Johnson's *Preface* and his *Lives*, the latter famously repudiated as *Johnson's Poets*, become in this light an early Biblioteca Britannica or prototype of *The Great Tradition*.

But viewed in the spirit of cultural jingoism of this kind Johnson's standards are once again narrowed down. They are something less than the 'cosmopolitan nationalism' recently observed by Clement Hawes,[31] and in ways that might seem to cause problems for critical history. Johnson's significance would be reduced to a struggle for power within the contending cultural totalities of his time and in a fashion that Pope had precisely warned the critic against. Be that as it may, a slide between the two conceptions of canonical value, the critical and the scriptural, almost always takes place when - as Guillory observes - the canon is 'opened'. In the one case, the 'canon' is a 'closed body of writing defined by the Church through its authority' (as Stein Haugom Olsen expresses it[32]), and is the place where those in doubt are referred for the truth. Their heresies are corrected. Disputes and controversies occur here under the aspect of the problem of *meaning*. But the contrast is with the inherited approbation of authors and literary works that are open to the flow of history. There is here an essentially *dynamic* tradition of literary change, revolution, re-creation, translation, the assertion of modernity through cultural transmission that has more accurately been compared to a *musée imaginaire*. The various exhibits are periodically rotated, spend time in the gallery basement, and are added to as new acquisitions are made or old ones disposed of. The 'canon' in this literary sense is then a whole that perpetually re-creates itself. Priests may interpret the meaning of scriptural texts for their religious communities; but such a canon is constantly subject to *evaluation* at the hands of the public: its contents and shape, its very definition as distinct from its meaning, is the business of the literary critic. No such freedom in the ultimate judgment of value is available in the case of religious texts without their religious status being called into question.

There is therefore no strong analogy between the canon of great literature, which Johnson is often assumed or accused to have conjured up for England and the English in the eighteenth century, and the conservationist canon of scriptural texts. Olsen has observed that: 'Only societies without a tradition have the need for a canon in the scriptural sense'.[33] And 'In our culture', writes W.W. Robson, 'the proposal to close the literary canon is not a live option'.[34] For Charles Hinnant, in the conclusion to his *Steel for the Mind*, Johnson 'sees absolutely no virtue in the kind of interpretive approach that sees the poetry of the past as a kind of secular scripture'. 'Poetry is not being understood', writes Hinnant correctly, 'if the critic regards its texts as canonical in a scriptural sense'.[35] Trevor Ross has noticed in his study of *The Making of the English Literary Canon* that Johnson 'steadfastly rejected any attempt to publicize his criticism ... as providing a definitive ordering of the English canon'.[36] Nevertheless, the sense that the canon, in common with the 'classics', has been constructed to defend indefensible judgments, is motivated only and always by the prejudices of race, gender and class, promotes authors and works that we now do not like, and gives an illusory power, endurance, unity and uniqueness to literature in which we do not believe, has remained potent. Similarly the tendency to place the 'canonical' in conflict with the 'marginal' misconstrues at the expense of Johnson the immanent spirit and corporate nature of poetic and critical activity in the eighteenth century. It ignores the collapse of cultural difference between classical, medieval, renaissance and eighteenth century through creative translation, and has ensured that the kind of enduring value Johnson identified in Shakespeare, and which then supplies a criterion for his commentary on poets in the *Lives*, seems merely narcissistic. Thus does the 'canon' become a term of opprobrium for *other people's* opinions and the grounds on which they hold them.

In this view, Johnson's criticism could not be thought to take its power and authority from the courage, conviction, subtlety, emotional profundity and articulateness of the judgments themselves. Its source is the supposed need to defend an establishment, sexual or class privilege and bigotry and hand it on. But the moral superiority assumed by this charge is not itself without moral flaws. It combines historically with the lingering half-truth, originating in the eighteenth century amongst Johnson's contemporaries and reviewers, but kept going through Macaulay on Johnson (in the nineteenth century) and F.R. Leavis on Johnson (in the twentieth), that Johnson had projected the values of his own poetry and drama into his assessment of the poets he criticized in the *Lives*. Where he approved of poets, he approved because they wrote as he did, and where he disapproved, it was because they differed. Johnson's selection of heroic couplets for the *Vanity of Human Wishes* thus guarantees the negative estimates of poets who adopted other metrical forms - Milton, Thomson, Akenside or Gray. The logical entailment is that Johnson did not and could not write much or very approvingly about female poets of the eighteenth century because he was not himself of their number.

'The literary canon of "great literature"', writes Toril Moi, 'ensures that it is this "representative experience" (one selected by male bourgeois critics) that is transmitted to future generations, rather than those deviant, unrepresentative experiences discoverable in much female, ethnic and working-class writing'.[37] The suggestion, once again, of course, is here that the 'representative experience' (what Johnson's older, more advanced theoretical model called 'general nature') is falsely so called, a sham of class, gender, racial or imperialist interests masquerading as 'general'. Such representativeness appears to blur the boundaries in demarcation disputes. It is not that there can be no communication across time or class, race or gender. Rather the accusation of double-dealing derives from the the uniformity of principle and opinion that is imputed to the past, and this in turn comes from the snobbery and protective sexism of the individual himself. It is a product of that smug part of élite society to which he belongs. The spirit of conduct in which the critic acts is then variously unconscious or actively conspiratorial. But my suggestion has been that this is a false dichotomy in historical thought about Johnson's critical judgment. It can be traced back to the badness of the analogy with the scriptural canon identified by Guillory, Olsen and others. Disowning the canon cannot reflect an intelligent or informed conception of change within the traditions of English literature. Why? - because literature and literary criticism interact and because the canon in the transferred scriptural sense applies to something other than literature. The value of the texts in question is assumed *a priori*. Literary works must be buried 'according to the canon' (in the usage applied by Johnson to the 'canoniz'd bones' of Hamlet's father [*Shakespeare*, 8: 968-69]), and the canon must remain frozen in time, must resist change through the flux of critical and literary history if it is to provide an adequate foil to the 'marginal' works the modern critic prefers. The critical and literary history described by the canon has then as its function the polemical characteristics of a necessary myth.[38]

For if Johnson had swallowed the version of critical and literary history imputed to the critical past by Moi and Herrnstein-Smith, then he would simply have transmitted the past, hermeneutically sealed. What we find, in fact, is Johnson's own radical inclination to expose the distinctions between synchronic and diachronic consensus. We discover that Johnson had a highly developed interest in stripping out the illusions of both past and contemporary taste. Had Johnson been willing to accept a pre-existing canon (on the same terms he accepted as an act of Faith the sacred texts of the Bible) he would likewise not have resisted the 'petty cavils' of Dennis, Rymer and other 'petty minds' on the value of Shakespeare. And in the light of the charge that the canon communicates a false sense of 'representative experience', a faked or coerced uniformity demystified as oppression, then the move that Johnson made to 'rejoice to concur with the common reader' at the conclusion of his 'Life of Gray' would not appear the exceptional judgment that it undoubtedly is in that 'Life' (*Lives*, 3: 441). Equally the attack that Johnson launched upon *Lycidas* in a 'Life of Milton', where *Paradise Lost* approaches the status of Homer, would have failed to produce the outcry that it did (*Lives*, 1: 163-64); and if Johnson's practice of literary and critical history merely *instanced* the theory of Herrnstein-Smith, where 'those with cultural power tend to be members of socially, economically, and politically established classes', and where 'the texts that survive will tend to be those that appear to reflect and reinforce establishment ideologies',[39] then Johnson would have had no significant motive to revive the reputation of Cowley. Readers today would then have nothing to learn from Johnson. Whether or not it is accurate to speak of Johnson as a 'bourgeois' critic, and whether Cowley's poetry does indeed reflect and reinforce 'established ideologies' (Royalism and so forth), arguments in both directions and on both counts could probably be made. In any event, Johnson's critical intervention in his 'Life of Cowley' has failed to ensure that Cowley's poetical text should survive.

But this is a missed opportunity for the cultural radicals; for just as a large part of a revivalist interest in Cowley's poetry might have rested on the analysis of its implied attitude to women, we have seen how Johnson's comments on Cowley's *Mistress* (and on 'The Chronicle') suggest in acute form the question of how a more consciously gendered reading of his literary criticism might take place.[40] Moreover the question raised for anti-canonical feminist materialism by Johnson's criticism of Cowley is not confined to the attitude *to* women - as an entire half of the human race - adopted by Samuel Johnson, but rather the masculinity, femininity or androgyny of Johnson's judicial statements themselves,[41] and how a definition of criticism conscious of gender might deal with Johnson's praise of Cowley's 'gaiety of fancy', with his lightness of touch, and with his unsolemnity, when concepts of masculine and feminine are persistently *a priori*. We have seen that Johnson complains of the love poems in Cowley's *Mistress* that they are cold. Their addressees exist only as the distant and denatured objects of the poet's affections, and an appropriating line is drawn around them. That Johnson is reacting *against* the imaginative strategies Cowley used to position the fictional women in his poems is reflected in his distaste for the *Mistress* and the vivid imagery of 'sluggish frigidity' whereby women inspire the same reactions as flowers. But if applying feminist critical frameworks to Johnsonian criticism would at the same time highlight his highly aggressive tone in judging the *Mistress*, it may be difficult to say whether a feminist criticism would favour Johnson's articulate statement of distaste for Cowley's collection, or would acknowledge a culpable failure of empathy with the poems.

In the case of 'The Chronicle', the poem is a list of all the girls in Cowley's heroically fantasized sexual past; the women are seen as a succession of different systems of personal control over men, and Cowley reduces his women to the level of names. Is Johnson's attitude *here* misogynistic?[42] Yes, if we take the lightness that Johnson finds in his judgment of Cowley as a sympathetic reflection of a tritely superior attitude - one that we ought to condemn moralistically on feminist grounds; no, if we want our literary judgments of English poetry free of the 'manly' censorious note that is commonly associated with Johnson's canonical tastes.[43] The ability of the critic to rise in aesthetic sympathy with the poet will point in one direction; the failure to condemn the poet for his moral offence against equity of gender, or female priority, may point in quite another.

The fact is, either way, that Johnson endorsed, or canonized, nothing in his literary criticism that he did not also express explicit or implicit reservations about. Much eighteenth-century poetry has perished in the fire of his ridicule. The texts that have survived since Johnson's day have done so often in the teeth of his critical disapproval. The texts that have not survived, as distinct from other texts by the same authors who overall have, may not have needed the active connivance of a major literary critic to wither and die, reduced to the 'phantoms that cannot be wounded' (*Rambler* 4: 134). Moreover the conception of the literary and critical past canonized by 'the established classes' is impossible to reconcile with the very vocal body of opinion that arose to defend Shakespeare, Milton and Gray, and many of the poets in the *Lives*. The agency of canon formation may dampen protest. But the nature of Johnson's judgments is perpetually controversial. They neither reflect nor promote the consensuality of any class, established or otherwise. Rather they provoke a shrill crescendo of massive admiration and massive dissent. Thus the criticism of Johnson has traditionally come from every possible angle and is self-cancelling in its conflicting claims.

By which I mean this: That Johnson can be seen as at one time the idealizing champion of the eighteenth-century poets *over and against* the seventeenth century; at another he is confined within the seventeenth-century modernizing model of refinement. It is here that he is slave to the philosophical conceptions of Bacon and Locke, the French criticism of Rapin and Boileau or the Waller-Denham-Dryden poetical line. At one moment Johnson is the founding father of a nationalist élitism based on the sanctification of Shakespeare - the symbol of the bourgeois values that have bedevilled the post-materialist moral and political world of Herrnstein-Smith. At another Johnson is grossly disrespectful toward Shakespeare. He is an enlightenment rationalist numb to the dramatic. Johnson on these grounds is thought to have downgraded Shakespeare vis-à-vis the linguistic polish of the eighteenth-century poets, with their superior model of tragedy, and their consonance with Johnson's personal practice. Johnson on the one hand attracts criticism for his own criticism of Milton as an extremely unpleasant man, the Republican and Puritan tenacious of political and religious views deeply hostile to his. On the other we can still hold Johnson to account for being too liberal and bourgeois in the *Lives*. He seizes on the human interest of each of his subjects. He links literature to events in individuals' lives in their finitude and imperfection, rich, poor, middling, Whig, Tory, Puritan, Royalist, monumental or minor.

Seen in this light, the cultural radicals' account of the critical past as a process of inventing canons that we in the present inherit blindly - till our eyes are opened by post-materialist Critical Theory - rests on self-exempting assumptions. These assumptions are concerned with what membership of a socially, politically and economically 'established' class might at any time actually be, and they evince a rather naïve conception - in terms of historical theory - of the relationship of the eighteenth-century critical text to the universe of its social context. This, the sum total of everything going on in society in a thousand different places and for a thousand different reasons at the time that Johnson composed the *Preface* or the *Lives*, is narrowed by an arbitrary criterion of relevance. The drama of contrasting cultural categories thus plays out yet again a very familiar mode of eighteenth-, nineteenth- and twentieth-century misrepresentation of Johnson, and a very unradical teleology of triumphal revelation. But what this account of the critical past also suggests is the sentimental optimism of the scriptural genre to which this radical discourse is itself in thrall. The canonical pieties of social control are read back into a critical past once inhabited by Samuel Johnson. They ensure that what is taken from the Johnsonian past in no way exceeds what the present brings to it. Such an idea of the canon does not suggest that the texts discussed by Johnson are connected symmetrically to the 'canonical' texts that are taught in the schools. But since such texts are literary works, human and not sacred artefacts, Johnson of all people would have found it amazing if they were.

Notes

[1] Johnson planned, but never wrote, a history of criticism. Boswell's catalogue of Johnson's 'Designs' includes a projected 'History of Criticism as it relates to judging of Authors from Aristotle to the present age. An account of the rise and improvements of that art, of the different Opinions of Authours ancient and Modern' (*Boswell's Life of Johnson*, 4: 381). For a full discussion of these unfinished or unstarted projects see Paul Tankard, '"That Great Literary Projector": Samuel Johnson's *Designs* of Projected Works', *AJ* 13 (2002), 103-80. Bate has pointed out that Johnson's project for a critical history was 'a strangely novel ambition to find in any writer before the later nineteenth century'. See *The Achievement of Samuel Johnson*, 180.

[2] Greg Clingham, *Johnson, Writing, Memory* (Cambridge: Cambridge University Press, 2002), 160.

[3] *Essays*, 1: 197.

[4] R.D. Hume, *Dryden's Criticism* (Ithaca and London: Cornell University Press, 1970) prints in the front-matter 'A Chronological List of Dryden's Major Critical Essays' which admits the 'Life of Plutarch' (1683). Edward Pechter, in *Dryden's Classical Theory of Literature* (Cambridge: Cambridge University Press, 1975) also includes 'literary biography' amongst Dryden's critical work (1).

[5] *Essays*, 2: 285.

[6] See 'History as Re-Enactment of Past Experience', in *The Idea of History*, 282-302. As observed in chapter 1, Collingwood's conception of 're-enactment' as a basis for knowing the past is discussed in detail by Paul Ricoeur, 'The Reality of the Past', *Time and Narrative*, 3: 142-56.

[7] See Hume: Dryden 'can maintain clear critical standards while remaining free of the fatal inflexibility which dogged his more literal-minded contemporaries' (230).

[8] Kermode recruits Dryden to the cause of those amongst critics of Shakespeare who - like Johnson - have remained 'on this side idolatry'. Preface, *Shakespeare's Language* (London: Allen Lane, 2000), viii.

[9] *Essays*, 2: 274-76.

[10] See, for example, *A Comparison between the Eloquence of Demosthenes and Cicero*, trans. anon. (Oxford, 1672); *Observations on the Poems of Homer and Vergil*, trans. John Davies); *The Comparison of Plato and Aristotle* (London, 1672 (London, 1673), trans. John Dancer; *Monsieur Rapin's Comparison of Thucydides and Livy*, trans. T. Taylor (Oxford, 1694).

[11] See *Les entretiens d'Ariste et d'Eugene*, 2nd ed. (Amsterdam, 1671) and *La manière de bien penser dans les ouvrages d'esprit*, 2nd ed. (Amsterdam, 1692).

[12] For details of the Johnson-Pope link in this concatenation see my 'Johnson's "Life of Pope" and Pope's Preface to the *Iliad*', *N&Q*, n.s. 27, no. 1 (February 1980): 50.

[13] R.S. Crane, *The Idea of the Humanities*, 2: 174-75. Both Hume and Pechter express

indebtedness to this essay, but do not, it seems to me, sufficiently develop its implications for their practice as critical historians.

[14] The comparison suggested on these grounds is with Johnson's Preface to *A Dictionary of the English Language* (1755). There, by an act of self-fashioning, Johnson had lifted the drudgery of compiling and introducing a dictionary above the mundane. Here too, in a different context, Hayden White writes of the 'Ironic mode of conceiving history' in the Enlightenment, and claims that 'the historiography of the age was necessarily impelled toward a purely Satirical mode of representation, in the same way that the literature of the age in general was'. See *Metahistory: The Historical Imagination in Nineteenth-Century Europe* (Baltimore and London: Johns Hopkins University Press, 1973), 65-66.

[15] Harold Bloom, *The Anxiety of Influence: A Theory of Poetry*, 2nd ed. (New York and Oxford: Oxford University Press, 1997). David Perkins in *Is Literary History Possible?* includes Bloom among the theorists of literary-historical 'immanent change', where there is 'the desire or necessity of writers to produce works unlike those of previous writers' (161), and where influence takes place 'not by reading but by misreading, by 'misprision' or misunderstanding the texts of the past' (169).

[16] In Montaigne, see, for example, 'Of Experience', *Essays*, 3, esp. 466-87, and the following: 'We must learn to suffer what we cannot evade. Our Life, like the harmony of the World, is compos'd of contrary things, of several Notes, sweet and harsh, sharp and flat, spritely and solemn; and the *Musician* who should only affect one of these, what would he be able to do? He must know how to make use of them all, and to mix them; and we likewise, the *goods* and *evils* which are consubstantial with Life: Our Being cannot subsist without this mixture, and the one are no less necessary to it than the other' (3: 510-11).

[17] See 'Human Nature and Human History', *The Idea of History*, esp. 226-27.

[18] See *Autobiography and Literary Essays* (1981), ed. John M. Robson and Jack Stillinger, *Collected Works of John Stuart Mill*, 33 vols. (Toronto and London: University of Toronto Press and Routledge, 1963-91), 1: esp. 53. Cf. Berlin, 'John Stuart Mill and the Ends of Life', *Four Essays on Liberty*, 184.

[19] Michel de Certeau, *The Writing of History*, 4. Other references are to H.R. Jauss, 'Literary History as a Challenge to Literary Theory', *Toward an Aesthetic of Reception*, 3-45; R.G. Collingwood, *The Idea of History* (1946); Hans-Georg Gadamer, *Truth and Method*, trans. Joel Weinsheimer and Donald G. Marshall (London: Sheed and Ward, 1989).

[20] Jacques Derrida, *Glas*, trans. John P. Leavey and Richard Rand (Lincoln and London: University of Nebraska Press, 1986), 1.

[21] John Guillory, *Cultural Capital: the Problem of Literary Canon Formation* (Chicago: Chicago University Press, 1993), 6.

[22] Harold Bloom, *The Western Canon*, Chapter 8, 183-202.

[23] Stefan Collini, 'Grievance Studies': How Not to Do Cultural Criticism', *English Pasts: Essays in History and Culture* (Oxford: Oxford University Press, 1999), Chapter 13, 252-68.

[24] Charles Altieri, 'An Idea and Ideal of a Literary Canon', *Canons*, ed. Robert von Hallberg (Chicago and London: University of Chicago Press), 41.

[25] Robert DeMaria, Jr., *The Life of Samuel Johnson*, 119. Alvin Kernan, *Samuel Johnson and the Impact of Print* (Princeton: Princeton University Press, 1987), has written on the canonizing role of Johnson's Literary Club. Kernan quotes Johnson's remarks from the *Preface to Shakespeare* to show that 'Fame and a place in the canon' are determined by no other 'test ... than the length of duration and continuance of esteem' and that 'What mankind have long possessed they have often examined and compared, and if they persist to value the possession, it is because frequent comparisons have confirmed opinion in its favour' (226).

[26] Barbara Hermstein-Smith, *Contingencies of Value: Alternative Perspectives for Critical Theory* (Cambridge, MA: Harvard University Press, 1988), 51. The emphasis on 'please long' is mine.

[27] Johnson may in turn have been echoing Pope. Cf. the 'Argument' to 'Epistle 4: To Richard Boyle, Earl of Burlington' (1735): 'How men are disappointed in their most expensive undertakings, for want of this true Foundation, without which [Nature] nothing can please long, if at all....' *Epistles*, 129.

[28] James E.G. Zetzel, 'Re-creating the Canon: Augustan Poetry and the Alexandrian Past', in *Canons*, 127, note 1, records that David Ruhnken, in 1768, 'was the first to use the word "canon" to describe a selective list of literary works'.

[29] Anne McDermott, 'Johnson's *Dictionary* and the Canon: Authors and Authority', *The Yearbook of English Studies* 28 (1998): 65.

[30] James Chandler, 'The Pope Controversy: Romantic Poets and the English Canon', *Canons*, 210.

[31] See Clement Hawes, 'Johnson's Cosmopolitan Nationalism', in *Johnson Re-Visioned*, 37-63.

[32] Stein Haugom Olsen, 'The Canon and Artistic Failure', *BJA* 41, no. 3 (July 2001), 276n.

[33] Olsen, 276n.

[34] W.W. Robson, 'The Definition of Literature', *The Definition of Literature and other essays* (Cambridge: Cambridge University Press, 1982), 2.

[35] Charles H. Hinnant *'Steel for the Mind': Samuel Johnson and Critical Discourse* (Newark, London and Toronto: University of Delaware Press and Associated University Presses), 210.

[36] Trevor Ross, *The Making of the English Literary Canon: From the Middle Ages to the Late Eighteenth Century* (Montreal and Kingston: McGill-Queen's University Press, 1998), 270.

[37] Toril Moi, *Sexual/Textual Politics: Feminist Literary Theory* (London and New York: Methuen, 1985), 78.

[38] Like much in history, its purpose is not just to explain but also to justify the present. It enacts a supremacist progress of criticism from the state of error in the past to today's pinnacle of correctness.

[39] *Contingencies of Value*, 51. 'We don't *choose* the great literature', writes Ian Robinson, 'it chooses itself on merit'. *The English Prophets: A Critical Defence of English Criticism* (Denton: Edgeways, 2001), 314.

[40] The question of Johnson's sexual politics (in relation to *Irene*, the *Rambler* and to *Rasselas*) has been most lucidly discussed by Kathleen Nulton Kemmerer, *'A Neutral Being Between the Sexes': Samuel Johnson's Sexual Politics* (Lewisburg: Bucknell University Press, 1998). At the same time, the pioneering work of such Johnsonian scholars as James G. Basker and Isobel Grundy over an alleged Johnsonian misogyny has made significant strides; but it is likely to lead to the most interesting conclusions when able to move beyond an ungainsayable refutation of the prejudice instanced by Johnson's famous remark that a woman preaching is like a dog walking on its hind legs. A further stage would be to grapple with the sexuality of Johnson's critical textuality, to interpret his metaphors, tone, manner and language in gendered terms. See Basker, 'Multicultural Perspectives: Johnson, Race, and Gender', *Johnson Re-Visioned*, 64-79, and 'Dancing Dogs, Women Preachers and the Myth of Johnson's Mysogyny', *AJ* 3 (1990): 63-90; Grundy, 'Samuel Johnson as Patron of Women', *AJ* 1 (1987): 59-77.

[41] This should not seem at all strange or unprecedented. The gendered nature of Coleridge's critical text has recently been discussed by Tim Fulford in his chapter on 'Masculinity in Coleridge's Criticism', *Romanticism and Masculinity: Gender, Politics and Poetics in the Writings of Burke, Coleridge, Cobbett, Wordsworth, De Quincey and Hazlitt* (Houndmills: Macmillan, 1999).

[42] '"Men", said Johnson, "know that women are an over-match for them, and therefore they choose the weakest or most ignorant'. *Boswell's Life of Johnson*, 5: 226.

[43] 'Manly' is among the 'several favourite epithets' or cant critical terms of Dick Minim, satirized by Johnson in the *Idler* 61 (192).

Bibliography

Amigoni, David. '"Borrowing Gargantua's Mouth": biography, Bakhtin and grotesque discourse - James Boswell, Thomas Carlyle and Leslie Stephen on Samuel Johnson', in *Victorian Culture and the Idea of the Grotesque*. Ed. Colin Trodd, Paul Barlow and David Amigoni. Aldershot: Ashgate, 1999, 21-36.

Anderson, Robert. *The Life of Samuel Johnson LLD. with Critical Observations on his Works*. London, 1795.

anon. *Pope Alexander's Supremacy and Infallibility Examin'd*. London, 1729.

Arac, Jonathan. *Critical Genealogies: Historical Situations for Postmodern Literary Studies*. New York: Columbia University Press, 1987.

Arnold, Matthew. 'Hamlet Once More'. *Pall Mall Gazette*. 23 October 1884. Rpt. in *Selected Criticism of Matthew Arnold*. London: New English Library, 1972, 309-10.

Arnold, Matthew. Ed. *The Six Chief Lives from Johnson's 'Lives of the Poets'*. London: Macmillan, 1879.

Athenaeum, The. October 1831, 632-33.

Bainbridge, Beryl. *According to Queeney*. London: Little, Brown, 2001.

Barnes, Julian. *England, England*. London: Picador/Jonathan Cape, 1998.

Barthes, Roland. 'What Is Criticism?' *Critical Essays*. Trans. Richard Howard. Evanston: Northwestern University Press, 1972.

Barthes, Roland. *Le Plaisir du texte*. Paris: Éditions du Seuil, 1973.

Basker, James G. 'Dancing Dogs, Women Preachers and the Myth of Johnson's Mysogyny'. *AJ* 3 (1990): 63-90.

Basker, James G. 'Multicultural Perspectives: Johnson, Race, and Gender.' In *Johnson Re-Visioned: Looking Before and After*. Ed. Philip Smallwood. Lewisburg: Bucknell University Press, 2001, 64-79.

Bate, W. J. *The Achievement of Samuel Johnson*. New York: Oxford University Press, 1955.

Berlin, Isaiah. 'Historical Inevitability'. 1954. *Four Essays on Liberty*. Oxford: Oxford University Press, 1969.

Blake, William. *William Blake's Writings*. Ed. G.E. Bentley, Jr. 2 vols. Oxford: Clarendon Press, 1978.

Bloom, Harold. *The Anxiety of Influence: A Theory of Poetry*. 2nd ed. 1973. New York and Oxford: Oxford University Press, 1997.

Bloom, Harold. *The Western Canon: The Books and School of the Ages*. New York: Harcourt Brace, 1994.

Bochner, Jay. 'Shakespeare in France: A Survey of Dominant Opinion, 1733-1830'. *Revue de Littérature Comparée* 39 (1965): 44-65.

Boileau-Despréaux, Nicolas. *L'Art Poétique*. 1674. Trans. Sir William Soame and John Dryden. London, 1683.

Boileau-Despréaux, Nicolas. *The Works of Monsieur Boileau*. Trans. J. Ozell et al. 3 vols. London, 1711-13.

Boswell, James. *Boswell's Life of Johnson*. Ed. George Birkbeck Hill and L.F. Powell, 6 vols. Oxford: Clarendon Press, 1934-50.

Bouhours, Dominique. *La manière de bien penser dans les ouvrages d'esprit*, 2nd. ed. Amsterdam, 1692.

Bouhours, Dominique. *Les entretiens d'Ariste et d'Eugene*, 2nd. ed. Amsterdam, 1671.

Bowie, Andrew. *From Romanticism to Critical Theory*. London: Routledge, 1997.

Brown, Alan. 'On the Subject of Practical Criticism'. *CQ* 28, no. 4 (1999): 293-327.

Brownell, Morris. '"Dr Johnson's Ghost": Genesis of a Satirical Engraving'. *HLQ* 50, no. 4 (1987): 338-57.

Brownell, Morris. *Samuel Johnson and the Arts*. Oxford: Oxford University Press, 1989.

Churchill, Charles. *The Ghost*. 1762. *The Poetical Works of Charles Churchill*. Ed. Douglas Grant. Oxford: Oxford University Press, 1956.

Clark, J.C.D. *Samuel Johnson: Literature, religion and English cultural politics from the Restoration to Romanticism*. Cambridge: Cambridge University Press, 1994.

Clark, Jonathan and Howard Erskine-Hill. Eds. *Samuel Johnson in Historical Context*. Houndmills: Palgrave, 2002.

Clark, Norma. *Dr Johnson's Women*. London and New York: Hambleton and London, 2000.

Clifford, James L. and Donald J. Greene. *Samuel Johnson: A Survey and Bibliography of Critical Studies*. Minneapolis: University of Minnesota Press, 1970.

Clingham, Greg. 'Resisting Johnson'. In *Johnson Re-Visioned: Looking Before and After*. Ed. Philip Smallwood. Lewisburg: Bucknell University Press, 19-36.

Clingham, Greg. Ed. *The Cambridge Companion to Samuel Johnson*. Cambridge: Cambridge University Press, 1997.

Clingham, Greg. *Johnson, Writing, Memory*. Cambridge: Cambridge University Press, 2002.

Coleridge, Samuel Taylor. *Coleridge's Shakespearean Criticism*. Ed. T.M. Raysor. 2 vols. London: Constable, 1930.

Collingwood, R.G. *The Idea of History*. 1946. Rev. ed. Jan van der Dussen. Oxford: Oxford University Press, 1993.

Collingwood, R.G. *The New Leviathan or Man, Society, Civilization and Barbarism*. 1942. Rev. ed. David Boucher. Oxford: Oxford University Press, 1992.

Collini, Stefan. 'Grievance Studies: How Not to Do Cultural Criticism'. In *English Pasts: Essays in History and Culture*. Oxford: Oxford University Press, 1999, 252-68.

Collini, Stefan. 'How the Critic came to be King'. *TLS*. 9th August 2000.

Cowley, Abraham. *Select Works*. Ed. Richard Hurd. London, 1772.

Cowley, Abraham. *The Collected Works of Abraham Cowley*. Ed. Thomas O. Calhoun et al. Newark: University of Delaware Press, 1989-.

Cowley, Abraham. *Works*. London, 1681.

Cowper, William. *The Correspondence of William Cowper*. Arranged by Thomas Wright. 4 vols. London: Hodder and Stoughton, 1904.

Crabb Robinson, Henry. *Diary*. In *Coleridge's Shakespearean Criticism*. Ed. T.M. Raysor. London: Constable, 1930.

Crane, R.S. *The Idea of the Humanities and other essays Critical and Historical*. 2 vols. Chicago and London: University of Chicago Press, 1967.

Critical Review, The. 20 (November 1765).

Damrosch Jr. Leopold. *Samuel Johnson and the Tragic Sense*. Princeton: Princeton University Press, 1972.

Damrosch Jr. Leopold. *The Uses of Johnson's Criticism*. Charlottesville: University of Virginia Press, 1976.

Davis, Philip. *In Mind of Johnson: A Study of Johnson the Rambler*. London: Athlone Press, 1989.

De Certeau, Michel, *The Writing of History*. Trans. Tom Conley. New York: Columbia University Press, 1988.

DeMaria Jr., Robert. *The Life of Samuel Johnson: A Critical Biography*. Oxford: Blackwell, 1993.

Dennis, John. *The Critical Works of John Dennis*. Ed. Edward Niles Hooker. 2 vols. Baltimore: Johns Hopkins University Press, 1939-43.

Derrida, Jacques. *Glas*. Trans. John P. Leavey and Richard Rand. Lincoln and London: University of Nebraska Press, 1986.

Donald, Diana. *The Age of Caricature: Satirical Prints in the Age of George III*. London: Yale University Press, 1996.

Duport, Paul. *Essais Littéraires sur Shakspeare*. 2 tom. Paris, 1828.

Dryden, John. *Of Dramatic Poesy and Other Critical Essays*. Ed. George Watson. 2 vols. London: Everyman, 1962.

Dryden, John. *The Poems of John Dryden*. Ed. James Kinsley. 4 vols. Oxford: Clarendon Press, 1958.

Eagleton, Terry. *Literary Theory: An Introduction*. Oxford: Blackwell, 1983.

Edinger, William. *Johnson and Detailed Representation: The Significance of the Classical Sources*. English Literary Studies Monograph Series, no. 72. Victoria, B.C.: University of Victoria, 1997.

Edinger, William. *Samuel Johnson and Poetic Style*. Chicago and London: University of Chicago Press, 1977.

Eliot, George. 'Worldliness and Other-Worldliness: The Poet Young'. 1857. *Essays of George Eliot*. Ed. Thomas Pinney. London: Routledge and Kegan Paul, 1963, 335-85.

Eliot, T.S. 'John Dryden'. 1921. In *Selected Essays*. London: Faber and Faber, 1932, 305-16.

Eliot, T.S. 'Johnson as Critic and Poet'. 1944. In *On Poetry and Poets*. London: Faber and Faber, 1957, 162-92.

Eliot, T.S. 'Tradition and the Individual Talent'. 1919. In *Selected Essays*. London: Faber and Faber, 1932, 13-22.

Elys, Edmund. *An Exclamation to All those that love the Lord Jesus in sincerity, against an apology written by an ingenious person for Mr. Cowley's lascivious and profane verses*. London, 1670.

Evans, Scott D. *Samuel Johnson's 'General Nature': Tradition and Transition in Eighteenth-Century Discourse*. Newark: University of Delaware Press, 1999.

Fruman, Norman. *The Damaged Archangel*. New York: George Braziller, 1971.

Fulford, Tim. *Romanticism and Masculinity: Gender, Politics and Poetics in the Writings of Burke, Coleridge, Cobbett, Wordsworth, De Quincey and Hazlitt*. Houndmills: Macmillan, 1999.

Fussell, Paul. *Samuel Johnson and the Life of Writing*. London: Chatto and Windus, 1972.

Gadamer, Hans-Georg. *Truth and Method*. 2nd. rev. ed. Trans. Joel Weinsheimer and Donald G. Marshall. London: Sheed and Ward, 1989.

Geller, Jaclyn. 'The Unnarrated Life: Samuel Johnson, Female Friendship, and the Rise of the Novel'. In *Johnson Re-Visioned: Looking Before and After*. Ed. Philip Smallwood. Lewisburg: Bucknell University Press, 80-98.

George, Dorothy Mary. *Hogarth to Cruickshank: Social Change in Graphic Satire*. London: Allen Lane, 1967.

Gillray, James. *The Works of James Gillray from the Original Prints with the addition of many subjects not before collected*. London, 1849.

Griffin, Robert J. *Wordsworth's Pope*. Cambridge: Cambridge University Press, 1995.

Griffiths, Elizabeth. *The Morality of Shakespeare's Drama Illustrated*. London, 1775.

Grundy, Isobel. 'On Reading Johnson for Laughs'. *The New Rambler* (1978): 21-25.

Grundy, Isobel. 'Samuel Johnson as Patron of Women'. *AJ* 1(1987): 59-77.

Guillory, John. *Cultural Capital: the Problem of Literary Canon Formation*. Chicago: University of Chicago Press, 1993.

Guizot, François Pierre Guillaume. *Shakespeare et son temps*. Paris, 1852.

Gunnell, Doris. *Stendhal et l'Angleterre*. Paris: Charles Bosse, 1909.

Hallberg, Robert von. Ed. *Canons*. Chicago and London: University of Chicago Press, 1983.

Harris, Wendell V. Ed. *Beyond Poststructuralism*. University Park, PA: Penn State University Press, 1996.

Hawes, Clement. 'Johnson's Cosmopolitan Nationalism'. In *Johnson Re-Visioned: Looking Before and After*. Ed. Philip Smallwood. Lewisburg: Bucknell University Press 37-63.

Hazlitt, William. *The Complete Works of William Hazlitt*. Ed P.P. Howe. 21 vols. Suffolk: Chaucer Press, 1930.

Hédelin, François (l'Abbé d'Aubignac). *The Whole Art of the Stage made English*. London, 1684.

Hill, Draper. *Mr. Gillray the Caricaturist: A Biography*. Greenwich, Conn: Greenwood Press, 1965.

Hinman, Robert B. *Abraham Cowley's World of Order*. Cambridge, MA: Harvard University Press, 1960.

Hinnant, Charles H. *'Steel for the Mind': Samuel Johnson and Critical Discourse*. Newark, London and Toronto: University of Delaware Press and Associated University Presses, 1994.

Hopkins, David and Tom Mason. Eds. *Abraham Cowley: Selected Poems*. Manchester: Carcanet Press, 1994.

Hopkins, David. *John Dryden*. Cambridge: Cambridge University Press, 1986.

Horace. *The Art of Poetry*. Trans. Daniel Bagot. Edinburgh and London: Blackwood, 1863.

Houston, Percy H. *Doctor Johnson: A Study in Eighteenth Century Humanism*. Cambridge MA: Harvard University Press, 1923.

Hume, David. *The History of England, from the Invasion of Julius Caesar to the Revolution in 1688*. 8 vols. London, 1770.

Hume, R. D. *Dryden's Criticism*. Ithaca and London: Cornell University Press, 1970.

Hunt, James Henry Leigh. *Leigh Hunt's Dramatic Criticism 1808-1831*. Ed. L.H. Houtchens and C. W. Houtchens. New York: Columbia University Press, 1949.

Jauss, Hans Robert. 'Literary History as a Challenge to Literary Theory', *Toward an Aesthetic of Reception*. Trans. Timothy Bahti (Minneapolis: University of Minnesota Press, 1982), 3-45.

Johnson, Samuel. *A Dictionary of the English Language*. London, 1755.

Johnson, Samuel. Ed. *The Plays of William Shakespeare*, 2nd. ed. 10 vols. London: C. Bathhurst, 1778.

Johnson, Samuel. *Lives of theEnglish Poets*. Ed. George Birkbeck Hill, 3 vols. Oxford: Clarendon Press, 1905.

Johnson, Samuel. *The Letters of Samuel Johnson*. Ed. Bruce Redford. 5 vols. Oxford: Clarendon Press, 1992-94.

Johnson, Samuel. *The Works of Johnson LL.D*. Ed. Arthur Murphy. 12 vols. London: T. Longman, 1792.

Johnson, Samuel. *The Yale Edition of the Works of Samuel Johnson*, Gen. Ed. John H. Middendorf. New Haven and London: Yale University Press 1958-.

Keast, W.R. 'Johnson's Criticism of the Metaphysical Poets'. *ELH* 17 (1950): 59-70.

Kemmerer, Kathleen Nulton. 'A Neutral Being Between the Sexes': Samuel Johnson's Sexual Politics. Lewisburg: Bucknell University Press, 1998.

Kenrick, William. 'The Plays of William Shakespeare'. *Monthly Review* 33 (October 1765): 285-301. (November 1765): 374-89.

Kermode, Frank. *Shakespeare's Language*. London: Allen Lane, 2000.

Kernan, Alvin. *Samuel Johnson and the Impact of Print*. Princeton: Princeton University Press, 1987.

Knight, G. Wilson. *The Wheel of Fire: Interpretations of Shakespearean Tragedy*. London: Methuen, 1972.

Korshin, Paul J. 'The Essay and *The Rambler'*. In *The Cambridge Companion to Samuel Johnson*. Ed. Greg Clingham. Cambridge: Cambridge University Press, 1997, 51-66.

Kramnick, Jonathan Brody. 'Reading Shakespeare's Novels: Literary History and Cultural Politics in the Lennox-Johnson Debate'. In *Eighteenth-Century Literary History: An MLQ Reader*. Ed. Marshall Brown. Durham and London: Duke University Press, 1999, 43-67.

Kunisch, J. Ed. G.G. Bredows nachgelassene Schriften. Breslau, 1816.

Lamarque, Peter. *Fictional Points of View*. Ithaca: Cornell University Press, 1996.

Lawrence, D.H. 'John Galsworthy'. In *Phoenix: The Posthumous Papers of D.H. Lawrence*. Ed. Edward D. McDonald. London: Heinemann, 1936, 539-50.

Leavis, F.R. 'Doctor Johnson'. *Kenyon Review* 8 (1946): 640-41.

Leavis, F.R. 'Johnson as Critic'. *Scrutiny* 12, no. 3 (1944): 187-200.

Leavis, F.R. '*Scrutiny*: A Retrospect'. 1963. Rpt. in *Valuation in Criticism and Other Essays*. Ed. G. Singh. Cambridge: Cambridge University Press, 1986, 218-43.

Leavis, F.R. *The Common Pursuit*. 1952. Harmondsworth: Penguin Books, 1969.

Leoni, Michele da. *Tragedie di Shakespeare*. Verona, 1819.

Liebert, Herbert W. *Lifetime Likenesses of Samuel Johnson, reissued with additional plates, to commemorate the two hundred and sixty-fifth birthday of Dr. Samuel Johnson*. Los Angeles: William Andrews Clark Memorial Library, 1974.

Lipking, Lawrence. *Samuel Johnson: the Life of an Author*. Cambridge MA: Harvard University Press, 1998.

Lloyd, Evan. *The Powers of the Pen. A Poem*. 2nd. ed. London, 1768.

Loiseau, Jean. *Abraham Cowley: Sa Vie, Son Oeuvre*. Paris: Didier, 1931.

Lynn, Steven. 'Johnson's Critical Reception'. In *The Cambridge Companion to Samuel Johnson*. Ed. Greg Clingham. Cambridge: Cambridge University Press, 1997, 240-53.

Lynn, Steven. *Samuel Johnson after Deconstruction: Rhetoric and The Rambler*. Carbondale: Southern Illinois University Press, 1992.

Macaulay, Thomas Babington. 'Boswell's Life of Johnson'. *Edinburgh Review* 54, no. 107 (September 1831): 1-38.

Macaulay, Thomas Babington. *Critical and Historical Essays contributed to the Edinburgh Review*. 2nd. ed., 3 vols. London, 1843.

Mack, Maynard. *Alexander Pope: A Life*. New Haven and London: Yale University Press, 1985.

Malone, Edmond. Ed. *The Plays and Poems of William Shakespeare*. 21 vols. London: Rivington, 1821.

Maner, Martin. *The Philosophical Biographer: Doubt and Dialectic in Johnson's Lives of the Poets*. Athens and London: University of Georgia Press, 1988.

Manning, Susan. 'Whatever Happened to Pleasure?' *CQ* 30, no. 3 (2001): 215-32.

Mason, H.A. 'An Introduction to Literary Criticism by way of Sidney's *Apologie for Poetrie'*. *CQ* 12, nos. 2 and 3 (1983): 79-173.

Mason, H.A. *The Tragic Plane*. Oxford: Clarendon Press, 1985.

Mason, H.A. *To Homer through Pope: An Introduction to Homer's Iliad and Pope's Translation*. London: Chatto and Windus, 1972.

Mason, Tom, 'Dryden's Chaucer'. Unpublished doctoral dissertation. University of Cambridge, 1981.

Mason, Tom. 'Cowley and the Wisdom of Anacreon'. *CQ* 19 (1990): 103-37.

Mason, Tom and Adam Rounce. '"Looking before and After"?: Reflections on the Early

Reception of Johnson's Critical Judgments'. In *Johnson Re-Visioned: Looking Before and After*. Ed. Philip Smallwood. Lewisburg: Bucknell University Press 134-66.

McDermott, Anne. 'Johnson's *Dictionary* and the Canon: Authors and Authority'. *The Yearbook of English Studies*, 28 (1998): 44-65.

Mill, John Stuart. *Autobiography and Literary Essays*. 1981. Ed. John M. Robson and Jack Stillinger. *Collected Works of John Stuart Mill*. 33 vols. Toronto and London: University of Toronto Press and Routledge, 1963-91.

Miller, John. *A Course of the Belles Lettres or the Principles of Literature*, *translated from the French*. 4 vols. London, 1761.

Mills, Howard. "'Wonderfully alert word usage'". *CQ* 1, no. 3 (Summer 1966): 298-306.

Moi, Toril. *Sexual/Textual Politics: Feminist Literary Theory*. London and New York: Methuen, 1985.

Money, David. 'Samuel Johnson and the Neo-Latin Tradition'. In *Samuel Johnson in Historical Context*. Ed. Jonathan Clark and Howard Erskine-Hill. Houndmills: Palgrave, 2002, 199-221.

Montaigne, Michel de. *Essays of Michael Seigneur de Montaigne*. Trans. Charles Cotton. 3rd ed. 3 vols. London, 1700.

Nethercott, A.H. 'The Reputation of Abraham Cowley (1660-1800)'. *PMLA* 38, (1923): 588-641.

Nisbet, H.B. and Claude Rawson. Eds. *The Cambridge History of Literary Criticism*. Vol. 4: *The Eighteenth Century*. Cambridge: Cambridge University Press, 1997.

Oldmixon, John. *The Arts of Logic and Rhetorick*. London, 1728.

Olsen, Stein Haugom. 'The Canon and Artistic Failure'. *BJA* 41, no. 3 (July 2001): 261-78.

Parker, G.F. *Johnson's Shakespeare*. Oxford: Clarendon Press, 1989.

Pechter, Edward. *Dryden's Classical Theory of Literature*. Cambridge: Cambridge University Press, 1975.

Penny, Nicholas. Ed. *Reynolds*. London: Weidenfeld and Nicholson, 1986.

Perkin, M.R. *Abraham Cowley: A Bibliography*. Folkstone: Dawson, 1977.

Perkins, David. *Is Literary History Possible?* Baltimore and London: Johns Hopkins University Press, 1992.

Peterfreund, Stuart. 'Blake's Attack on Johnson'. *Transactions of the Johnson Society of the North West* 7 (1974): 44-57.

Philips, Katherine. *Poems: By the most deservedly Admired Mrs Katherine Philips: The Matchless Orinda*. London, 1667.

Piozzi, Hester Lynch (Mrs. Thrale). *Anecdotes of the Late Samuel Johnson, LL.D.*, *Johnsonian Miscellanies*. 2 vols. Ed. George Birkbeck Hill. London: Clarendon Press, 1897.

Pope, Alexander, *The Dunciad: An Heroic Poem*. 'The Second Edition in Three Books'. Dublin. Reprinted for A. Dodd, London, 1728.

Pope, Alexander. *The Correspondence of Alexander Pope*. Ed. George Sherburn, 5 vols. Oxford: Clarendon Press, 1956.

Pope, Alexander. *The Dunciad Variorum with the Prolegomena of Scriblerus*. London: A. Dod, 1729.

Pope, Alexander. *The Dunciad with Notes Variorum*. London: 'Printed for Lawton Gilliver', 1729.

Pope, Alexander. *The Twickenham Edition of the Poems of Alexander Pope*. Ed. John Butt et al. 11 vols. London: Methuen, 1939-1969.

Pope, Alexander. *The Works of Alexander Pope, Esq.: In nine Volumes Complete with Notes and Illustrations*. London, 1797.

Powell, L.F. 'The Portraits of Johnson'. In *Boswell's Life of Johnson*. Ed. George Birkbeck

Hill. Rev. L. F. Powell, 6 vols. Oxford: Clarendon Press, 1934-50. Vol. 4, Appendix H, 447-64.

Rapin, René. *A Comparison between the Eloquence of Demosthenes and Cicero.* Trans. anon. Oxford, 1672.

Rapin, René. *Monsieur Rapin's Comparison of Thucydides and Livy.* Trans. T. Taylor. Oxford, 1694.

Rapin, René. *Observations on the Poems of Homer and Vergil.* Trans. John Davies. London, 1672.

Rapin, René. *Reflections on Aristotle.* Trans. Thomas Rymer. London, 1674.

Rapin, René. *The Comparison of Plato and Aristotle.* Trans. John Dancer. London, 1673.

Richardson, William. *A Philosophical Analysis of some of Shakespeare's Remarkable Characters.* 3rd ed. London, 1784.

Ricoeur, Paul. *Time and Narrative.* Trans. Kathleen Blamey and David Pellauer. 3 vols. Chicago and London: University of Chicago Press, 1988.

Robinson, Ian. *The English Prophets: A Critical Defence of English Criticism.* Denton: Edgeways, 2001.

Robson, W.W. *The Definition of Literature and other essays.* Cambridge: Cambridge University Press, 1982.

Ross, Trevor. *The Making of the English Literary Canon: From the Middle Ages to the Late Eighteenth Century.* Montreal and Kingston: McGill-Queen's University Press, 1998.

Rosslyn, Felicity. *Tragic Plots: Aeschylus to Lorca.* Aldershot: Ashgate, 2001.

Rymer, Thomas. *The Critical Works of Thomas Rymer.* Ed. Curt A. Zimansky. New Haven: Yale University Press, 1956.

Sachs, Arieh. *Passionate Intelligence: Imagination and Reason in the Work of Samuel Johnson.* Baltimore: Johns Hopkins University Press, 1967.

Saintsbury, George. *A History of Criticism and Literary Taste in Europe.* 2nd. ed. 3 vols. Edinburgh and London: William Blackwood, 1902-1906.

Schlegel, A.W. *A Course of Lectures on Dramatic Art and Literature.* Trans. John Black. Rev. ed. 1809. London: Bohn's Standard Library, 1846.

Scruton, Roger. *A Short History of Modern Philosophy.* 2nd. ed. London and New York: Routledge, 2002.

Seward, Anna. *The Letters of Anna Seward written between the years 1784 and 1807.* 6 vols. Edinburgh, 1811.

Sherbo, Arthur. *Samuel Johnson: Editor of Shakespeare. With an Essay on The Adventurer.* Urbana: University of Illinois Press, 1956.

Smallwood, Philip. 'Ironies of the Critical Past: Historicizing Johnson's Criticism'. In *Johnson Revisioned: Looking Before and After.* Ed. Philip Smallwood. Lewisburg: Bucknell University Press, 2001, 114-33.

Smallwood, Philip. 'Johnson's Life of Pope and Pope's Preface to the *Iliad*'. *N&Q*, n.s. 27, no. 1 (February 1980): 50.

Smallwood, Philip. 'Shakespeare: Johnson's Poet of Nature'. In *The Cambridge Companion to Samuel Johnson.* Ed. Greg Clingham. Cambridge: Cambridge University Press, 1997, 143-60.

Smallwood, Philip. 'The Johnsonian Monster and the *Lives of the Poets*: James Gillray, Critical History and the Eighteenth-Century Satirical Cartoon'. *BJECS* 25, no. 2 (2002): 217-45.

Smallwood, Philip. Review of *The Cambridge History of Literary Criticism 4: The Eighteenth Century.* In *AJ* 10 (1999): 392-99.

Smith, Barbara Herrnstein. *Contingencies of Value: Alternative Perspectives for Critical Theory.* Cambridge, MA: Harvard University Press, 1988.

Smith, D. Nichol. Ed. *Eighteenth Century Essays on Shakespeare*. 2nd. ed. Oxford: Clarendon Press, 1963.

Spectator, The. Ed. Donald F. Bond. 5 vols. Oxford: Clarendon Press, 1965.

Spector, Robert D. *Samuel Johnson and the Essay*. Westport, Conn.: Greenwood Press, 1997.

Spittal, John Ker. Ed. *Contemporary Criticisms of Dr. Samuel Johnson, his Works, and his Biographers*. London: John Murray, 1923.

Stendhal (Henri Beyle). 'Des Unités de Temps et de Lieu'. In 'Qu'est-ce que le Romanticisme?' (1818). *Oeuvres Complètes*. 35 toms. Ed. Pierre Martino. *Journal Littéraire*. Nouvelle edition. 3 toms. Champion: Paris, Genève, 1970, 3: 106-109.

Stendhal (Henri Beyle). *Racine et Shakspeare* (1823/25), *Oeuvres Complètes* 37.

Stendhal (Henri Beyle). *Traité de L'Art de Faire des Comédies*. In *Journal Littéraire* (1813), 3: 1-53.

Stock, R.D. *Samuel Johnson and Neoclassical Dramatic Theory: The Intellectual Context of the* Preface to Shakespeare. Lincoln: University of Nebraska Press, 1973.

Suard, Jean-Baptiste Antoine. 'Observations sur Shakespeare' (1769). In tom. 4 of *Variétés littéraires*. 4 toms. Lacombe: Paris, 1768-69, 65-94.

Tankard, Paul. '"That Great Literary Projector": Samuel Johnson's *Designs* of Projected Works'. *AJ* 13 (2002): 103-80.

Tinker, C.B. *Dr Johnson and Fanny Burney: Being the Johnsonian Passages from the Works of Mme. D'Arblay*. New York: Andrew Melrose, 1911.

Trotter, David. *The Poetry of Abraham Cowley*. London: Macmillan, 1979.

Venturo, David F. *Johnson the Poet: The Poetic Career of Samuel Johnson*. Newark: University of Delaware Press, 1999.

Voltaire. *Oeuvres Complètes de Voltaire*. 52 toms. Paris: Garnier, 1877-85.

Wain, John. *Johnson as Critic*. London and Boston: Routledge and Kegan Paul, 1973.

Waller, A.R. Ed. *The English Writings of Abraham Cowley*. 2 vols. Cambridge: Cambridge University Press, 1905-106.

Warton, Joseph. 'Observations on Shakespeare's *King Lear*'. *The Adventurer*. 4 vols. London, 1778.

Warton, Joseph. *Essay on the Genius and Writings of Pope*, London, 1756 and 'Volume the Second' 1782.

Warton, Joseph. Ed. *The Works of Alexander Pope, Esq.: In nine Volumes Complete with Notes and Illustrations*. London, 1797.

Watson, George. *The Literary Critics: A Study of English Descriptive Criticism*. Harmondsworth: Penguin Books, 1962.

Wellek, René. *A History of Modern Criticism, 1750-1900*, 1: *The Later Eighteenth Century*. London: Jonathan Cape, 1955.

White, Hayden. *Metahistory: the Historical Imagination in Nineteenth-Century Europe*. Baltimore and London: Johns Hopkins University Press, 1973.

White, Ian. 'On *Rasselas*'. *CQ* 6, no. 1 (July 1972): 6-31.

Wimsatt, W.K. *The Portraits of Alexander Pope*. New Haven and London: Yale University Press, 1965.

Wimsatt, W.K. *The Prose Style of Samuel Johnson*. New Haven: Yale University Press, 1941.

Winn, James A. 'Past and Present in Dryden's *Fables*'. *HLQ* 63 (2000): 157-74.

Wordsworth, William. *Letters of William and Dorothy Wordsworth*. Ed. E. de Selincourt. 2nd. ed. rev. C.L. Shaver. Oxford: Clarendon Press, 1967-69.

Wordsworth, William. *The Poetical Works of William Wordsworth*. Ed. E. de Selincourt and Helen Darbishire. 5 vols. Oxford: Clarendon Press, 1949.

Wordsworth, William. *The Prose Works of William Wordsworth*. Ed. W.J.B. Owen and J.W. Smyser, 3 vols. Oxford: Clarendon Press, 1974.

Works of the English Poets. 3rd ed. London: J. Heath. 1802.

Zetzel, James E.G. 'Re-creating the Canon: Augustan Poetry and the Alexandrian Past'. In *Canons*. Ed. Robert von Hallberg. Chicago and London: Chicago University Press, 1984, 107-29.

Index

Abraham Cowley: A Bibliography
(Perkin) 92
Abraham Cowley's World of Order
(Hinman) 93
According to Queeney (Bainbridge) 113
Achievement of Samuel Johnson (Bate)
36, 91, 93, 153
Addison, Joseph 50, 56, 77-9, 99, 128,
135, 140-142
aesthetics of reception 3; *see also*
reader-reception
Age of Caricature (Donald) 115
Akenside, Mark 149
Alexander, Michael 91
Altieri, Charles 146
Amigoni, David 101
Anderson, Robert 110
anxiety of influence xii, 144
Arac, Jonathan 133
Aristotle 22, 25-6
Arnold, Matthew 2, 32
Ars Poetica (Horace) 61, 102
Arts of Logick and Rhetorick (Oldmixon)
93
Atkins, J.W.H. 4, 57
Austen, Jane 96, 99

Bacon, Francis 30, 152
Bainbridge, Beryl 113
Baridon, Michel 133
Barnes, Julian 112-113
Barthes, Roland 90
Basker, James G. 155
Bate, W.J. 36, 91, 93, 153
Batteux, Abbé 62
Beattie, James 95
Berlin Isaiah x, 6, 10, 13, 144, 154
Blair, Hugh 95
Blake, William 107
Bloom, Harold 95, 119, 144, 146
Bochner, Jay 132
Boileau-Despréaux, Nicolas 58, 68, 78,
88, 95-6, 111, 123, 125-6,
133, 135, 140, 152

Boswell, James 22, 50, 93, 96, 101, 107,
109, 113, 115, 134, 153
Boswell's Life of Johnson 153
Bouhours, Dominique 77, 123, 125-6,
135, 140
Bray, René 4
Brownell, Morris 104, 114, 116
Burney, Fanny 92
Butler, Samuel 23-4, 51

Calhoun, Thomas O. 91
Callendar, James Thomson 107
Cambridge Companion to Johnson
(Clingham) xiii
Cambridge History of Literary Criticism
ix, 2, 4, 8, 9, 10, 11, 114, 131,
133
Carter, Elizabeth 92
Cato (Addison) 26, 50, 56, 79, 140-141
Certeau, Michel de 2, 4, 145
Chandler, James 148
Chaucer, Geoffrey, 40, 59, 138, 148
Churchill, Charles 109
Clark, Jonathan (J.C.D.) xii, 115
Clarke, Norma 34, 92
Cleveland, John 65
Clifford, James L. xiii
Clingham, Greg xiii, 13, 138
Coleridge, Samuel Taylor xii, 2, 54, 96,
127, 130, 134, 136
Collings, Samuel 101, 109
Collingwood, R.G. x, 2, 3, 5, 10, 138,
144-5
Collini, Stefan 146
comedy 38, 42, 43-5, 60, 76, 95, 127-8
Cotton, Charles 32
*Course of Lectures on Dramatic Art and
Literature* (Schlegel) 60
Course of the Belles Lettres (Miller) 62
Cowley, Abraham, xi, 32, 99, 101, 137,
151; *see also* Johnson
Anacreontiques 64, 73-6, 86-7,
89, 92, 133
Davideis 86-9, 92

Miscellanies 64-9, 82, 86-8, 91-2
Mistress 64, 69, 76-85, 87, 92-3,
    151
Pindarique Odes 72, 82, 85, 86-8,
    92
Cowper, William 101, 110-111
Cox, C.B. 35
Crane, R.S. 13, 57, 141
Crashaw, Richard 69, 93
Crews, Frederick 22
Critical Genealogies (Arac)
Critical Review 59-60
Cultural Capital (Guillory) 145-6

d'Aubignac, François Hédelin, Abbé 58
Damaged Archangel (Fruman) 135
Damrosch Jr., Leopold 13, 61-2, 113
Davis, Philip 63
Defence of Poetry (Shelley) 117
Deformities of Samuel Johnson 107, 109
DeMaria, Robert 34, 146
Dennis, John 40, 58, 60, 131, 141, 150
Derrida, Jacques 96, 145
Doctor Johnson (Houston) 132
Donald, Diana 102, 114-115
Donne, John 65, 84, 99
Dr. Johnson's Women (Clarke) 92
Dr. Johnson and Fanny Burney (Tinker)
    114
Dryden x, xii, 2, 6, 21, 25, 28, 32, 35,
    39-40, 51, 61, 88-9, 91, 95-7,
    100-101, 113, 115, 119-120,
    122-5, 130, 133, 138-42, 144-
    5, 148
    'Absalom and Achitophel' 61
    'Author's Apology for Heroic
        Poetry' 138
    compared with Pope 140-141
    Eleonora 58
    Essay on Dramatic Poesy 139
    Fables Ancient and Modern 29-
        30
    Indian Emperor 24, 125
    'The Knight's Tale' 59
    'Preface to *Fables*' 81, 139-40
    The Tempest 97
    translation of Horace 31, 73
        of Lucretius 31, 73
        of Ovid's *Metamorphoses* 29-
        30

Dryden's Classical Theory of Literature
    (Pechter) 153
Dryden's Criticism (Hume) 153
Duport, Paul 132
Dyson, A.E. 35

Eagleton, Terry 4, 58
Edinger, William 3, 93
*Eighteenth Century Essays on
    Shakespeare* (Nichol-Smith)
    36, 62
Eliot, George 33, 99
Eliot, T.S. 1, 14, 51, 91, 96
Elys, Edmund 92
England, England (Barnes) 112-113
English Prophets (Robinson) 155
Erasmus 33, 96, 111
Erskine-Hill, Howard xii
Essais Littéraires sur Shakspeare
    (Duport) 132
Essay on Poetry (Sheffield) 68
Essay on Pope (Warton) 26, 109, 111,
    113
Evans, Scott D. 58

Fielding, Henry 34
Four Essays on Liberty (Berlin) 13, 154
Fruman, Norman 135
Fulford, Tim 155
Function of Criticism (Eagleton) 4
Fussell, Paul 61

Gadamer, Hans-Georg x, 7, 145
Garrick, Eva 92
Geller, Jaclyn 34, 92
George, Mary Dorothy 114
Gerard, Alexander 95
Gillray, James xi, 100-113
Gray, Thomas 109-111, 113, 115, 131,
    149, 152; *see also* Johnson
Greene, Donald J. xiii
Griffin, Robert 134
Griffiths, Elizabeth 61
Grundy, Isobel 34, 92, 113, 155
Guillory, John 145-6, 148, 150
Guizot, François Pierre Guillaume 132
Gunnell, Doris 118

Hagstrum, Jean 12, 99
Hall, John 106

Hammond, James 100
Hart, Kevin xiii
Hawes, Clement 148
Hazlitt, William xii, 58, 60, 129-30, 136
Herrnstein-Smith, Barbara 146-7,
    150, 152
Heyworth, Lawrence 91
Hill, Draper 102, 104, 106
Hinman, Robert B. 91, 93
Hinnant, Charles 99, 149
History and Criticism (LaCapra) 1
History of England (Hume) 92
History of English Literature
    (Alexander) 91
History of English Poetry (Warton
    T.) 148
Hobbes, Thomas 85, 133
Hogarth to Cruickshank (George)
    114
Homer 35, 148, 150, compared with
    Virgil 139-40; *see also* Pope
Hopkins, David 36, 91
Horace 31, 35, 61, 69, 78, 102, 148
Houston, Percy H. 132
Hudibras (Butler) 23-4, 51, 61
Hume, David 92-3, 133
Hume, R.D. 153
Hunt, James Henry Leigh 129
Hunter, William B. 91

Idea of History (Collingwood) 5
Idea of the Humanities (Crane) 13
idealist 2, 3
In Mind of Johnson (Davis) 63
Is Literary History Possible? (Perkins) 7,
    13, 154

Jauss, Hans Robert x, 3, 145
John Dryden (Hopkins) 36
Johnson as Critic (Wain) 58
Johnson the Poet (Venturo) 133
Johnson, Samuel
    conception of genius, 10
    Dedication to *Shakespear Illustrated*
        28, 60
    Dictionary 82, 104, 106, 110, 113,
        147-8, 154
    Idler x, 11, 16, 22-4, 33-5, 50, 76,
        96, 106-107, 134, 156
    Irene 22, 29, 34, 42, 45, 47, 50, 110-
        111, 155

letters, diaries and prayers 90
Lives of the Poets x-xi, 8, 11, 14,
    17, 19, 22, 24-5, 33-5, 44,
    46, 49-51, 64, 69, 79, 93, 97-
    8, 100-101, 104, 107, 109,
    111-113, 115, 117-118, 122,
    125, 138, 141-2, 149, 152
    'Addison' 46, 98-9, 134, 141-2,
        148
    'Akenside' 110
    'Blackmore' 96-7, 115
    'Butler', 40, 51, 61
    'Collins' 110
    'Cowley' xi, 3, 18, 34, 39, 47,
        61, 65-94, 99, 123, 126, 131,
        133, 135, 148, 151
    'Denham' 148
    'Dorset' 97
    'Dryden' 35, 58, 61, 83, 97,
        100, 110, 124, 139, 148
    'Fenton' 148
    'Gay' 97, 112
    'Gray' 96, 100-101, 109-11,
        116, 122, 150
    'Hammond' 99, 100, 110
    'Lyttelton' 110
    'Milton' 62, 91, 100, 104,
        109-11, 114, 116, 122, 134,
        148, 150
    'Otway' 110
    'Philips' 98
    'Pomfret' 148
    'Pope', 10, 18, 21, 35, 37, 39,
        46, 100, 104, 107, 110, 114,
        120-121, 125, 140-141, 148
    'Prior' 46, 100, 109-10, 114,
        116
    'Roscommon' 61, 148
    'Savage' 97
    'Shenstone' 110, 112
    'Smith' 98
    'Sprat' 148
    'Stepney' 148
    'Thomson' 44, 61, 111, 125
    'Waller' 34, 65, 88, 91, 97,
        110, 147-8
    'Yalden' 148
    'Young' 44
*Miscellaneous Observations on
    the Tragedy of Macbeth* 24,
    28, 33

Poems 16, 113
   'The Ant', 119
   London 29, 96-7, 111
   Vanity of Human Wishes 24,
      29, 42, 96-7, 111, 121, 149
   Preface to Shakespeare x-xi, 7, 8,
      10-11, 16-18, 22, 24-5, 27-8,
      33-5, 38-40, 42-3, 45, 47-8,
      50-51, 54-6, 58-9, 61,
      76, 87, 93, 100, 106, 122, 125-
      6, 128-29, 131, 133, 135,
      139-40, 142-4, 152, 154
   Proposals (for his edition of
      Shakespeare) 28
   Rambler x-xi, 8, 11, 15-18, 20-22,
      24-8, 33-5, 40, 42-3, 81, 107,
      152, 155
   Rasselas x, 8, 29-30, 32-3, 38,
      42-3, 50, 58, 90, 106, 113,
      117, 129, 142-3, 155
Johnson, Writing, Memory (Clingham)
   138
Johnson's Shakespeare (Parker) 13
Juvenal 148

Kames, Henry Home, Lord 95
Kant, Immanuel 133
Keast W.R. 91, 99
Keats, John 91
Kemmerer, Kathleen Nulton 34, 155
Kenrick, William 60
Kermode, Frank 139
Kernan, Alvin 154
Kramnick, Jonathan Brody 34
Krutch, J.W. xii, 99

l'Art Poétique (Boileau) 58
LaCapra, Dominick 1
Lamarque, Peter 53, 56, 62
Lawrence, D.H. 6-7
Leavis, F.R., viii, xii-xiii, 3, 6-7, 27, 35,
   149
Lectures on Drama (Schlegel) 127
Lennox, Charlotte 34, 92
Life of Dryden (Scott) 117
Life of Johnson (Anderson) 110
Life of Johnson (Boswell) 50, 93, 96, 107
*Life of Samuel Johnson: A Critical
   Biography* (DeMaria) 34
Lipking, Lawrence 34
Literary Critics (Watson) 4

Literary Theory: An Introduction
   (Eagleton) 58
Locke, John 133, 152
Lodge, David 22
Longinus 140
Lucretius 31, 144, 148; *see also* Dryden
Lynn, Steven xiii, 34
Lyttelton, George 110, 120

Macaulay, Thomas Babington viii, 9, 43,
   100, 102, 109-10, 112, 149
Making of the English Literary Canon
   (Ross) 149
Malone, Edmond 60
Maner, Martin 37
manners 38-9, 40, 42, 44, 58
Manning, Susan 93
Marx, Karl 23
Mason, H.A. 57, 134
Mason, Tom 36, 91-2, 116
McDermott, Anne 148
Metahistory (White) 154
Metamorphoses (Ovid) 29-30
Mill, John Stuart 113, 144
Miller, John 62
Mills, Howard 35
Milton, John 17, 21-2, 28, 36, 50-51,
   64, 87-8, 91, 100-101, 107,
   109-11, 113, 115, 149, 152;
   see also Johnson
   Comus 122
   compared with Philips
   Lycidas 150
   Paradise Lost 150
   Samson Agonistes 25-6, 50
Moi, Toril 149-50
Money, David 133
Montagu, Elizabeth 92
Montaigne, Michel de x, 32-3, 38, 140,
   144
Monthly Review 60, 109
moral purpose 38, 45-6, 55
*Morality of Shakespeare's Drama
   Illustrated* (Griffiths) 61
More, Hannah 92
Morgan, Maurice 95

nature 38-9, 40-44, 46-7, 49, 57, 76, 78,
   95, 119-125, 128-31, 134, 147
Nethercott, Arthur H. 93

Neutral Being Between the Sexes
        (Kemmerer) 155
Newton, John M. 36
Newton, Thomas 91

Oldmixon, John 93
Olsen, Stein Haugom 148-50
On Poetry and Poets (Eliot, T.S.) 14
Osborne, John 114
Otway, Thomas 110
Ovid 29-30, 144, 148

Park, Thomas 109
Parker, G.F. 13, 134-5
Passionate Intelligence (Sachs) 63
pastoral 97, 100, 111; pastoral poetry 18-
        19, 21
Pechter, Edward 153
Penny, Nicholas 115
Perkins, David x, 4, 7, 13, 92, 154
Philips, John 98
Philips, Katherine 91
*Philosophical Analysis of some of
        Shakespeare's Remarkable
        Characters* (Richardson) 37
Philosophical Biographer (Maner) 37
Piozzi, Hester Lynch (Mrs. Thrale) 92,
        96, 101, 106-7, 112-114
Plato 144
Pliny 35
poetical diction xii, 21, 119-120, 131
poetical justice 10, 38, 47, 52, 54-7,
        131-2
Poetry of Abraham Cowley (Trotter) 93
Pope, Alexander, xii, 2, 10, 19, 21, 25,
        28, 39, 51, 88, 91, 95-6, 100-
        101, 107, 110, 113, 119-120,
        122-6, 128, 130, 133
    compared with Dryden 140-141
    Dunciad Variorum 115
    Epistle to Arbuthnot 102, 106
    Epistle to Burlington 107, 155
    Essay on Criticism, 10-11, 22, 69,
        81, 109, 111, 116, 133, 148
    Essay on Man 116
    Preface to Shakespeare 36, 54, 62
    translation of Homer 6, 10, 28,
        35-6, 75, 78, 121-3, 125,
        134, 140
Portraits of Alexander Pope (Wimsatt)
        114

postmodern viii, 145
    postmodern literary history 13
*Practical Criticism of Poetry: A
        Textbook* 35
Prior, Matthew 100, 109; *see also*
        Johnson
Pritchard, Allen 91
Prose Style of Samuel Johnson
        (Wimsatt) 113

Racine et Shakspeare (Stendhal) 118
Rapin, René 58-9, 123, 125-6, 135, 140,
        152
reader-reception 2; reception aesthetics
        145; *see also* aesthetics of
        reception
*Reflections on Aristotle's Treatise of
        Poesie* (Rymer) 58-9
Réflexions (Rapin) 58-9
Revaluation (Leavis) xiii
    Wellek's review of 6
Reynolds (Penny) 115
Reynolds, Sir Joshua 104, 106-7, 112-
        113
Richardson, William 37
Ricoeur, Paul x, 2-3, 5, 8, 10, 13, 153
Robinson, Henry Crabb 128, 135
Robinson, Ian 155
Robson, W.W. 149
Rochester, John Wilmot, Earl of 30
Rogers, Pat 2, 82, 93
Romanticism and Masculinity (Fulford)
        155
Roscommon, Wentworth Dillon, Earl of
        61, 69
Ross, Trevor 149
Rosslyn, Felicity 55
Rounce, Adam 116
Rowlandson, Thomas 109, 101
Rymer, Thomas 35, 40, 58, 125, 131,
        140, 150
    Short View of Tragedy 59-60

Sachs, Arieh 63
Sacred Wood (Eliot, T.S.) 1
Saintsbury, George ix, 4, 8-10, 43
Samuel Johnson (Krutch) xii
Samuel Johnson after Deconstruction
        (Lynn) 34
*Samuel Johnson and Neoclassical
        Dramatic Theory* (Stock) xiii

Samuel Johnson and Poetic Style
(Edinger) 93
Samuel Johnson and the Arts (Brownell)
114
Samuel Johnson and the Culture of
Property (Hart) xiii
Samuel Johnson and the Essay (Spector)
35
Samuel Johnson and the Impact of Print
(Kernan) 154
Samuel Johnson and the Life of Writing
(Fussell) 61-2
Samuel Johnson and the Tragic Sense
(Damrosch) 13, 62
Samuel Johnson: A Survey and
Bibliography of Critical
Studies (Clifford and Greene)
xiii
Samuel Johnson: Literature, religion and
English cultural politics
(Clark) 115
Samuel Johnson: The Life of an Author
(Lipking) 34
Samuel Johnson's 'General Nature'
(Evans) 58
Samuel Johnson's Literary Criticism
(Hagstrum) 12
Savage, Richard 97
Schlegel, A.W. xii, 60, 126-30, 136
Scott, Sir Walter 117, 123
Scrutiny xii
Scruton, Roger xiii
Searle, John 95
Selected Essays (Eliot, T.S.) 91
Seneca 35
Seward, Anna 109-10, 115
Shakespeare et son temps (Guizot)
132
Shakespeare, William 28, 64, 91, 101,
115, 130, 135, 137, 139-40,
144, 148-50, 152
compared with Dorset 97
compared with other dramatists
44
compared with Dryden 24-5
faults of 54
his labour 45
All's Well that Ends Well
Johnson's notes on 60
As You Like It
Johnson's notes on 59

Comedy of Errors
Johnson's notes on 61
Cymbeline
Johnson's notes on 27
Hamlet 24, 55
character of Polonius 41
'celebrated soliloquy' 28
in the essays 21
Johnson's defence of 16
Johnson's notes on 43, 48-9,
150
mix of elements in 43
Voltaire on 59
Henry IV
Johnson's notes on 41, 43, 60-
61
Henry V
Johnson's notes on 58
Henry VI
Johnson's notes on 58
Julius Caesar, Johnson's notes on
40
King John
Johnson's notes on 27-8
King Lear
Johnson's notes on x, 1, 6, 10,
19, 41, 43, 48, 52, 54, 56
Macbeth 26-28
Johnson's notes on 30-31, 43,
45
Measure for Measure
Johnson's notes on 32
Merchant of Venice 106-7
Othello
comparison with *Cato* 50, 79,
140
Johnson's notes on 6, 43-4
Rymer on 59
Richard II
Hazlitt on 58
Johnson's notes on 58
Romeo and Juliet
Johnson's notes on 61
Tempest
compared with Dryden's
version, 97
Johnson's notes on 41, 134
Schlegel on 129
Timon of Athens
Johnson's notes on 61
Troilus and Cressida

Johnson's notes on 41, 60
representation of Romans and
kings 41
Sheffield, John, Earl of Mulgrave 68
Shelley, Percy Bysshe 117
Shenstone, William 110
Sherbo, Arthur 55
Short History of Modern Philosophy
(Scruton) xiii
Smith, Edmund 98
Sophocles 33
Spacks, Patricia Meyer 34
Spectator (Addison) 77-8, 135
Spector, Robert D. 35
Spenser, Edmund 65
Spingarn, J.E. 4
'Steel for the Mind' (Hinnant) 149
Stendhal (Henri Beyle) xii, 117-118,
130, 132
Stendhal et l'Angleterre (Gunnell) 118
Stock, R.D. xiii
Suard, Jean-Baptiste 117
Suckling, Sir John 71
Swift, Jonathan 3

Tancred and Sigismunda (Thomson)
61
Tate, Nahum 1, 52, 56, 62
The Whole Art of the Stage (d'Aubignac)
58
Thomson, James 61, 111, 125, 149; *see
also* Johnson
Timaeus (Plato) 144
Time and Narrative (Ricoeur) 5
Tinker, C.B. 114
To Homer through Pope (Mason) 134
Tour to the Hebrides (Boswell) 101, 109,
115
tragedy 38, 42-5, 47, 60, 127-8, 152
Tragic Plots (Rosslyn) 55
transfusion 138-42
Trotter, David 93

Unwin, William 101
Uses of Johnson's Criticism (Damrosch)
13, 61, 113

Venturo, David F. 133
Virgil 35, 120-121, 123, 148, compared
with Homer 139-40
Voltaire 7, 40, 59, 132

Wain, John 3, 58, 99
Waller, Edmund 110
Walpole, Horace 109
Warburton, William 28, 35
Warton, Joseph 26, 52, 54, 60, 95, 100-
101, 109-13
Warton, Thomas 34, 95, 148
Watson, George 4, 100
Wellek, René ix, 4-5, 8-10, 34, 64, 99,
126-7, 131-2
Western Canon (Bloom) 95
White, Hayden 154
White, Ian 36
Wilson Knight, G. 56
Wimsatt, W.K. 113-114
Winn, James A. 36
Wittgenstein, Ludwig viii
Wollstonecraft, Mary 117
Wordsworth, xii, 90-91, 96, 119-126,
127, 130-131, 133-4, 140,
143
Appendix to *Lyrical Ballads* 119,
122
'Essay Supplementary to the
Preface' 120, 125, 134
'Essays upon Epitaphs' 120, 125,
135
Preface to *Lyrical Ballads* 124
Wordsworth's Pope (Griffin) 134

Young, Edward 33